RENAL DIET COOKBOOK FOR BEGINNERS

300+ KIDNEY-FRIENDLY RECIPES WITH LOW SODIUM, LOW POTASSIUM, AND LOW PHOSPHORUS. INCLUDES A 4-WEEK MEAL PLAN

DARLENE BARTON

Table of Contents

Introduction

A s you know, the Renal Diet Cookbook helped you learn more about your condition, make excellent choices, and keep up with the basics. We hope that you have enjoyed learning more about your Renal Diet. At Renal Diet Cookbook, we understand that the quality of our products and services is just as important as the quality of our information.

Okay, so you're an HCT patient and you want to learn more about how you can improve your quality of life through diet. That's great! I know how tough it can be to adjust one's diet daily, but a few of these tips will help you in your quest.

Research shows that by incorporating certain protein sources into your daily diet, you'll find it easier to produce an adequate amount of the amino acids necessary for cellular function. Not only that, but proper food selection also contributes to better renal function. Here are some diet tips that will help you get started:

Increase the number of fruits and vegetables in your daily intake. Having a wonderful variety of foods is the easiest way to get enough nutrients for your body. A diet high in carbohydrates can cause the kidneys to store extra water, which may increase the risk of edema or swelling because of fluid retention. Here, having a low-carbohydrate diet is more important than ever! Make sure that you are drinking enough water. You need around 3 liters per day, which is equivalent to 1 gallon. You should also avoid caffeinated and sugary beverages as they can lead to dehydration and loss of electrolytes. Drink enough fluids with each meal. Patients with chronic HCT often complain about constipation or diarrhea, especially when they are on dialysis. However, they may not be aware that constipation occurs because of nutrient absorption being hindered because of fluid volume loss in the gut. Here are some dietary tips for patients who often complain about constipation: Include fiber-rich foods in your daily diet. This includes vegetables and fruits such as orange juice (juice contains vitamin C) and applesauce (which contains pectin). Avoid consuming medications containing aspirin (it is a potent inhibitor of prostaglandin synthesis). Eat more calcium-rich foods such as milk products and vegetables such as broccoli and spinach (calcium facilitates.

The Renal Diet Cookbook is a guide to help you choose the right foods for your patient's diet. If you are unfamiliar with a renal diet, it is a regimen that reduces the amount of protein in your patient's diet. This guide makes it easy to understand the purpose of a renal diet and how to get your patient started with a renal diet plan.

The Renal Diet Cookbook is the only cookbook specifically created to help people with chronic kidney disease eat a healthier diet.

Renal Diet Cookbook is designed specifically for those diagnosed with chronic kidney disease (CKD) who want to follow a healthy diet. The book provides simple, step-by-step, and easy-to-follow recipes that include specific instructions for kidney patients. This guide was designed specifically to help those with CKD gain back lost weight and enjoy their favorite foods. It's also ideal for patients who are trying to avoid having dialysis three times a week or more

Chapter 1: What is Kidney Disease?

Kidney disease (also called Renal Disease or Kidney Failure) is a type of condition where kidneys gradually lose their ability to function properly. The kidney's primary role is to filter out toxins and waste from the bloodstream, make urine, and control the balance of minerals within the system. However, when, for whatever reason, their function slows down or declines, the kidneys are unable to do all the above tasks as effectively as before, in their healthy and optimal condition. If the condition is left untreated, it will gradually get worse and the patient will ultimately reach the stage of kidney failure, which will demand urgent medical care for the survival of the patient.

Types and Stages of Kidney Disease

- <u>1st stage: Normal function</u>: A stage where the patient has lost only 10% of his/her renal capacity e.g., due to having only one kidney or other reasons. The stage is considered to be normal and there are no heavy symptoms noted but some preventive measures e.g., diet may be suggested by your doctor to control the risk of losing further renal function.

- <u>2nd stage: Mild-loss of function</u>. At this stage, the patient has lost around 11-40% of their kidney function. This stage, similar to stage 1, does not require urgent medical care but preventive measures e.g., renal diet or alcohol avoidance, may be suggested.

- <u>3rd stage: Moderate to a severe loss of function</u>. A stage where the patient has lost 41-70% of their renal function. Most patients are diagnosed at this stage because they start to display symptoms and visit their doctor to find out the cause.

- <u>4th stage: Severe loss of function</u>. At this stage, the patient has lost 71-85% of renal function. Due to the severity of the stage, the patient will need to follow a special diet plan, take meds, and be under the supervision of the doctor.

- <u>5th stage: Kidney failure</u>. The most severe and serious stage of all as the patient has already lost 85%+ of their kidney function and will need urgent medical care to survive.

Each stage and the percentage % of kidney function is measured by an index called GFR (Glomerular Filtration Rate), which is performed by a specialty renal doctor. The glomeruli are renal filters that filter out excess liquid and waste and are equal to kidney function. This means that if you have glomeruli reaching 60, your kidney function is 60% as well.

Now when it comes to managing your stage of renal failure, your doctor will typically administer some medication to control your symptoms e.g., diuretics to control liquid retention or blood pressure control medication to prevent blood pressure raise as a result of kidney dysfunction. Depending on your stage, you will have to make some diet and lifestyle changes e.g., quit smoking and perform mild exercises.

Causes of Kidney Disease

The following conditions have been associated with the onset of kidney diseases and the presence of one condition, will significantly increase the risk of developing the second condition as they are interrelated:

- <u>Diabetes (Type I and II)</u>. Diabetes makes immune system cells attack other cells of the system (auto-immunity attacks) and the kidney cells might be targeted as well.

- <u>Polycystic Organ Disease</u>. When cysts develop around an organ, e.g., kidneys, there will be increased fluid buildup and damage to the function of the affected organ.

- <u>Tumors/Cancer</u>. Cancer in the kidneys, especially at a developed stage, will dramatically worsen kidney function.

- Lupus and Autoimmune Disorders. Lupus and other similar autoimmune disorders will make the immune system attack various tissue cells and kidneys may also be under attack.

- Birth Defects. A child can rarely be born with decreased kidney function as a result of a congenital disability or complication e.g., the mother excessively taking NSAIDs during pregnancy.

- Accidents. Accidents that affect the lower back region can also damage the kidneys and decrease their function.

Kidney stones, urinary infections, as well as alcohol and drug/substance abuse, are also negatively associated with renal disease. It has also been found in several studies that obese adults over 45 with heart problems have a higher risk of developing the renal disease compared to younger people within a normal weight range.

The main problem with kidney disease is that, as a result of decreased kidney function, the kidneys will accumulate waste and fluid and there will be an electrolyte and mineral imbalance which may also trigger other health problems such as elevated blood pressure, elevated cholesterol, fluid buildup in several organs, anemia, infections and decrease immunity.

Risks

In contrast to ONN, during this disease entity kidney damage occurs gradually, primarily within the course of chronic diseases, such as:

- Diabetes mellitus (diabetic nephropathy),
- Hypertension (hypertensive nephropathy),
- Glomerulonephritis and tubulointerstitial inflammatory processes,
- Polycystic degeneration,
- Systemic diseases, including sarcoidosis and amyloidosis
- Less often long-term impaired blood flow or outflow of urine,
- Plasma myeloma,
- HIV nephropathy
- Genetically determined syndromes, e.g., apart syndrome.

Symptoms

Kidney failure is a progressive disease; it does not happen overnight. Some people in the early stages of kidney disease do not show any symptoms. Symptoms usually appear in the later stages of kidney disease. Some people may not even show any symptoms of kidney disease until their kidneys fail (end-stage).

When the kidneys are damaged, wastes and toxins can build up in your body. Once the buildup occurs, you may feel sick and experience the following symptoms:

- Nausea
- Poor appetite
- Weakness
- Trouble sleeping
- Tiredness
- Itching
- Weight loss
- Muscle cramps (especially in the legs)
- Swelling of your feet and ankles
- Anemia (low red blood cell count)

The good news is that once you begin treatment for kidney disease, your symptoms, and general health will improve.

Chapter 2: What is Renal Diet?

A renal diet is actually a diet that is low in sodium, phosphorus, and potassium, which are three minerals that the system cannot metabolize properly and filter out (in excess levels) when renal function is compromised.

Benefits of Renal Diet

The role of diet in kidney disease, therefore, is very important as eating certain foods with varying levels of these minerals can either improve or worsen renal function. Specifically, the renal diet includes the following benefits:

- Decreased fluid buildup in kidneys and other organs
- Mineral balance
- Regulated blood pressure

All these three major benefits will help ease many symptoms of the disease and even limit dependency on certain drugs e.g., diuretics, which may often lead to side effects when abused.

Diabetes and heart disease patients who also suffer from some type of kidney failure may also benefit from the renal diet as these problems are interconnected and factors that influence one disorder, e.g., diet, will influence the other and vice versa.

Therefore, if you are diagnosed with decreased kidney function, a renal diet will help you keep your kidney activity levels stable and help you avoid dialysis-which is the final and most difficult stage of renal failure and may put your health at serious risk.

A proper renal diet plan that is low in phosphorus, potassium, and sodium can slow down the progression of the disease and control accompanying symptoms that often come with the renal disease such as elevated blood pressure and mineral imbalance.

Lifestyle to Adopt

The chronic renal disease does not make it to end-stage renal failure. There are some options to help possibly prevent or even decrease the rate of your progress. By adopting healthy habits, many people with CKDs have a better quality of life. Well-being is a complete physical, mental, and social state. Ask the members of your health care team to explain how to strive for wellness and adopt principles such as:

- A well-balanced diet
- Physical activities at regular intervals (ideally 30 to 60 minutes four to five times a week)
- Well-controlled blood pressure
- Balanced blood glucose (in the presence of diabetes)
- Stop smoking
- Control of anemia (maintenance of a normal blood count)
- Maintaining a healthy weight
- Moderation in alcohol consumption
- Taking medication according to the doctor's instructions

It is also essential to be familiar with your kidney disease and to listen to the information and advice given to you by your doctor and medical care team.

Tips and advice

Birthdays, weddings, graduations, picnics, and barbecues are wonderful occasions for getting together with family and friends. For people with kidney disease, these social gatherings can also mean tough choices about what to eat and drink. It is possible to enjoy them if you have a good plan in place and keep a positive attitude. Below are some kidney-healthy diet tips for social gatherings:

1. **Don't go hungry.** Have a snack before you leave the house. Going to any event hungry will only set you up for disaster and will most likely lead to overeating. Having a high-protein snack beforehand—for example, half of a tuna sandwich—will make you feel a little full and help you make healthier choices.

2. **Avoid high-sodium foods.** Salty foods will only make you thirsty, which will make you want to drink more than you probably should. Rather than choosing hot dogs or sausages, choose lower-sodium foods such as chicken and hamburgers. Go easy on the barbecue sauce and salad dressing, because they are very high in salt. If available, you can even ask for vegetables to be grilled.

3. **Limit alcohol.** It is best to speak with your physician first about drinking alcohol. Alcoholic beverages also count toward your fluid intake.

4. **Food safety is important.** Having kidney disease puts you at a higher risk for food-borne illnesses. Keep food at safe temperatures, wash produce well, and use separate cutting boards for raw and cooked meats.

5. **Plan.** Ask your family or friends about the menu. This way you can decide exactly what you want to eat. If it's not to your liking and doesn't fit with your diet, you can bring your own dish.

Nutrients Needed

A renal diet involves consuming certain nutrients while limiting or avoiding other nutrients which may worsen kidney function. The following macro and micro-nutrients play a major role in renal diet and the management of kidney disease:

1. **Potassium.** Potassium is a key mineral responsible for regulating heartbeats and the health of the muscle tissue. In normal people with no kidney damage, experts recommend consuming 4700mg/daily, however, those with decreased kidney function should consume ideally only 2000mg per day, as anything beyond this limit cannot be properly metabolized by the kidneys.

2. **Phosphorus.** Phosphorus is another key mineral responsible for bone and connective tissue, e.g., joint, and works similarly to calcium. However, when someone has renal disease, excess amounts of phosphorus can damage the kidneys and won't be expelled properly by the system, leading to calcium deposits in organs and connective tissue and causing further health problems.

3. **Calories.** There is no strict limit for calories in the renal diet, however, your doctor may advise you to limit your consumption of calories to lose weight or increase the consumption of calories to keep a healthy weight and avoid any health complications e.g., too low or too high blood cholesterol.

4. **Protein.** As the building blocks of our muscles and connective tissue, proteins are essential in our diet. Still, those with CKD may be advised to consume certain amounts by their doctors, depending on the disease's stage. In most cases, taking 37-41 grams of protein daily (from all daily meals) is recommended.

5. **Fats.** Fats often act as an alternative energy source. In renal damage, healthy fats can be taken without any limits, as long as they come from low phosphorus and low potassium resources e.g., wheat germ oil instead of avocado oil.

6. **Sodium.** Sodium, a key mineral known as "salt" is responsible for regulating blood pressure and electrolyte as well as liquid balance in the system. However, excess amounts of sodium cannot be metabolized by renal disease patients properly. The doctor will often advise its limitation, which is typically up to 1500mg/daily.

7. **Carbohydrates.** Carbs are the primary source of fuel in our body and often come with other minerals that may benefit our system. Generally, there is no limitation to the number of carbs one can consume when on a renal pre-dialysis diet, however, those with diabetes or heart problems should limit the consumption of simple carbs e.g., bread and pies, and go for more complex carbs which have fiber and other nutrients e.g., sweet potatoes or brown rice.

8. **Sugars.** Sugars, similar to carbs, act as a quick and temporary fuel for the body but excessive consumption can often lead to inflammatory diseases like diabetes and heart problems. In the renal diet, sugar is not on the list of non-permitted foods, however, excess consumption should be avoided for general health reasons.

9. **Fiber.** Fiber is essential for the regulation of the digestive tract and also plays a role in the protection of vital organs e.g., liver and kidneys from damage. This is why it is a staple in the renal diet, as long as it comes from low potassium and phosphorus sources e.g., peppers.

10. **Vitamins & Minerals.** The human system, in general, needs more than 13 vitamins and minerals to function properly and patients with kidney disease are no exception to this rule. Since some foods that are low in phosphorus and potassium may be low in other minerals as well, some doctors recommend the supplementation of vitamins like Vitamin C and B-complex, which are often depleted in kidney disease patients.

11. **Fluids.** Water is essential for the hydration of your system, but too much water and fluids can place an extra burden on the kidneys, which is something that CKD patients don't want. This is why doctors will often suggest the consumption of no more than 32 ounces of fluids (around 1 liter) daily.

Chapter 3: What to Eat

Many foods work well within the renal diet, and once you see the available variety, it will not seem as restrictive or difficult to follow. The key is focusing on foods with a high level of nutrients, which makes it easier for the kidneys to process waste by not adding too much that the body needs to discard. Balance is a major factor in maintaining and improving long-term renal function.

Garlic

A portion of excellent, vitamin-rich food for the immune system, garlic is a tasty substitute for salt in a variety of dishes. It acts as a significant source of vitamin C and B6 while aiding the kidneys in ridding the body of unwanted toxins. It's a great, healthy way to add flavor for skillet meals, pasta, soups, and stews.

Berries

All berries are considered a good renal diet food due to their high level of fiber, antioxidants, and delicious taste, making them an easy option to include as a light snack or as an ingredient in smoothies, salads, and light desserts. Just one handful of blueberries can provide almost one day's vitamin C requirement, as well as a boost of fiber, which is good for weight loss and maintenance.

Bell Peppers

Flavorful and easy to enjoy both raw and cooked, bell peppers offer a good source of vitamin C, vitamin A, and fiber. Along with other kidney-friendly foods, they make the detoxification process much easier while boosting your body's nutrient level to prevent further health conditions and reduce existing deficiencies.

Onions

This nutritious and tasty vegetable is excellent as a companion to garlic in many dishes, or on its own. Like garlic, onions can provide flavor as an alternative to salt, and provides a good source of vitamin C, vitamin B, manganese, and fiber, as well. Adding just one quarter or half of the onion is often enough for most meals, because of its strong, pungent flavor.

Macadamia Nuts

If you enjoy nuts and seeds as snacks, you may soon learn that many contain high amounts of phosphorus and should be avoided or limited as much as possible. Fortunately, macadamia nuts are an easier option to digest and process, as they contain much lower amounts of phosphorus and make an excellent substitute for other nuts. They are a good source of other nutrients, as well, such as vitamin B, copper, manganese, iron, and healthy fats.

Pineapple

Unlike other fruits that are high in potassium, a pineapple is an option that can be enjoyed more often than bananas and kiwis. Citrus fruits are generally high in potassium. If you find yourself craving an orange or grapefruit, choose pineapple instead. In addition to providing high levels of vitamin B and fiber, pineapples can reduce inflammation thanks to an enzyme called bromelain.

Mushrooms

Mushrooms are a safe option for the renal diet, especially the shiitake variety, high in nutrients such as selenium, vitamin B, and manganese. They contain a moderate amount of plant-based protein, which is easier for your body to digest and use than animal proteins. Shiitake and Portobello mushrooms are often used in vegan diets as a meat substitute, because of their texture and pleasant flavor.

What to Avoid?

Eating restrictions might be different depending upon your level of kidney disease. If you are in the early stages of kidney disease, you may have different restrictions as compared to those who are at the end-stage renal disease, or kidney failure. In contrast to this, people with an end-stage renal disease requiring dialysis will face different eating restrictions. Let's discuss some foods to avoid while being on the renal diet.

1. **Dark-Colored Colas** contain calories, sugar, phosphorus, etc. They contain phosphorus to enhance flavor, increase its life, and avoid discoloration. Which can be found in a product's ingredient list? This addition of phosphorus varies depending on the type of cola. Mostly, the dark-colored colas contain 50–100 mg in a 200-ml serving. Therefore, dark colas should be avoided on a renal diet.

2. **Canned Foods** including soups, vegetables, and beans, are low in cost but contain high amounts of sodium because of the addition of salt to increase its life. Because of this amount of sodium inclusion in canned goods, people with kidney disease should avoid consumption. Opt for lower-sodium content with the label "no salt added." One more way is to drain or rinse canned foods, such as canned beans and tuna, which could decrease the sodium content by 33–80%, depending on the product.

3. **One cup of already cooked brown rice** possesses about 150 mg of phosphorus and 154 mg of potassium, whereas one cup of already cooked white rice has about 69 mg of phosphorus and 54 mg of potassium. Bulgur, buckwheat, pearled barley, and couscous are equally beneficial, low-phosphorus options and might be a suitable alternative instead of brown rice.

4. **Bananas** are high potassium content, low in sodium, and provides 422 mg of potassium per banana. It might disturb your daily balanced potassium intake to 2,000 mg if a banana is a daily staple.

5. **Whole-Wheat Bread** may harm individuals with kidney disease. But for healthy individuals, it is recommended over refined, white flour bread. White bread is recommended instead of whole-wheat varieties for individuals with kidney disease because it has phosphorus and potassium. If you add more bran and whole grains to the bread, then the amount of phosphorus and potassium contents increases.

6. **Oranges and Orange Juice** are enriched with vitamin C content and potassium. 184 grams provides 333 mg of potassium and 473 mg of potassium in one cup of orange juice. With these calculations, oranges and orange juice must be avoided or used in a limited amount while being on a renal diet.

If you are suffering from or living with kidney disease, reducing your potassium, phosphorus, and sodium intake is an essential aspect of managing and tackling the disease. The foods with high-potassium, high-sodium, and high-phosphorus content listed above should always be limited or avoided. These restrictions and nutrients intakes may differ depending on the level of damage to your kidneys. Following a renal diet might be a daunting procedure and a restrictive one most of the time. But, working with your physician and nutrition specialist and a renal dietitian can assist you to formulate a renal diet specific to your individual needs.

Chapter 4: Breakfast Recipes

1. Garlic Mayo Bread

Preparation Time: 10 minutes
Cooking Time: 5 minutes
Servings: 1-2
Ingredients:

- 1 tbsp. vegetable oil
- 2 cloves garlic, minced
- 1 tsp. paprika
- Dash cayenne pepper
- ½ tsp. lemon juice
- 1 tbsp. Parmesan cheese, grated
- ¼ cup mayonnaise
- French bread, sliced
- ½ tsp. Italian herbs

Directions:

1. Mix the garlic with the oil in a small bowl and leave it overnight.
2. Discard the garlic from the bowl and keep the garlic-infused oil.
3. Mix the garlic-oil with cayenne, paprika, lemon juice, mayonnaise, and Parmesan.
4. Place the bread slices in a baking tray lined with parchment paper.
5. Top these slices with the mayonnaise mixture and drizzle the Italian herbs on top.
6. Broil these slices for 5 minutes until golden brown.
7. Serve warm.

Nutrition:
Calories 217, Total Fat 7.9g, Sodium 423mg, Dietary Fiber 1.3g, Sugars 2g, Protein 7g, Calcium 56mg, Phosphorous 347mg, Potassium 72mg

2. Strawberry Topped Waffles

Preparation Time: 15 minutes
Cooking Time: 20 minutes
Servings: 2
Ingredients:

- 1 cup flour
- ¼ cup Swerve
- 1 ¾ tsp. baking powder
- 1 egg separated
- ¾ cup milk
- ½ cup butter, melted
- ½ tsp. vanilla extract
- Fresh strawberries, sliced

Directions:

1. Prepare and preheat your waffle pan following the instructions of the machine.
2. Begin by mixing the flour with Swerve and baking soda in a bowl.
3. Separate the egg yolks from the egg whites, keeping them in two separate bowls.
4. Add the milk and vanilla extract to the egg yolks.
5. Stir the melted butter and mix well until smooth.
6. Now beat the egg whites with an electric beater until foamy and fluffy.
7. Fold this fluffy composition in the egg yolk mixture.
8. Mix it gently until smooth, then add in the flour mixture.
9. Stir again to make a smooth mixture.
10. Pour a ½ cup of the waffle batter into a preheated pan and cook until the waffle is cooked.
11. Cook more waffles with the remaining batter.
12. Serve fresh with strawberries on top.

Nutrition:
Calories 342, Total Fat 20.5g, Sodium 156mg, Dietary Fiber 0.7g, Sugars 3.5g, Protein 4.8g, Calcium 107mg, Phosphorous 126mg, Potassium 233mg

3. Cheese Spaghetti Frittata

Preparation Time: 10 minutes
Cooking Time: 10 minutes
Servings: 2
Ingredients:

- 2 cups whole-wheat spaghetti, cooked
- 2 tsp. olive oil and 1 medium onion, chopped
- 2 large eggs
- ¼ cup milk
- ¼ cup Parmesan cheese, grated
- 2 tbsp. fresh parsley, chopped
- 2 tbsp. fresh basil, chopped
- ½ tsp. black pepper
- 1 tomato, diced

Directions:

1. Set a suitable non-stick skillet over moderate heat and add in the olive oil.
2. Place the spaghetti in the skillet and cook by stirring for 2 minutes on moderate heat. Whisk the eggs with milk, parsley, and black pepper in a bowl.
3. Pour this milky egg mixture over the spaghetti and top it all with basil, cheese, and tomato.

4. Cover the spaghetti frittata again with a lid and cook for approximately 8 minutes on low heat. Slice and serve.

Nutrition: Calories 230, Total Fat 7.8g, Sodium 77mg, Dietary Fiber 5.6g, Sugars 4.5g, Protein 11.1g, Calcium 88mg, Phosphorous 368 mg, Potassium 214mg,

4. Shrimp Bruschetta

Preparation Time: 15 minutes
Cooking Time: 10 minutes
Servings: 2
Ingredients:

- 6 oz. shrimps, peeled
- ½ tbsp. tomato sauce
- ¼ tsp. Splenda
- ⅛ tsp. garlic powder
- ½ tsp. fresh parsley, chopped
- ¼ tsp. olive oil
- ½ tsp. lemon juice
- 2 whole-grain bread slices
- ½ cup water, for cooking

Directions:
1. In the saucepan, pour water and bring it to a boil.
2. Add shrimps and boil them over high heat for 5 minutes.
3. After this, drain shrimps and chill them to the room temperature.
4. Mix up together shrimps with Splenda, garlic powder, tomato sauce, and fresh parsley. Add lemon juice and stir gently.
5. Preheat the oven to 360°F.
6. Coat the slice of bread with olive oil and bake for 3 minutes.
7. Then place the shrimp mixture on the bread. Bruschetta is cooked.

Nutrition: Calories 199, Fat 3.7, Fiber 2.1, Carbs 15.3, Protein 24.1

5. Strawberry Muesli

Preparation Time: 10 minutes
Cooking Time: 30 minutes
Servings: 2
Ingredients:

- 1 cup Greek yogurt
- ½ cup strawberries, sliced
- ½ cup Muesli
- 2 tsp. maple syrup
- ¼ tsp. ground cinnamon

Directions:
1. Put Greek yogurt in the food processor.

2. Add 1 cup of strawberries, maple syrup, and ground cinnamon.
3. Blend the ingredients until you get a smooth mass.
4. Transfer the yogurt mass to the serving bowls.
5. Add Muesli and stir well.
6. Leave the meal for 30 minutes in the fridge.
7. After this, decorate it with the remaining sliced strawberries.

Nutrition:
Calories 149, Fat 2.6, Fiber 3.6, Carbs 21.6, Protein 12

6. Yogurt Bulgur

Preparation Time: 10 minutes
Cooking Time: 15 minutes
Servings: 2
Ingredients:

- 1 cup bulgur
- 2 cups Greek yogurt
- 1 ½ cup water
- ½ tsp. salt
- 1 tsp. olive oil

Directions:
1. Pour olive oil into the saucepan and add bulgur.
2. Roast it over medium heat for 2-3 minutes. Stir it from time to time.
3. After this, add salt and water.
4. Close the lid and cook bulgur for 15 minutes over medium heat.
5. Then chill the cooked bulgur well and combine it with Greek yogurt. Stir it carefully.
6. Transfer the cooked meal onto the serving plates. The yogurt bulgur tastes the best when it is cold.

Nutrition:
Calories 274, Fat 4.9, Fiber 8.5, Carbs 40.8, Protein 19.2

7. Bacon and Cheese Crust less Quiche

Preparation Time: 10 minutes
Cooking Time: 4 hours
Servings: 2
Ingredients:

- 1 tbsp. butter
- 10 beaten eggs
- 8 oz. shredded cheddar cheese, reduced-fat
- 1 cup light cream
- ½ tbsp. black pepper
- 10 pieces chopped bacon, cooked

Directions:
1. Grease your slow cooker with butter and set aside.
2. Combine eggs, cheese, cream, and pepper in a mixing bowl. Add mixture into the slow cooker.

3. Splash bacon over the mixture and cover the slow cooker.
4. Cook for about 4 hours on low. Make sure the quiche is not over-cooked.
5. Serve and enjoy.

Nutrition:
Calories: 436, Total fat: 36g, Saturated fat: 16g, Total carbs: 4g, Protein: 24g, Sugars: 1.6g, Fiber: 0.5g, Sodium: 631mg, Potassium: 30.8g

8. Mushroom Crust less Quiche

Preparation Time: 15 minutes
Cooking Time: 4 hours
Servings: 2

Ingredients:
- 3 tbsp. butter, divided
- 1 package, 10-oz., sliced mushrooms
- 1 red bell pepper, 1-inch strips
- ¼ tbsp. kosher salt
- 1 tbsp. minced onion, dried
- 10 beaten eggs
- ½ tbsp. black pepper
- 1 cup light cream
- 1 package, 10-oz., shredded cheddar cheese, reduced-fat

Directions:
1. Grease your slow cooker with 1 tablespoon butter.
2. Heat 2 tablespoon butter in a skillet for about 30 seconds over medium heat then add mushrooms, peppers, salt, and onions.
3. Sauté for about 5 minutes until mushrooms lose water and pepper softens. Drain vegetables and transfer to the slow cooker.
4. Whisk together eggs, black pepper, cream, and cheese in a mixing bowl.
5. Add the egg mixture to vegetables into the slow cooker, then stir to combine.
6. Cover the slow cooker and cook for about 4 hours on low. Make sure it's not to overcook.
7. Serve and enjoy

Nutrition:
Calories: 429, Total fat: 35g, Saturated fat: 20g, Total carbs: 5.3g, Protein: 23.2g, Sugars: 2.7g, Fiber: 0.9g, Sodium: 738mg, Potassium: 362mg

9. Maple Glazed Walnuts

Preparation Time: 15 minutes
Cooking Time: 2 hours
Servings: 3-4

Ingredients:
- 8 oz. walnuts
- ¼ cup butter
- ¼ cup maple syrup, sugar-free
- ½ tbsp. vanilla extract, pure

Directions:
1. Add all the ingredients to the slow cooker and turn it to low.
2. Cook for 2 hours, stirring occasionally to ensure all the nuts are well coated.
3. When the time has elapsed, transfer the walnuts onto a parchment paper. Let sit for a few minutes to cool.
4. Serve and enjoy.

Nutrition:
Calories 328, Total Fat 24g, Saturated Fat 6g, Total Carbs 10g, Net Carbs 8g, Protein 4g, Sugar: 7g, Fiber: 2g, Sodium: 2mg, Potassium 127g

10. Ham and Cheese Strata

Preparation Time: 10 minutes
Cooking Time: 3 hours
Servings: 2

Ingredients:
- 1 tbsp. butter
- 8 slices low-carb Ezekiel bread divided into 16 triangles remove crust and save
- 6 oz. thinly sliced ham, chopped
- 8 oz. Monterey jack cheese, shredded,
- 2 tbsp. minced onions, dried
- 6 eggs
- 3 ¼ cups half-and-half
- ½ tbsp. salt
- ¼ tbsp. Tabasco sauce
- ¾ tbsp. black pepper

Directions:
1. Grease your slow cooker with butter, then put 8 triangles of bread at the bottom. Sprinkle the trimmed off crust pieces to cover the bottom of your slow cooker with bread fully.
2. Sprinkle ham over the bread to make a thick layer, then add cheese preserving ½ cup.
3. Sprinkle half of the onions over cheese, then top with remaining bread slices. Set aside.
4. Mix eggs, half-and-half, salt, tabasco sauce, and pepper in a mixing bowl until well blended.
5. Pour the egg mixture over bread, then sprinkle the remaining onions on top. Let sit for about 15 minutes.
6. Sprinkle preserved cheese and cover your slow cooker.
7. Cook for about 3 hours on low and when time has elapsed, uncover your slow cooker.
8. Let the strata sit for about 10 minutes before cutting.
9. Serve and enjoy.

Nutrition:
Calories: 481.4, Total fat 37.8g, Saturated fat 20.5g, Total carbs 11.4g, Protein 23.9g, Sugar 1.1g, Fiber 1g, Potassium 382mg, Sodium 1334mg.

11. Breakfast Salad from Grains and Fruits

Preparation Time: 5 minutes
Cooking Time: 15 minutes
Servings: 2

Ingredients:

- 18 oz. low-fat vanilla yogurt
- 1 cup raisins
- 1 orange
- 1 red delicious apple
- 1 Granny Smith apple
- ¾ cup bulgur
- ¾ cup quick-cooking brown rice
- ¼ tsp. salt
- 3 cups water

Directions:

1. On high fire, place a large pot and bring water to a boil.
2. Add bulgur and rice. Lower fire to a simmer and cooks for 10 minutes while covered.
3. Turn off fire, set aside for 2 minutes while covered.
4. In the baking sheet, transfer and dispersed grains to cool.
5. Meanwhile, peel oranges and cut into sections. Chop and core apples.
6. Once grains are cool, transfer to a large serving bowl along with fruits.
7. Add yogurt and mix well to coat.
8. Serve and enjoy.

Nutrition:
Calories: 187; Carbs: g; Protein: g; Fats: g; Phosphorus: mg; Potassium: mg; Sodium: 117mg

12. French Toast with Applesauce

Preparation Time: 5 minutes
Cooking Time: 15 minutes
Servings: 2

Ingredients:

- ¼ cup unsweetened applesauce
- ½ cup milk
- 1 tsp. ground cinnamon
- 2 eggs
- 2 tbsp. white sugar
- 6 slices whole-wheat bread

Directions:

1. Mix well applesauce, sugar, cinnamon, milk, and eggs in a mixing bowl.

2. Soak the bread, one by one, into the applesauce mixture until wet.
3. On medium fire, heat a nonstick skillet greased with cooking spray.
4. Add soaked bread one at a time and cook for 2-3 minutes per side or until lightly browned.
5. Serve and enjoy.

Nutrition:
Calories: 57; Carbs: 6g; Protein: 4g; Fats: 4g; Phosphorus: 69mg; Potassium: 88mg; Sodium: 43mg

13. Bagels Made Healthy

Preparation Time: 5 minutes
Cooking Time: 25 minutes
Servings: 2

Ingredients:

- 2 tsp. yeast
- 1 ½ tbsp. olive oil
- 1 ¼ cups bread flour
- 2 cups whole-wheat flour
- 1 tbsp. vinegar
- 2 tbsp. honey
- 1 ½ cups warm water

Directions:

1. In a bread machine, mix all ingredients, and then process on dough cycle.
2. Once done or end of the cycle, create 8 pieces shaped like a flattened ball.
3. In the center of each ball, make a hole using your thumb, then create a donut shape.
4. In a greased baking sheet, place donut-shaped dough then covers and let it rise for about ½ hour.
5. Prepare about 2 inches of water to boil in a large pan.
6. In a boiling water, drop one at a time the bagels and boil for 1 minute, then turn them once.
7. Remove them and return them to the baking sheet and bake at 350°F (175°C) for about 20 to 25 minutes until golden brown.

Nutrition: Calories: 221; Carbs: 42g; Protein: 7g; Fats: g; Phosphorus: 130mg; Potassium: 166mg; Sodium: 47mg

14. Cornbread with Southern Twist

Preparation Time: 15 minutes
Cooking Time: 60 minutes
Servings: 2

Ingredients:

- 2 tbsp. shortening
- 1 ¼ cups skim milk
- ¼ cup egg substitute
- 4 tbsp. sodium-free baking powder
- ½ cup flour

- 1 ½ cups cornmeal

Directions:
1. Prepare an 8 x 8-inch baking dish or a black iron skillet, then add shortening.
2. Put the baking dish or skillet inside the oven at 425°F. Once the shortening has melted that means the pan is hot already.
3. In a bowl, add milk and egg, then mix well.
4. Take out the skillet and add the melted shortening into the batter and stir well.
5. Pour all mixed ingredients into the skillet.
6. For 15 to 20 minutes, cook in the oven until golden brown.

Nutrition:
Calories: 166; Carbs: 35g; Protein: 5g; Fats: 1g; Phosphorus: 79mg; Potassium: 122mg; Sodium: 34mg

15. Grandma's Pancake Special

Preparation Time: 5 minutes
Cooking Time: 15 minutes
Servings: 3

Ingredients:
- 1 tbsp. oil
- 1 cup milk
- 1 egg
- 2 tsp. sodium-free baking powder
- 2 tbsp. sugar
- 1 ¼ cups flour

Directions:
1. Mix all the dry ingredients such as flour, sugar, and baking powder.
2. Combine oil, milk, and egg in another bowl. Once done, add them all to the flour mixture.
3. Make sure that as you stir the mixture, blend them until slightly lumpy.
4. In a hot greased griddle, pour in at least ¼ cup of the batter to make each pancake.
5. To cook, ensure that the bottom is brown, then turn and cook the other side, as well.

Nutrition:
Calories: 167; Carbs: 50g; Protein: 11g; Fats: 11g; Phosphorus: 176mg; Potassium: 215mg; Sodium: 70mg

16. Very Berry Smoothie

Preparation Time: 3 minutes
Cooking Time: 5 minutes
Servings: 2

Ingredients:
- 2 quarts water
- 2 cups pomegranate seeds
- 1 cup blackberries

- 1 cup blueberries

Directions:
1. Mix all ingredients in a blender.
2. Puree until smooth.
3. Transfer to a serving glass and enjoy.

Nutrition:
Calories: 464; Carbs: 111g; Protein: 8g; Fats: 4g; Phosphorus: 132mg; Potassium: 843mg; Sodium: 16mg

17. Pasta with Indian Lentils

Preparation Time: 5 minutes
Cooking Time: 35 minutes
Servings: 2

Ingredients:
- ¼-½ cup fresh cilantro (chopped)
- 3 cups water
- 2 small dry red peppers (whole)
- 1 tsp. turmeric
- 1 tsp. ground cumin
- 2-3 cloves garlic (minced)
- 1 can (15-oz.) cubed tomatoes (with juice)
- 1 large onion (chopped)
- ½ cup dry lentils (rinsed)
- ½ cup orzo or tiny pasta

Directions:
1. In a skillet, combine all ingredients except for the cilantro, then boil on medium-high heat.
2. Ensure to cover and slightly reduce heat to medium-low and simmer until pasta is tender for about 35 minutes.
3. Afterward, take out the chili peppers, then add cilantro and top it with low-fat sour cream.

Nutrition: Calories: 175; Carbs: 40g; Protein: 3g; Fats: 2g; Phosphorus: 139mg; Potassium: 513mg; Sodium: 61mg

18. Pineapple Bread

Preparation Time: 20 minutes
Cooking Time: 1 hour
Servings: 2

Ingredients:
- ⅓ cup Swerve
- ⅓ cup butter, unsalted
- 2 eggs
- 2 cups flour
- 3 tsp. baking powder
- 1 cup pineapple, undrained
- 6 cherries, chopped

Directions:
1. Whisk the Swerve with the butter in a mixer until fluffy.

2. Stir in the eggs, then beat again.
3. Add the baking powder and flour, then mix well until smooth.
4. Fold in the cherries and pineapple.
5. Spread this cherry-pineapple batter in a 9x5 inch baking pan.
6. Bake the pineapple batter for 1 hour at 350°F.
7. Slice the bread and serve.

Nutrition:
Calories 197, Total Fat 7.2g, Sodium 85mg, Dietary Fiber 1.1g, Sugars 3 g, Protein 4g, Calcium 79mg, Phosphorous 316mg, Potassium 227mg

19. Parmesan Zucchini Frittata

Preparation Time: 10 minutes
Cooking Time: 35 minutes
Servings: 2

Ingredients:
- 1 tbsp. olive oil
- 1 cup yellow onion, sliced
- 3 cups zucchini, chopped
- ½ cup Parmesan cheese, grated
- 8 large eggs
- ½ tsp. black pepper
- ⅛ tsp. paprika
- 3 tbsp. parsley, chopped

Directions:
1. Toss the zucchinis with the onion, parsley, and all other ingredients in a large bowl.
2. Pour this zucchini-garlic mixture into an 11x7 inches pan and dispersed it.
3. Bake the zucchini casserole for approximately 35 minutes at 350°F.
4. Cut in slices and serve.

Nutrition:
Calories 142, Total Fat 9.7g, Saturated Fat 2.8g, Cholesterol 250mg, Sodium 123mg, Carbohydrate 4.7g, Dietary Fiber 1.3g, Sugars 2.4g, Protein 10.2g, Calcium 73mg, Phosphorous 375mg, Potassium 286mg

20. Texas Toast Casserole

Preparation Time: 10 minutes
Cooking Time: 30 minutes
Servings: 2

Ingredients:
- ½ cup butter, melted
- 1 cup brown Swerve
- 1 lb. Texas Toast bread, sliced
- 4 large eggs
- 1 ½ cup milk
- 1 tbsp. vanilla extract
- 2 tbsp. Swerve
- 2 tsp. cinnamon
- Maple syrup for serving

Directions:
1. Layer a 9x13 inches baking pan with cooking spray.
2. Spread the bread slices at the bottom of the prepared pan.
3. Whisk the eggs with the remaining ingredients in a mixer.
4. Pour this mixture over the bread slices evenly.
5. Bake the bread for 30 minutes at 350°F in a preheated oven.
6. Serve.

Nutrition:
Calories 332, Total Fat 13.7g, Sodium 350mg, Dietary Fiber 2g, Sugars 6g, Protein 7.4g, Calcium 143mg, Phosphorous 186mg, Potassium 74mg

21. Fluffy Homemade Buttermilk Pancake

Preparation Time: 10 minutes
Cooking Time: 30 minutes
Servings: 2

Ingredients:
- ¼ cup olive oil
- 2 cups low-fat buttermilk
- 2 cups all-purpose flour
- 1 tsp. lemon juice
- 2 tbsp. sugar
- 2 large egg whites
- 1 ½ tsp. baking powder

Directions:
1. Put a pan over medium flame.
2. In a large bowl, add all the dry ingredients. In another bowl, add oil, buttermilk, and egg whites mix and mix with dry ingredients.
3. Mix it well.
4. Spray oil on the pan. Pour the batter into the pan in a pancake shape.
5. Cook until brown on both sides.
6. Repeat with the rest of the batter, enjoy.

Nutrition:
Calories 217| Total Fat 9 g| Saturated Fat 1 g| Cholesterol 44 mg| Sodium 330 mg| Carbohydrates 27 g| Protein 6 g| Phosphorus 100 mg| Potassium 182 mg| Fiber 1 g| Calcium 74 mg

22. Blueberry Muffins

Preparation Time: 10 minutes
Cooking Time: 30 minutes
Servings: 2

Ingredients:

- 2 ½ cups fresh blueberries
- ½ cup low-fat unsalted butter
- 1 ¼ cups artificial sweetener
- 2 cups soy milk
- 2 cups all-purpose flour
- ½ tsp. salt
- 3 eggs' white
- 2 tsp. baking powder

Directions:

1. In a food mixer, add sugar alternative and margarine, blend it on low until smooth.
2. Add eggs, mix until combined well.
3. Add dry ingredients after sifting and add milk.
4. Take ½ cup of berries and mash them. Mix in the mixture with your clean hands. Add the rest of the berries.
5. Spray oil on the muffin cups.
6. Pour muffin mixture into muffin cups.
7. Bake in the oven for ½ hour at 375°F.

Nutrition: Calories 275| Total Fat 9 g| Saturated Fat 5 g| Cholesterol 53 mg| Sodium 210 mg| Carbohydrates 44 g| Protein 5 g| Phosphorus 100 mg| Potassium 121 mg| Dietary Fiber 1.3 g| Calcium 108 mg

23. Easy Turkey Breakfast Burritos

Preparation Time: 10 minutes
Cooking Time: 30 minutes
Servings: 2
Ingredients:

- ¼ cup chopped bell peppers
- 4 cups ground turkey
- ¼ cup olive oil
- 8 egg whites, whisked
- ¼ cup chopped onions
- ½ tsp. chili powder
- 2 tbsp. jalapeño peppers (seeded)
- 8 pieces flour burrito shells
- 2 tbsp. scallions, diced
- ½ tsp. smoked paprika
- 1 cup shredded vegan cheese

Directions:

1. In a pan over medium heat, sauté peppers, cilantro, turkey, scallions, and onions. Until translucent.
2. In another pan, cook the whisked eggs.
3. In burrito, add turkey and vegetable mix, eggs, and cheese.
4. Fold and serve.

Nutrition: Calories 407| Total Fat 24 g| Saturated Fat 7 g| Trans Fat 0 g| Cholesterol 237 mg| Sodium 513 mg|

Carbohydrates 23 g| Protein 25 g| Phosphorus 359 mg |Potassium 285 mg| Dietary Fiber 2 g| Calcium 209 mg

24. Loaded Veggie Eggs

Preparation Time: 10 minutes
Cooking Time: 30 minutes
Servings: 2
Ingredients:

- ¼ cup diced onion
- 6-7 egg whites
- 3 cups fresh kale
- 1 clove pressed garlic
- 1 tbsp. oil
- ¼ cup diced bell pepper
- 1 cup cauliflower
- ¼ tsp. black pepper
- Spring onion for garnish

Directions:

1. Whisk the egg whites.
2. In a pan, over medium flame, add peppers and onions and sauté for 3 minutes.
3. Then add garlic and cauliflower—Cook well on low heat for 5 minutes.
4. Add egg whites, mix with vegetables.
5. When eggs are cooked, garnish with spring onion, black pepper. Serve hot.

Nutrition: Calories 240| Total Fat 16.6g| Cholesterol 372mg| Sodium 195mg| Total Carbohydrate 7.8g| Dietary Fiber 2.7g| Protein 15.3g| Potassium 605.2mg| Phosphorus 253.6mg

25. Diet Breakfast

Preparation Time: 10 minutes
Cooking Time: 30 minutes
Servings: 2
Ingredients:

- 3 egg whites
- ¼ tsp. garlic, minced
- 2 tbsp. bell pepper, chopped
- ¼ cup cabbage, chopped
- ¼ cup mushrooms
- Black pepper
- 2 tbsp. jalapeno, chopped

Directions:

1. In a saucepan, sauté all ingredients, add the mushroom to the last.
2. Do not overcook vegetables.
3. Then add pepper and garlic to the eggs.
4. Scramble on Low Heat.
5. Sprinkle with basil and serve

Nutrition:
Calories 176 | Protein 7.3 g | Carbohydrates 9.2 g | Fat 8.2 g | Cholesterol 132 mg | Sodium 162 mg | Potassium 211 mg | Phosphorus 115 mg | Calcium 17.4 mg | Fiber 3 g

26. Breakfast Burrito

Preparation Time: 10 minutes
Cooking Time: 30 minutes
Servings: 2
Ingredients:

- 2 flour tortillas
- 4 egg whites
- 3 tbsp. green chilies, chopped
- ½ tsp. hot pepper sauce
- ¼ tsp. ground cumin

Directions:

1. In a skillet over medium flame, spray cooking oil.
2. In a mixing bowl, add eggs, cumin, green chilies, hot sauce, and whisk well.
3. Add whisked eggs into a skillet. Let it cook for two minutes until eggs are cooked.
4. Now, lay burritos on a hot skillet and or microwave them and place egg mixture on them.
5. Roll and fold on sides.
6. Serve hot

Nutrition:
Calories 366 | Protein 18 g | Carbohydrates 33 g | Fat 18 g | Cholesterol 372 mg | Sodium 394 mg | potassium 215 mg | Phosphorus 254 mg | Calcium 117 mg | Fiber 2.5 g

27. Maple Pancakes

Preparation Time: 10 minutes
Cooking Time: 30 minutes
Servings: 2
Ingredients:

- 1 cup 1 % low-fat milk
- 1 cup all-purpose flour
- 1 tbsp. honey
- 2 pinches salt
- 1 tbsp. maple extract
- 2 large egg whites
- 2 tsp. baking powder
- 2 tbsp. olive oil

Directions:

1. In a mixing bowl, mix flour, baking powder, salt. Mix well.
2. Set it aside.
3. In a big mixing bowl, mix egg whites, oil, maple extract, honey, and milk.
4. Now mix dry ingredients and wet ingredients. Do not over mix. It should be lumpy.
5. Put a skillet over medium flame, spray cooking oil, and pour the batter and cook pancakes until brown on both sides.
6. Serve hot

Nutrition:
Calories 178 | Protein 6 g | Carbohydrates 25 g | Fat 6 g | Cholesterol 2 mg | Sodium 267 mg | Potassium 126 mg | Phosphorus 116 mg | Calcium 174 mg | Fiber 0.7 g |

28. Mini Frittatas

Preparation Time: 10 minutes
Cooking Time: 30 minutes
Servings: 2
Ingredients:

- ¼ cup low fat shredded cheese
- ⅓ cup chopped red bell pepper
- ⅓ cup zucchini, chopped
- ⅓ cup broccoli, diced
- 2-3 tbsp. fresh basil
- ¼ tsp. pepper
- ½ tbsp. seasoning (salt-free)
- 10-12 eggs' whites and 3 yolks

Directions:

1. Let the oven Preheat to 375°F.
2. Spray the muffin pan with oil.
3. In a mixing bowl, mix zucchini, basil, red bell pepper, and broccoli.
4. In another bowl, mix pepper, cheese, seasoning (salt-free), eggs, and salt.
5. Mix the egg mix with vegetables.
6. Pour the egg mixture into muffin cups, at least ⅓ cup.
7. Bake for 18-20 minutes at 375°F or until cooked.
8. Serve right away.

Nutrition: Calories 245 | Protein 11 g | Carbohydrates 9.2 g | Fat 7.7 g | Cholesterol 121 mg | Sodium 99.2 mg | Potassium 201 mg | Phosphorus 109 mg | Calcium 27.9 mg | Fiber 2 g

29. Dilly Scrambled Eggs

Preparation Time: 10 minutes
Cooking Time: 30 minutes
Servings: 2
Ingredients:

- 1 tsp. dried dill weed
- 3 large egg white
- 1 tbsp. crumbled goat cheese
- ⅛ tsp. black pepper

Directions:

1. In a bowl, mix eggs.

2. Pour the egg mixture into the skillet over medium flame.
3. Sprinkle dill weed and black pepper to eggs.
4. Cook until eggs are done.
5. Garnish with goat cheese.
6. Serve right away.

Nutrition:
Calories 194|Protein 16 g| Carbohydrates 1 g| Fat 14 g| Cholesterol 334 mg| Sodium 213 mg| Potassium 162 mg| Phosphorus 50 mg| Calcium 214 mg| Fiber 0.2 g

30. Start Your Day Bagel

Preparation Time: 10 minutes
Cooking Time: 30 minutes
Servings: 2

Ingredients:
- 1 bagel
- 2 red onion slices
- 2 tbsp. low-fat cream cheese
- 1 tsp. lemon-pepper seasoning (low-sodium)
- 2 small tomato slices

Directions:
1. Slice the bagel and toast to your liking
2. Spread cream cheese on each ½ bagel.
3. Add tomato slice, onion slice.
4. Sprinkle with lemon pepper.

Nutrition:
Calories 134|Protein 5 g| Carbohydrates 19 g| Fat 6 g| Cholesterol 15 mg| Sodium 219 mg| Potassium 162 mg| Phosphorus 50 mg| calcium 9 mg| Fiber 1.6 g

31. Egg Muffins

Preparation Time: 10 minutes
Cooking Time: 30 minutes
Servings: 2

Ingredients:
- 10 large eggs, whites
- 1 cup bell peppers
- 2 cups ground pork
- 1 cup onion
- ½ tsp. garlic minced
- ½ tsp. herb seasoning
- ¼ tsp. poultry seasoning (no salt)
- 2 pinches salt to taste
- 2 tbsp. milk substitute

Directions:
1. Let the oven and preheat to 350°F and spray cooking oil on the muffin tin
2. Chop the vegetables finely.
3. In a bowl, mix garlic pork, herb seasoning, poultry seasoning to make sausage.

4. In a skillet, cook the sausage until done and drain the liquid, if any
5. Whisk the eggs with salt and milk.
6. Add vegetables and sausage crumbles, mix well.
7. Add egg mixture into muffin tins, leave some space on top.
8. Bake for 18 to 20 minutes or until done.
9. Serve hot.

Nutrition:
Calories 154|Protein 12 g| Carbohydrates 3 g| Fat 10 g| Cholesterol 230 mg| Sodium 155 mg| Potassium 200 mg| Phosphorus 154 mg| Calcium 37 mg| Fiber 0.5 g

32. Quick & Easy Apple Oatmeal Custard

Preparation Time: 10 minutes
Cooking Time: 30 minutes
Servings: 2

Ingredients:
- ½ cup almond milk
- ⅓ cup quick-cooking oatmeal
- ¼ tsp. cinnamon
- ½ apple
- 2 egg whites

Directions:
1. Finely diced the ½ apple.
2. In a large mug, add almond milk, egg, and oats. Mix well with a fork.
3. Add apple and cinnamon. Mix well.
4. Microwave for two minutes on high.
5. Fluff it with a fork.
6. Cook for another sixty-second if required.
7. Add in a little milk or water if the consistency is too thick.

Nutrition:
Calories 248|Protein 11 g| Carbohydrates 33 g| Fat 8 g| Cholesterol 186 mg| Sodium 164 mg| Potassium 362 mg| phosphorus 240 mg| Calcium 154 mg| Fiber 5.8 g

33. Microwave Coffee Cup Egg Scramble

Preparation Time: 10 minutes
Cooking Time: 30 minutes
Servings: 2

Ingredients:
- 2 tbsp. 1 % low-fat milk
- 2 large egg whites

Directions:
1. Spray the coffee cup with oil. Add eggs and milk and whisk.
2. Put the coffee cup in the microwave, let it cook for 45 seconds, then remove and fluff with a fork.
3. Cook for an additional 30-45 seconds, until eggs are almost done.

4. Add pepper and enjoy.

Nutrition:
Calories 117 | Protein 15 g| Carbohydrates 3 g| Fat 5 g| Cholesterol 188 mg| Sodium 194 mg| Potassium 226 mg| Phosphorus 138 mg| Calcium 72 mg| Fiber 0 g

34. No-Fuss Microwave Egg White French Toast

Preparation Time: 10 minutes
Cooking Time: 30 minutes
Servings: 2

Ingredients:
- ½ cup egg whites
- 1 slice bread
- 2 tbsp. sugar-free syrup
- 1 tsp. unsalted butter, softened

Directions:
1. Add bread to the slice. Cut into cubes.
2. Add cubed slices into a bowl.
3. Add egg whites over bread pieces
4. Add syrup on top. Microwave for 60 seconds or more until eggs are set.

Nutrition:
Calories 200 | Protein 15 g| Carbohydrates 24 g| Fat 5 g| Cholesterol 11 mg| Sodium 415 mg| Potassium 235 mg| Phosphorus 54 mg| Calcium 50 mg| Fiber 0.7 g

35. Tofu Scrambler

Preparation Time: 10 minutes
Cooking Time: 30 minutes
Servings: 2

Ingredients:
- 1 tsp. onion powder
- 1 tsp. olive oil
- ¼ cup diced green bell pepper
- ¼ cup red bell pepper, diced
- ⅛ tsp. turmeric
- 1 cup Firm tofu (less than 10 % calcium)
- 2 clove garlic, minced

Directions:
1. In a non-stick pan, add bell peppers and garlic in olive oil.
2. Rinse the tofu and add in the skillet to break it into pieces with hands.
3. Add all the remaining ingredients.
4. Stir often, and cook on medium flame until the tofu becomes a light golden brown, for almost 20 minutes.
5. Serve warm.

Nutrition:
Calories 213 Cal | Total Fat 13 g| Saturated Fat 2 g| Trans Fat 0 g| Cholesterol 0 mg| Sodium 24 mg| Carbohydrates 10 g |Protein 18 g| Phosphorus 242 mg| Potassium 467 mg| Dietary Fiber 2 g| Calcium 274 mg

36. Southwest Baked Egg Breakfast Cups

Preparation Time: 10 minutes
Cooking Time: 30 minutes
Servings: 2

Ingredients:
- 3 cups rice, cooked
- ½ cup shredded cheddar cheese
- ½ cup chopped green chilies
- ¼ cup cherry peppers diced
- ½ cup skim milk
- 3 egg whites whisked
- ½ tsp. ground cumin
- ½ tsp. black pepper

Directions:
1. In a bowl, mix chilies, cherry peppers, eggs, cumin, 2 ounces of cheese, rice, black pepper.
2. Spray the muffin tins with oil
3. Pour mix into muffins tin. Garnish with cheese.
4. Bake for 15 minutes at 400°F or until set.

Nutrition:
Calories 109 Cal | Total Fat 4 g| Saturated Fat 2 g| Trans Fat 0 g| Cholesterol 41 mg| Sodium 79 mg| Carbohydrates 13 g| Protein 5 g| Phosphorus 91 mg| Potassium 82 mg| Dietary Fiber 0.5 g| Calcium 91 mg

37. Stuffed Breakfast Biscuits

Preparation Time: 10 minutes
Cooking Time: 30 minutes
Servings: 2

Ingredients:
- ½ tsp. baking powder
- 1 tbsp. honey
- 1 tbsp. lemon juice
- 8 tbsp. softened unsalted butter
- ¾ cup milk
- 2 cups flour

Filling:
- 1 cup shredded cheddar cheese
- 5 egg whites
- ¼ cup scallions, thinly sliced
- 1 cup chopped bacon (reduced-sodium)

Directions:
1. Let the oven Preheat to 425°F.

For Filling:
1. Cook the eggs, scrambled

2. Cook bacon to a crisp.
3. Mix filling ingredients and set it aside

The Dough:
1. In a big bowl, add all the dry ingredients.
2. Add in butter and cut with a fork, and add in lemon juice and milk. Knead well.
3. Spray muffin tin with oil generously.
4. Pour ¼ cup of mixture into the muffin tins.
5. Bake for 10-12 minutes at 425°F until golden brown.

Nutrition:
Calories 330 Cal| Total Fat 23 g| Saturated Fat 11 g| Trans Fat 0.6 g| Cholesterol 105 mg|Sodium 329 mg| Carbohydrates 19 g| Protein 11 g| Phosphorus 170 mg| Potassium 152 mg| Dietary Fiber 1 g| Calcium 107 mg

38. Cheesesteak Quiche

Preparation Time: 10 minutes
Cooking Time: 30 minutes
Servings: 2

Ingredients:
- 2 tbsp. olive oil
- 2 cups trimmed sirloin steak, roughly chopped
- 1 cup onion, chopped
- ½ cup cheese, shredded
- 6 egg whites, whisked
- ½ tsp. ground black pepper
- 1 cup low-fat cream
- Par-cooked prepared piecrust

Directions:
1. In a pan with oil, Sauté onions, and chopped steak. Cook until meat is cooked. Let it cool for ten minutes. Mix in cheese, set it aside.
2. In a bowl, whisk cream eggs with black pepper, mix it well.
3. Add cheese mix and steak on pie crust, then add the egg mixture on top and ½ hour bake at 350°F. and turn off the oven and cover the quiche with foil.
4. Let it sit for ten minutes, then serve.

Nutrition:
Calories 527 Cal| Total Fat 19 g| Saturated Fat 17 g| Trans Fat 1 g| Cholesterol 240 mg| Sodium 392 mg| Carbohydrates 22 g| Protein 22 g| Phosphorus 281 mg| Potassium 308 mg| Dietary Fiber 1 g| Calcium 137 mg

39. Chocolate Pancakes with Moon Pie Stuffing

Preparation Time: 10 minutes
Cooking Time: 30 minutes
Servings: 2

Ingredients:
Moon Pie Stuffing:
- ¼ cup heavy cream
- 1 tbsp. cocoa powder (unsweetened)
- ½ cup low-fat softened cream cheese
- 2 tbsp. honey

Chocolate Pancakes:
- 1 large egg white
- 1 cup flour
- 3 tbsp. cocoa powder (unsweetened)
- ½ tsp. baking powder
- 2 tbsp. olive oil
- 1 tbsp. lemon juice
- 3 tbsp. honey
- 2 tsp. vanilla extract
- 1 cup almond milk

Directions:
Moon Pie Filling:
1. Beat cocoa and heavy cream together until stiff peaks are formed.
2. Whip in cream cheese, marshmallow cream, and whey protein powder for about a minute or until well blended, but don't overheat. Cover and set aside in the fridge.

Pancakes:
1. Mix all the dry ingredients in a large bowl and set aside.
2. Mix all the wet ingredients in a medium-size bowl.
3. Slowly fold in wet ingredients to the dry ingredients just until wet, but don't over mix.
4. Cook the pancakes on a lightly oiled griddle on medium heat or 375°F.
5. Use about ⅛ cup of batter to form 4-inch pancakes, flipping when they bubble.

Nutrition:
Calories 194 Cal |Total Fat 9 g| Saturated Fat 4 g| Trans Fat 0 g| Cholesterol 36 mg| Sodium 121 mg| Carbohydrates 22 g| Protein 7 g| Phosphorus 134 mg| Potassium 135 mg| Dietary Fiber 1 g| Calcium 67 mg

40. Apple Muffins

Preparation Time: 10 minutes
Cooking Time: 30 minutes
Servings: 2

Ingredients:
- 1 ½ tsp. cinnamon
- 1 ½ cups raw apple
- ½ cup water
- 1 cup honey
- ½ cup olive oil
- 2 large egg white
- 1 tbsp. vanilla

- 1 ½ cup all-purpose white flour
- 1 tsp. baking powder

Directions:
1. Let the oven and preheat to 400°F. add muffin papers in a muffin tin.
2. Peel and chop the apple into small pieces.
3. In a bowl, whisk eggs with water, honey, oil, vanilla and mix well
4. In another bowl, mix baking powder, one teaspoon cinnamon, flour.
5. Sift the flour mixture into the egg mix.
6. The batter should be lumpy. Add in the apple pieces.
7. Pour batter into muffin cups, sprinkle cinnamon on top. Enjoy warm.

Nutrition: Sodium 177 mg| Protein 3 g| Potassium 46 mg| Phosphorus 34 mg |Calcium 10 mg| Calories 162 kcal| Fat 10 g| Water 60 g |Carbohydrates 15 g

41. Breakfast Casserole

Preparation Time: 10 minutes
Cooking Time: 30 minutes
Servings: 2

Ingredients:
- 1 cup 1 % low-fat milk
- 1 cup pork sausage (reduced-fat)
- 5 large egg whites
- ½ tsp. dry mustard
- 1 cup cream cheese (low-fat)
- ½ chopped onion
- 4 slices white bread, cut into cubes

Directions:
1. Let the oven and preheat to 325°F
2. Break the sausage and cook in a pan, set it aside
3. In a blender, pulse the rest of the ingredients. Do not add bread yet.
4. Add the cooked sausage to the mix.
5. In a 9 by 9 dish, add the bread, and add sausage mix on top
6. Bake for 55 minutes.
7. Serve hot and enjoy.

Nutrition:
Calories 224 | Protein 11 g| Carbohydrates 9 g| Fat 16 g| Cholesterol 149 mg| Sodium 356 mg| Potassium 201 mg| Phosphorus 159 mg| Calcium 97 mg |fiber 0.4 g|

42. Apple Onion Omelet

Preparation Time: 10 minutes
Cooking Time: 30 minutes
Servings: 2

Ingredients:
- 1 tbsp. butter

- 3 large eggs whites
- 1 tbsp. water
- ⅛ tsp. black pepper
- ¼ cup 1 % low-fat milk
- 2 tbsp. shredded cheddar cheese
- ¾ cup sweet onion
- 1 big apple

Directions:
1. Let the oven Preheat to 400°F.
2. Peel and clean apple. Thinly slice the onion and apples
3. In a bowl, whisk the egg with milk, pepper, water. Set it aside.
4. In a pan, over a low flame, melt the butter.
5. Add apple and onion to the butter, cook for five minutes.
6. Add egg mix on top cook on medium flame until the edges are set.
7. Add the cheese on the top.
8. Put the skillet in the oven and bake for 10-12 minutes, or until set.
9. Serve hot

Nutrition: Calories 284 | Protein 13 | Carbohydrates 22 | Fat 16 | Cholesterol 303| Sodium 169| potassium 341|Phosphorus 238 |Calcium 147 |Fiber 3.5

43. Beach Boy Omelet

Preparation Time: 10 minutes
Cooking Time: 30 minutes
Servings: 2

Ingredients:
- 2 tbsp. green bell pepper, chopped
- 1 tsp. canola oil
- 2 tbsp. (shredded) hash browns
- 2 tbsp. soy milk
- 1 egg and 2 egg whites
- 2 tbsp. onion, chopped

Directions:
1. In a pan, heat the oil over medium flame. Sauté green pepper and onion for two minutes
2. Then add hash browns, cook for five minutes.
3. Whisk eggs with non-dairy creamer or soy milk
4. In another pan, cook the eggs until set.
5. Add the hash brown mixture in the center of eggs, wrap with eggs, and serve

Nutrition: Calories 228 | Protein 15 g |Carbohydrates 12 g |Fat 13 g |Cholesterol 165 mg |Sodium 180 mg |Potassium 307 mg| Phosphorus 128 mg |Calcium 38 mg |Fiber 0.9 g

44. Mushroom & Red Pepper Omelet

Preparation Time: 10 minutes
Cooking Time: 30 minutes
Servings: 2

Ingredients:

- ½ cup raw mushroom
- 3 large egg white
- 2 tbsp. onion
- ¼ cup red peppers
- 2 tbsp. whipped cream cheese
- 2 tsp. butter
- ¼ tsp. black pepper

Directions:

1. Chop up the red peppers, onion, and mushroom
2. In a pan, melt the butter (one teaspoon). Sauté red peppers, onion, and mushroom. Set it aside.
3. Melt another teaspoon of butter in a pan. Cook eggs. When eggs are half cooked, pour vegetable mix with cream cheese on top. Cook eggs until set
4. Continue cooking until eggs are set.
5. Fold the half omelet on top of the cream cheese mix. Add black pepper and serve

Nutrition:

Calories 178 | Protein 8.8 g | Carbohydrates 8.2 g | Fat 6.7 g | Cholesterol 132 mg | Sodium 156 mg | Potassium 201 mg | Phosphorus 121 mg | Calcium 21 mg | Fiber 0.4 g

45. Peach Berry Parfait

Preparation Time: 5 minutes
Cooking Time: 0 minutes
Servings: 2

Ingredients:

- 1 cup plain, unsweetened yogurt, divided
- 1 tsp. vanilla extract
- 1 small peach, diced
- ½ cup blueberries
- 2 tbsp. walnut pieces

Directions:

1. In a small bowl, mix the yogurt and vanilla. Add 2 tablespoons of yogurt to each of 2 cups. Divide the diced peach and the blueberries between the cups and top with the remaining yogurt.
2. Sprinkle each cup with 1 tablespoon of walnut pieces.

Cooking Tip: Make these up to three days in advance, cover, and refrigerate until ready to eat.

Nutrition:

Calories: 191; Total Fat: 10g; Saturated Fat: 3g; Cholesterol: 15mg; Carbohydrates: 14g; Fiber: 14g; Protein: 12g; Phosphorus: 189mg; Potassium: 327mg; Sodium: 40mg.

46. Open-Faced Bagel Breakfast Sandwich

Preparation Time: 5 minutes
Cooking Time: 0 minutes
Servings: 2

Ingredients:

- 1 multigrain bagel, halved
- 2 tbsp. cream cheese, divided
- 2 slices tomato
- 1 slice red onion
- Freshly ground black pepper
- 1 cup micro-greens

Ingredients:

1. In a toaster or oven, lightly toast the bagel.
2. Spread 1 tablespoon of cream cheese on each of the bagel halves, and top each half with 1 slice of tomato and a couple of rings of onion. Season with black pepper. Top each half with ½ cup of micro greens and serve.

Substitution Tip: Swap out the red onion for scallions or chives, the tomato for red bell pepper strips, or the micro greens for sprouts as needed to fit what you have on hand. You can also substitute the cream cheese with feta or Brie; just be sure to keep the portion size around 1 tablespoon per serving.

Nutrition:

Calories: 156; Total Fat: 6g; Saturated Fat: 3g; Cholesterol: 18mg; Carbohydrates: 22g; Fiber: 3g; Protein: 5g; Protein: 5g; Phosphorus: 98mg; Potassium: 163mg; Sodium: 195mg.

47. Bulgur Bowl with Strawberries and Walnuts

Preparation Time: 15 minutes
Cooking Time: 10 minutes
Servings: 2

Ingredients:

- 1 cup bulgur
- 1 cup strawberries, sliced
- 4 tbsp. (¼-cup) Homemade Rice Milk or unsweetened store-bought rice milk
- 4 tsp. brown sugar
- 4 tsp. extra-virgin olive oil
- 4 tbsp. (¼-cup) walnut pieces
- 4 tbsp. (¼-cup) cacao nibs (optional)

Directions:

1. In a small pot, combine the bulgur with 2 cups of water. Bring to a boil, then lower the heat and let simmer, covered, for 12 to 15 minutes, until tender. Remove from the heat and drain any excess water.
2. In each of four bowls, add a quarter of the bulgur and top with ¼ cup of strawberries, 1 tablespoon of rice milk, 1 teaspoon of brown sugar, 1 teaspoon

of olive oil, 1 tablespoon of walnut pieces, and 1 tablespoon of cacao nibs (if using).

Cooking Tip: Bulgur can be made up to five days in advance and stored in an airtight container in the refrigerator. To serve, heat in the microwave or, on a warm day, serve cold for a refreshing breakfast bowl.

Nutrition: Calories: 190; Total Fat: 9g; Saturated Fat: 1g; Cholesterol: 0mg; Carbohydrates: 26g; Fiber: 5g; Protein: 4g; Phosphorus: 66mg; Potassium: 153mg; Sodium: 13mg.

48. Overnight Oats Three Ways

Preparation Time: 5 minutes
Cooking Time: 0 minutes
Servings: 2
Ingredients:

- ¾ cup Homemade Rice Milk or unsweetened store-bought rice milk
- ½ cup plain, unsweetened yogurt
- ½ cup rolled oats
- 1 tbsp. ground flaxseed
- 1 tsp. vanilla extract
- 2 tsp. honey

VARIATION 1: CHOCOLATE PEANUT BUTTER

- 2 tbsp. natural unsalted peanut butter
- 2 tbsp. cocoa powder

VARIATION 2: BLUEBERRY CHEESECAKE

- ¼ cup blueberries
- 2 tbsp. cream cheese, at room temperature,
- Zest and juice of ½ lemon

Directions:

1. In a medium bowl, mix the rice milk, yogurt, oats, flaxseed, vanilla, and honey.
2. Add the ingredients to make your preferred variation and stir to blend.
3. Divide between two jars, cover, and refrigerate for at least 4 hours or overnight.

Substitution Tip: These oats can be flavored to suit your tastes. Strawberries, raspberries, blackberries, and peaches all go well with oats. For an extra nutritional boost, try adding a handful of unsalted nuts, or a teaspoon of chia seeds or hemp seeds to your bowl.

Nutrition: Calories: 196; Total Fat: 7g; Saturated Fat: 2g; Cholesterol: 7mg; Carbohydrates: 25g; Fiber: 3g; Protein: 8g; Phosphorus: 99mg; Potassium: 114mg; Sodium: 63mg.

49. Buckwheat Pancakes

Preparation Time: 10 minutes
Cooking Time: 15 minutes
Servings: 2
Ingredients:

- 1 ¾ cups Homemade Rice Milk or unsweetened store-bought rice milk
- 2 tsp. white vinegar
- 1 cup buckwheat flour
- ½ cup all-purpose flour
- 1 tbsp. sugar
- 2 tsp. Phosphorus-Free Baking Powder
- 1 large egg
- 1 tsp. vanilla extract
- 2 tbsp. butter for the skillet

Directions:

1. In a small bowl, combine the rice, milk, and vinegar. Let sit for 5 minutes.
2. Meanwhile, in a large bowl, mix the buckwheat flour and all-purpose flour. Add the sugar and baking powder, stirring to blend.
3. Add the egg and vanilla to the rice milk and stir to blend. Add the wet ingredients to the dry and stir until just mixed.
4. In a large skillet over medium heat, melt 1 ½ teaspoon of butter. Use a ¼-cup measuring cup to scoop the batter into the skillet. Cook for 2 to 3 minutes, until small bubbles form on the surface of the pancakes. Flip and cook on the opposite side for 1 to 2 minutes.
5. Transfer the pancakes to a serving platter, and in batches, continue cooking the remaining batter in the skillet, adding more butter as needed.

Lower Sodium Tip: There are several low-sodium and no-sodium baking powders on the market, but they can be hard to find in grocery stores. If you need to lower your sodium further, purchase low-sodium or no-sodium baking powder online.

Nutrition:
Calories: 264; Total Fat: 9g; Saturated Fat: 3g; Cholesterol: 58mg; Carbohydrates: 39g; Fiber: 3g; Protein: 7g; Phosphorus: 147mg; Potassium: 399mg; Sodium: 232mg.

Chapter 5: Lunch Recipes

50. Mint Couscous

Preparation Time: 10 minutes
Cooking Time: 15 minutes
Servings: 2
Ingredients:

- 1 cup (225-g.) couscous
- 1 pint (600-ml.) water
- 3 tbsp. fresh mint leaves, chopped
- 2 tbsp. olive oil
- Salt

Directions:

1. Bring the water to a boil in a pan and stir in the salt.
2. Add the couscous, lower the heat, cover the pan, and let cook for 5 minutes.
3. Take off the heat and leave covered to set for another 5 minutes.
4. Drizzle the olive oil and add the fresh mint leaves on top.

Nutrition:
Calories: 85kcal, Carbs: 13.6g, Protein: 2.3g, Sodium: 10mg, Potassium: 56mg, Phosphorus: 16mg, Fat: 2.4g, Dietary Fiber: 1.1g, Sugars: 0.1g

51. Lettuce Hot Dogs

Preparation Time: 10 minutes
Cooking Time: 15 minutes
Servings: 2.
Ingredients:

- 4 big lettuce leaves
- 4 low-sodium frankfurter sausages
- 1 small onion, chopped
- 1 slice bacon, cut into bits
- Drizzle of mustard

Directions:

1. Cook the sausages on the grill for 2-3 minutes on each side.
2. While the frankfurters are cooked, sauté the bacon bits in a small pan until nice and crisp.
3. Assemble each hot dog by layering one dog on each lettuce leaf, and adding the onion, bacon bits on top. Drizzle with mustard to finish.
4. Serve while hot.

Nutrition:
Calories: 215kcal, Carbs: 3.1g, Protein: 8.1g, Sodium: 252mg, Potassium: 177mg, Phosphorus: 73mg, Fat: 18.9g, Dietary Fiber: 0.5g, Sugars: 0.9g

52. Tofu & Quinoa Salad

Preparation Time: 20 minutes
Cooking Time: 0 minutes
Servings: 2
Ingredients:

- 12 oz. (336-g.) extra firm tofu, pat dried, and cut into small cubes
- 1 big Boston lettuce head, roughly chopped
- ½ cup (125-g.) cooked quinoa
- ½ cup (112-ml.) olive oil
- 1 tbsp. mustard
- 1 tsp. honey
- Salt-pepper

Directions:

1. Combine all the liquid ingredients in a small bowl to make your dressing.
2. Toss the tofu cubes over the lettuce leaves and stir in the quinoa.
3. Pour the dressing and toss everything well to combine.
4. Serve.

Nutrition:
Calories: 367kcal, Carbs: 10.7g, Protein: 10.5g, Sodium: 92mg, Potassium: 204mg, Phosphorus: 196 mg, Fat: 32.1g, Dietary Fiber: 2.7g, Sugars: 2.5g

53. Easy Pasta with Vodka & Tomato Sauce

Preparation Time: 18 minutes
Cooking Time: 15 minutes
Servings: 2
Ingredients:

- 10 oz. (280-g.) dry fettuccine pasta
- 1 cup (240-ml.) low sodium tomato pasta sauce
- ½ cup (120-ml.) vodka
- 1 tbsp. butter, melted
- 2 tbsp. parmesan cheese, grated
- Dash of salt
- Pepper

Directions:

1. Cook the fettuccine pasta approx. for 12 minutes in boiling water or according to package instructions. Drain and add the butter to prevent it from sticking
2. Return the pasta to a deep pan and add the vodka. Let evaporate for a couple of minutes.
3. Add the tomato sauce and cook on medium heat until the sauce has started to bubble (approx. 5 minutes). Add a dash of salt and pepper.

4. Serve with the parmesan cheese on top.

Nutrition:
Calories: 170kcal, Carbs: 22.2g, Protein: 5.3g, Sodium: 162mg, Potassium: 226mg, Phosphorus: 75mg, Fat: 5.7g, Dietary Fiber: 2.7g, Sugars: 3.5g

54. Spaghetti with Pesto & Chicken

Preparation Time: 15 minutes
Cooking Time: 15 minutes
Servings: 2

Ingredients:

- 12 oz. (340-g.) whole-wheat spaghetti
- ⅔ cup (200-g.) cooked chicken meat (no skin or bones)
- 2 tbsp. pesto sauce
- Dash of pepper

Directions:

1. Cooked the whole-wheat spaghetti in boiling water for 15 minutes or according to package instructions. Drain and set aside.
2. Add the pesto sauce to the pasta and toss to combine. Add the chicken meat and season with a dash of pepper.
3. Serve.

Nutrition:
Calories: 184kcal, Carbs: 22.9g, Protein: 11.6g, Sodium: 87mg, Potassium: 107mg, Phosphorus: 145mg, Fat: 5.8g, Dietary Fiber: 3.9g, Sugars: 1g

55. Broccoli Salad

Preparation Time: 15 minutes
Cooking Time: 15 minutes
Servings: 2

Ingredients:

- 4 cups (1-kg.) broccoli florets
- 1 large carrot, peeled and shredded
- 1 ½ cups (280-g.) red cabbage, thinly sliced
- 4 scallions, thinly sliced
- ¼ cup raisins
- 2 tbsp. sesame seeds
- 1 liter/4 cups water

For the dressing:

- 1 tbsp. vinegar
- 2 ½ tbsp. light mayo
- 1 tbsp. dry basil
- 1 tsp. garlic flakes
- ½ tsp. cayenne pepper

Directions:

1. Pre-boil the broccoli florets in boiling water until slightly soft but still firm (around 7-8 minutes). Drain and keep in a big bowl.

2. Meanwhile, combine all the dressing ingredients in a small bowl.
3. Combine the broccoli florets with carrot, cabbage, scallion's raisins, and sesame seeds.
4. Pour the dressing over the veggie and seed mixture and toss well to combine.
5. Place in the fridge for 20 minutes for the flavors to merge and serve.

Nutrition:
Calories: 58kcal, Carbs: 8.7g, Protein: 1.6g, Sodium: 88mg, Potassium: 295mg, Phosphorus: 141 mg, Fat: 1.2g, Dietary Fiber: 1.8, Sugars: 1.2g

56. Slow Cooked Chuck

Preparation Time: 10 minutes
Cooking Time: 1 hour
Servings: 2

Ingredients:

- 2 ½ lbs. (700-g.) beef chuck (for roasting)
- 1 large onion, sliced into thin rounds
- 2 tbsp. canola oil
- 1 tsp. garlic powder
- ½ tsp. cayenne pepper
- 1 tbsp. dried basil

Directions:

1. Add the canola oil into the slow cooker and add the onions.
2. Season the chuck with the spices and place them on top of the onions inside the slow cooker. Reduce the heat to medium-low.
3. Cover the lid and cook for 40 minutes undisturbed.
4. Open the lid and cook for another 20 minutes. Take off the heat and serve with the roasted onions around the meat.

Nutrition:
Calories: 575kcal, Carbs: 4.2g, Protein: 59.1, Sodium: 216mg, Potassium: 226 mg, Phosphorus: 107 mg, Fat: 24.6g, Dietary Fiber: 0.9g, Sugars: 1.6g

57. Baked Tuna

Preparation Time: 10 minutes
Cooking Time: 25 minutes
Servings: 3

Ingredients:

- 14 oz. (400-g.) can of tuna in water, drained
- ⅔ cup (200-g.) white onion, chopped
- ¼ cup (15-g.) green pepper, diced
- ¼ cup (15-g.) pimento
- ½ cup (115-g.) low sodium mayonnaise
- 2 tbsp. parmesan cheese, grated
- ¼ cup (30-g.) breadcrumbs

- Non-stick cooking spray

Directions:
1. Preheat your oven to 375°F/190°C.
2. Coat a square baking dish with the cooking spray.
3. Combine the tuna, peppers, pimento, onion, and mayo in a large bowl.
4. In a smaller bowl, combine the breadcrumbs with the parmesan cheese.
5. Place the tuna mixture into the baking dish and top with the breadcrumb/cheese mixture.
6. Bake in the oven for 20-25 minutes or until the topping/crust is golden brown.

Nutrition:
Calories: 271mg, Carbs: 10.1, Protein: 17.1g, Sodium: 299mg, Potassium: 209mg, Phosphorus: 254mg, Fat: 6.1, Dietary Fiber: 0.8g, Sugars: 1.7g

58. Vidalia Onion Pie

Preparation Time: 10 minutes
Cooking Time: 30 minutes
Servings: 2

Ingredients:
- 1 ½ cup (160-g.) crackers, crushed
- 2 cups (104-g.) sweet Vidalia onions, sliced
- ¼ cup (56-g.) cheddar cheese
- ¾ cup (180-ml.) ½-and-½
- ⅓ cup (76-g.) lightly salted butter, melted
- 2 tbsp. butter
- ⅛ tsp. black pepper
- 2 eggs

Directions:
1. Preheat your oven at 350°F/175°C.
2. Combine the crushed crackers with the melted butter and press the mixture into a 9" baking pan.
3. Heat a medium pan over medium heat and add the 2 tablespoons of butter to melt together with the onions. Sauté the onions until transparent, but not brown.
4. Meanwhile, combine the eggs with the ½-and-½ and the pepper.
5. Spread the onions over the crust. Pour the egg mixture over the onions and top with the cheddar cheese.
6. Bake for 30 minutes or until eggs and cheese are set.

Nutrition: Calories: 307kcal, Carbs: 16.7g, Protein: 5.6g, Sodium: 404mg, Potassium: 197mg, Phosphorus: 142mg, Fat: 24.6g, Dietary Fiber: 1g, Sugars: 7.1g

59. Runza Lamb Pocket

Preparation Time: 10 minutes
Cooking Time: 25 minutes
Servings: 2

Ingredients:
- 1 lb. (½ -kg.) ground lamb
- 4 cups (350-g.) cabbage, shredded
- 1 loaf bread dough, frozen
- ¼ cup (25-g.) onion, chopped
- ¼ tsp. pepper
- Dash of salt
- Cooking spray
- 1 liter water

Directions:
1. Thaw the bread dough according to package instructions.
2. Preheat your oven at 350°F/175°C. Meanwhile, boil the cabbage in water until tender.
3. Grease the bottom of the pan with cooking spray and cook the ground lamb, onion, and pepper until brown. Add the cabbage to the meat mixture.
4. Roll the bread dough into a rectangular shape and cut it into 12 square pieces of equal size.
5. Add the meat mixture to the center of each square and press the edges with a fork to seal.
6. Bake the pockets for 20-25 minutes.
7. Serve hot.

Nutrition:
Calories: 139kcal, Carbs: 4.2g, Protein: 7.1g, Sodium: 240mg, Potassium: 165mg, Phosphorus: 72mg, Fat: 10.4g, Dietary Fiber: 0.8g, Sugar: 0.7g

60. Quick BBQ Chicken Pizza

Preparation Time: 10 minutes
Cooking Time: 20 minutes
Servings: 2

Ingredients:
- 2 medium-sized corn tortillas (around 8 inches each)
- 4 oz. (115-g.) leftover cooked chicken, shredded
- 2 tbsp. spicy barbeque sauce
- 1 large red onion, sliced
- ¼ cup (30-g.) shredded Monterey jack cheese

Directions:
1. Spread 2 tablespoons of barbeque sauce over each tortilla.
2. Top with the shredded chicken and a few onion slices over each tortilla.
3. Finally, sprinkle and distribute the cheese on the tortillas.

4. Bake in the oven at 300°F/160°C for 12-15 minutes.

Nutrition:
Calories: 261kcal, Carbs: 24.1g, Protein: 22.64g, Sodium: 316mg, Potassium: 305 mg, Phosphorus: 335 mg, Fat: 8.5g, Dietary Fiber: 2.4g, Sugar: 4.1g

61. Butter Crab Risotto

Preparation Time: 10 minutes
Cooking Time: 18-20 minutes
Servings: 2

Ingredients:
- ⅔ cup (130-g.) white risotto rice
- ½ cup (60-g.) white crabmeat
- 2 tbsp. butter
- 2 long shallots, sliced
- ¼ cup (125-ml.) white wine
- 2 ½ cups (½-lt.) low sodium chicken stock or water
- 1 tbsp. Parmesan cheese, grated
- 1 tsp. salt
- ½ tsp. nutmeg

Directions:
1. Melt 1 tablespoon of butter in a deep skillet and once the butter is melted, add the crabmeat and shallots. Add the white wine and let cook until all the wine is evaporated.
2. Add the rice and give everything a good stir. Slowly incorporate the chicken stock into the rice mixture in small parts of ½ cup each time, while stirring. Stir for around a minute before you add the next part.
3. Once all the chicken stock has been added, cover the lid of the skillet and let cook until rice is cooked but creamy.
4. Add the remaining 1 tablespoon of butter in the mix, just a few moments before you take the risotto off the heat to add even more creaminess. Season with salt and nutmeg.
5. Sprinkle some parmesan cheese and serve.

Nutrition:
Calories: 217 kcal, Carbs: 30.37g, Protein: 3.54g, Sodium: 1149mg, Potassium: 113mg, Phosphorus: 63mg, Fat: 23.4g, Dietary Fiber: 1.3g, Sugars: 2.1g

62. Kale, Apple & Goat Cheese Salad

Preparation Time: 10 minutes
Cooking Time: 0 minutes
Servings: 2

Ingredients:
- 1 enormous bunch of kale
- 1 medium green apple, sliced
- 2 oz. (55-g.) goat cheese, crumbled
- 1 tbsp. white bread croutons
- 2 tbsp. Dijon mustard
- 1 tbsp. olive oil
- 1 tbsp. lemon
- 1 tsp. honey
- ½ tsp. thyme
- Salt/Pepper

Directions:
1. Cut the kale into big and rough parts (with your hands or with a knife).
2. Add the slices of the apple and the goat cheese and toss everything together.
3. In a small bowl or food processor, mix the olive oil, lemon, mustard, honey, thyme, salt, and pepper until smooth.
4. Pour the dressing over the salad and toss well.
5. Add the croutons on top and lightly toss again. Serve.

Nutrition: Calories: 256kcal, Carbs: 23.21g, Protein: 8.75g, Sodium: 304mg, Potassium: 242mg, Phosphorus: 205mg, Fat: 17.9g, Dietary Fiber: 4g, Sugars: 12.3g

63. Pinto Bean Burger Patties

Preparation Time: 10 minutes
Cooking Time: 10 minutes
Servings: 2

Ingredients:
- 1 can pinto beans (410-g.), drained
- 2 large spring onions, chopped
- 2 tbsp. gluten-free breadcrumbs
- 1 tbsp. olive oil (plus a drizzle for greasing your hands)
- 1 tsp. Italian seasoning
- 2 tbsp. fresh parsley, chopped
- Salt/Pepper
- Lettuce salad (optionally)

Directions:
1. Smash the pinto beans with a fork until you end up with a mushy paste (the beans don't have to be completely smashed).
2. In a small skillet, sauté the onions with olive oil until transparent.
3. Add the sautéed onions to the mashed beans. Stir and add the breadcrumbs, the Italian seasoning, and the parsley. Season with salt and pepper.
4. Grease your hands with some extra olive oil and take the mixture to form some medium flat patties with your hand (around 4-5 inches each).
5. Bake in a non-stick grilling pan for 3 minutes on each side.
6. Serve optionally with some lettuce salad.

Nutrition: Calories: 129kcal, Carbs: 18.98g, Protein: 5.67g, Sodium: 194mg, Potassium: 252mg, Phosphorus: 83mg, Fat: 4.2g, Dietary Fiber: 4.5g, Sugars: 0.8g

64. Jalapeno Popper Mushrooms

Preparation Time: 10 minutes
Cooking Time: 25 minutes
Servings: 2
Ingredients:

- 20 small white mushrooms, cleaned and stems trimmed
- 8 oz. (230-g.) cream cheese, at room temperature
- ⅔ cup (200-g.) shredded cheddar cheese
- 4 oz. (110-g.) can or jar jalapenos, finely chopped
- 2 cloves garlic, minced
- A drizzle olive oil
- Salt
- Pepper

Directions:

1. Combine the cream cheese with half of the cheddar cheese, garlic, and jalapenos. Season lightly with salt and pepper and stir everything together.
2. Drizzle the mushrooms lightly with the olive oil and begin stuffing the mushrooms with the mixture using a spoon (around 1 tbsp. for each mushroom).
3. Sprinkle the remaining cheddar cheese on top of the mushrooms.
4. Bake in the oven for 20-25 minutes at 350°F/175°C or until mushrooms have cooked, and the cheese is nicely melted.

Nutrition:
Calories: 163kcal, Carbs: 3.29g, Protein: 5.26g, Sodium: 186mg, Potassium: 160mg, Phosphorus: 97mg, Fat: 21.7g, Dietary Fiber: 0.7g, Sugars: 2.1g

65. Cranberry Glazed Turkey Meatballs

Preparation Time: 10 minutes
Cooking Time: 35 minutes
Servings: 2
Ingredients:

- 1 ¼ lb. (700-g.) ground turkey
- 2 large slices of whole-wheat bread, cut into small cubes
- 1 whole egg
- 2 tbsp. milk
- ¼ cup (30-g.) ricotta cheese
- 1 tbsp. dried thyme
- White flour (for dusting)
- ⅔ cup (160-g.) sugar-free cranberry sauce
- 3 tbsp. vegetable oil e.g., rapeseed oil
- Salt/Pepper

Directions:

1. Combine the white bread cubes with the milk and let them saturate. Add the egg, thyme, and ricotta cheese. Season with salt/pepper and mix well with your hands.
2. Form around 30 small balls with your hands (a tad smaller than a golf ball)
3. Lightly coat and roll the meatballs in flour and arrange them on a large baking sheet with parchment/wax paper.
4. Spray with some cooking spray on top and bake in the oven for 20 minutes at 350°F/175°C.
5. Heat a medium deep skillet with the vegetable oil over medium heat. Add the meatballs in batches of 8-10 each time. Add one part of the cranberry glaze in each batch and make sure all balls are evenly coated with the cranberry sauce glaze. Leave on the heat for 2 minutes (with the glaze), take off, and repeat the same step with the next two batches.
6. Transfer in a big shallow dish and serve warm.

Nutrition:
Calories: 91 kcal, Carbs: 10.08g, Protein: 4.6g, Sodium: 107mg, Potassium: 72mg, Phosphorus: 46mg, Fat: 6.8g, Dietary Fiber: 0.7g, Sugars: 2.5g

66. Kine Wontons

Preparation Time: 10 minutes
Cooking Time: 20 minutes
Servings: 2
Ingredients:

- 8 oz. (230-g.) cream cheese, softened at room temperature
- 5 green onions, chopped
- 2 tbsp. soy sauce
- 1 pack (340-g.) imitation crab meat
- 15 oz. (430-g.) can of water chestnuts, washed, drained, and finely chopped
- 2 packs (400-g.) wonton wrappers
- Vegetable oil (for frying)

Directions:

1. Combine the cream cheese, green onions, imitation crab meat, soy sauce, and water chestnuts in a medium bowl.
2. Place around 1 full tsp. of the cream cheese mix in the center of each wonton wrapper. Take the edges and fold each into a triangle, with slightly dampened hands.
3. Heat the oil in a large and deep skillet until hot and lightly smoking.
4. Fry the wontons in batches of 10 each time until golden brown.

5. Drain in a large paper towel-covered dish and serve hot.

Nutrition:
Calories: 63kcal, Carbs: 5.17g, Protein: 1.84g, Sodium: 122mg, Potassium: 41mg, Phosphorus: 45mg, Fat: 2.6g, Dietary Fiber: 0.2g, Sugars: 1.4g

67. Vegan Mac-and-Cheese

Preparation Time: 10 minutes
Cooking Time: 40 minutes
Servings: 2
Ingredients:

- 1 ½ cups (225-g.) elbow macaroni, cooked and drained
- 2 cups (580-ml.) soy or another vegetable cream
- 5 tbsp. vegan cheddar cheese imitation, grated
- 1 tbsp. mustard
- 1 tsp. paprika
- 1 clove garlic, minced
- 1 tbsp. margarine, melted
- Salt/Pepper

Directions:

1. Grease the bottom of a 3-quart Pyrex dish with margarine and add the cooked macaroni.
2. In a small mixing bowl, combine the soy cream with the garlic, mustard, paprika, and salt/pepper to taste.
3. Sprinkle the grated cheese on top.
4. Cook in the oven for 20-25 minutes at 350°F/175°C.

Nutrition:
Calories: 195kcal, Carbs: 11.7g, Protein: 4.7g, Sodium: 216mg, Potassium: 302 mg, Phosphorus: 120mg, Fat: 8.9g, Dietary Fiber: 0.7g, Sugars: 7.7g

68. Beef & Pepper Meatloaf

Preparation Time: 10 minutes
Cooking Time: 45 minutes
Servings: 2
Ingredients:

- 1 ½ lbs. (700-g.) ground beef (around 90% lean)
- 1 medium red bell pepper, diced
- 1 scallion, chopped
- 1 clove garlic, minced
- 1 tbsp. mustard
- 1 tsp. paprika
- ⅓ cup (36-g.) oats
- 1 egg white
- 1 tbsp. vegetable oil
- Salt/Pepper

Directions:

1. Heat the oil in a small skillet and add the red bell pepper, scallion, and garlic. Sauté for a couple of minutes.
2. In a large bowl, combine the ground beef with the peppers and the rest of the ingredients. Season with salt and pepper to taste.
3. Shape into a meatloaf on a large shallow baking sheet lined with wax paper.
4. Bake in the oven at 350°F/175°C for 40 minutes.

Nutrition: Calories: 180kcal, Carbs: 5.77g, Protein: 18.02g, Sodium: 88mg, Potassium: 263mg, Phosphorus: 161mg, Fat: 15.5g, Dietary Fiber: 1.3g, Sugars: 0.8g

69. Curried Rice Salad

Preparation Time: 10 minutes
Cooking Time: 0 minutes
Servings: 2
Ingredients:

- ½ cup (120-g.) cooked white rice e.g., basmati
- ¼ small red onion, finely chopped
- ½ green bell pepper, diced
- ½ red bell pepper, diced
- 1 stalk celery
- 1 cup white cabbage, shredded
- 1 small carrot, peel and shredded

For the dressing:

- 2-3 tbsp. balsamic vinegar
- 2-3 tbsp. rice vinegar
- 2 tbsp. mustard
- 2 cloves garlic, minced
- 1 tsp. light soy sauce
- 2 tsp. curry powder

Directions:

1. Combine the cooked rice with the diced peppers and the rest of the vegetables.
2. In a small dressing bowl, combine the ingredients of the dressing and stir well or blend in a food processor.
3. Add the dressing to the rice and vegetable salad, toss, and serve.

Nutrition:
Calories: 520kcal, Carbs: 23g, Protein: 3g, Sodium: 156 mg, Potassium: 240 mg, Phosphorus: 79 mg, Fat: 0.2g, Dietary Fiber: 1.3g, Sugars: 4.2g

70. Stuffed Zucchini

Preparation Time: 10 minutes
Cooking Time: 30 minutes
Servings: 2

Ingredients:

- 2 medium zucchinis
- ½ small white onion, chopped
- 1 egg, lightly beaten
- ¼ cup (30-g.) dry breadcrumbs
- ¼ cup (30-g.) grated parmesan cheese
- 1 tbsp. parsley, finely chopped
- 1 tbsp. cooking oil

Directions:

1. Cut the zucchini in half, lengthwise.
2. Scoop out the pulp with a spoon or ice cream scooper and reserve, leaving out an approx. ⅓-inch-thick shell. Cut the pulp into extra small chunks.
3. Heat the oil in a pan over medium heat and add the onion and zucchini pulp. Sauté until tender.
4. Remove from heat and combine with the rest of the ingredients. Fill the zucchini shells with the mixture. Place in a baking sheet lined with wax paper.
5. Bake for 20-25 minutes at 350°F/175°C
6. Serve warm.

Nutrition: Calories: 78kcal, Carbs: 5.5g, Protein: 3.4g, Sodium: 165 mg, Potassium: 240 mg, Phosphorus: 79 mg, Fat: 4.8g, Dietary Fiber: 1.2g, Sugars: 3.8g

71. Pad Kee Mao

Preparation Time: 10 minutes
Cooking Time: 15 minutes
Servings: 2

Ingredients:

- 8 oz. (230-g.) cooked rice noodles
- 2 shallots, diced
- 1 scallion, julienned
- 4 Thai red chili peppers, deseeded and sliced
- 1 cup (47-g.) holy basil leaves, washed and drained
- 6 pieces baby corn, cut in ½ lengthwise
- 3 tbsp. light soy sauce
- 2 tsp. oyster sauce
- 1 tbsp. fish sauce
- 1 ½ tsp. brown sugar
- 3 cloves garlic, minced
- 1 tsp. ginger
- 2 tbsp. white wine
- 3 tbsp. canola oil

Directions:

1. Heat the oil over medium heat in a wok until it's lightly smoking and sauté the garlic and ginger first for a minute so they release their natural aromas. Add the scallions and the shallot and sauté for another minute.
2. In a small bowl, combine all the liquid sauces e.g., soy sauce with the sugar and wine.
3. Add the baby corns, holy basil, and peppers to the wok and stir. Add the rice noodles, stir well, and top with the prepared soy sauce mixture. Stir with a flat spatula and make sure the sauce covers everything.
4. Serve warm.

Nutrition:
Calories: 211kcal, Carbs: 24.37g, Protein: 3.38g, Sodium: 512mg, Potassium: 229mg, Phosphorus: 75mg, Fat: 13.1g, Dietary Fiber: 2g, Sugars: 5.3g

72. Tuna Dip

Preparation Time: 10 minutes
Cooking Time: 15 minutes
Servings: 2

Ingredients:

- 1 can of tuna (100-g.), drained
- 1 cup (120-g.) cream cheese, softened at room temperature
- 1 tsp. prepared horseradish
- ½ cup (60-g.) sour cream
- 1 tsp. Worcestershire sauce
- 2 tbsp. onion, finely chopped
- ½ clove garlic
- Pitta chips or corn tortilla chips (optionally)

Directions:

1. Combine the Worcestershire with the horseradish sauce and add the cream cheese, onion, and garlic.
2. Add in the sour cream and stir well.
3. Add the tuna and mix again with a fork or spatula.
4. Serve with some dips of your choice e.g., pitta chips or corn tortilla chips.

Nutrition:
Calories: 700kcal, Carbs: 2g, Protein: 6g, Sodium: 169mg, Potassium: 130mg, Phosphorus: 146mg, Fat: 10.3g, Dietary Fiber: 0.4g, Sugars: 1.3g

73. Lemon Dill Rice

Preparation Time: 10 minutes
Cooking Time: 20 minutes
Servings: 2

Ingredients:

- 1 cup (200-g.) long-grain rice
- 2 ½ cups (500-ml.) water

- 1 tbsp. dried dill
- 1 tsp. lemon zest
- 1 tbsp. olive oil
- 1 small red onion, chopped
- Salt/Pepper

Directions:
1. Heat the olive oil and add the chopped red onion. Sauté for a few minutes until transparent.
2. Add the rice and stir. Add the water and a bit of salt and pepper to taste. Let cook until all water has been absorbed (around 15 minutes).
3. Add the dill and lemon zest and stir.
4. Serve warm.

Nutrition:
Calories: 171kcal, Carbs: 30.6g, Protein: 3.1g, Sodium: 238mg, Potassium: 120mg, Phosphorus: 131mg, Fat: 3.8g, Dietary Fiber: 1.8g, Sugars: 0.8g

74. Curried Pork Empanadas

Preparation Time: 10 minutes
Cooking Time: 45 minutes
Servings: 28 Empanadas

Ingredients:
Pastry:
- 16 oz. (450-g.) cream cheese
- 8 oz. (230-g.) unsalted butter, at room temperature
- 3 cups all-purpose flour
- 1 egg beaten

Filling:
- 1 ½ lbs. (700-g.) ground pork
- 2 tbsp. olive oil
- 1 cup white onion, finely chopped
- 4 shiitake mushrooms, finely chopped
- 1 clove garlic, minced
- 2 tbsp. sherry
- 1 tsp. light soy sauce
- 2 tsp. sugar
- 1 tsp. cornstarch
- ¼ cup raisins
- 1 tsp. curry powder
- ½ tsp. ground coriander
- Salt/Pepper

Directions:
1. In a mixing bowl, beat together the cream cheese with the butter. Slowly add in the flour and mix well with your hands.
2. Make two large dough balls with your hands and place them in the fridge covered with plastic foil for up to an hour.
3. Meanwhile, prepare your pork filling. Heat half of the oil in a deep and large skillet and add the

ground pork. Let cook for 3 minutes and then stir to cook from the other side with the help of a spatula.
4. Add the rest of the olive oil and the chopped onion. Sauté with the ground pork for 2 more minutes. Add the minced garlic and let cook until fragrant. Add the mushrooms and cook for another couple of minutes.
5. Season with curry, coriander, salt, and pepper. Add the sherry, soy sauce, sugar, cornstarch, and stir well. Finally, add the raisins. Make sure there are no big chunks of ground pork left and use a spatula to break any large pieces into smaller parts. Remove from the heat and set aside for 10 minutes.
6. Take the chilled dough and roll out on a lightly dusted surface until you are left with ⅛-inch-thick dough. Use a wide opening mason jar to cut even rounds (around 3" wide).
7. Beat the egg in a bowl to make your egg wash. Use a brush to brush lightly each pastry round with the egg wash. Place a teaspoon of the ground pork mixture in the center of each circle and fold in the edges with your hands. Press the outer edges with a fork to flute and seal.
8. Arrange in a baking sheet with wax paper and bake in the oven (in 2 batches) at 375°F/190°C for 15 to 20 minutes.

Nutrition:
Calories: 113kcal, Carbs: 7.69g, Protein: 2.63g, Sodium: 116mg, Potassium: 55mg, Phosphorus: 106mg, Fat: 7.6g, Dietary Fiber: 0.4g, Sugars: 0.5g

75. Baked Haddock

Preparation Time: 10 minutes
Cooking Time: 20 minutes
Servings: 2

Ingredients:
- ½ cup bread crumbs
- 3 tbsp. chopped fresh parsley
- 1 tbsp. lemon zest
- 1 tsp. chopped fresh thyme
- ¼ tsp. ground black pepper
- 1 tbsp. melted unsalted butter
- 12-oz. haddock fillets, deboned and skinned

Directions:
1. Preheat the oven to 350°F.
2. In a bowl, stir together the parsley, breadcrumbs, lemon zest, thyme, and pepper until well combined.
3. Add the melted butter and toss until the mixture resembles coarse crumbs.
4. Place the haddock on a baking sheet and spoon the bread crumb mixture on top, pressing down firmly.

5. Bake the haddock in the oven for 20 minutes or until the fish is just cooked through and flakes off in chunks when pressed.

Nutrition:
Calories: 143, Fat: 4g, Carb: 10g, Phosphorus: 216mg, Potassium: 285mg, Sodium: 281mg, Protein: 16g

76. Herbed Chicken

Preparation Time: 20 minutes
Cooking Time: 15 minutes
Servings: 2

Ingredients:
- 12 oz. boneless, skinless chicken breast, cut into 8 strips
- 1 egg white
- 2 tbsp. water, divided
- ½ cup breadcrumbs
- ¼ cup unsalted butter, divided
- Juice of 1 lemon
- Zest of 1 lemon
- 1 tbsp. fresh chopped basil
- 1 tsp. fresh chopped thyme
- Lemon slices, for garnish

Directions:
1. Place the chicken strips between 2 sheets of plastic wrap and pound each flat with a rolling pin.
2. In a bowl, whisk together the egg and 1 tablespoon of water.
3. Put the breadcrumbs in another bowl.
4. Dredge the chicken strips, one at a time, in the egg, then the breadcrumbs, and set the breaded strips aside on a plate.
5. In a large skillet over medium heat, melt 2 tablespoons of the butter.
6. Cook the strips in the butter for 3 minutes, turning once, or until they are golden and cooked through. Transfer the chicken to a plate.
7. Add the lemon zest, lemon juice, basil, thyme, and the remaining 1 tablespoon of water to the skillet and stir until the mixture simmers.
8. Remove the sauce from the heat and stir in the remaining 2 tablespoons of butter.
9. Serve the chicken with the lemon sauce drizzled over the top and garnished with lemon slices.

Nutrition:
Calories: 255, Fat: 14g, Carb: 11g, Phosphorus: 180mg, Potassium: 321mg, Sodium: 261mg, Protein: 20g

77. Pesto Pork Chops

Preparation Time: 20 minutes
Cooking Time: 20 minutes
Servings: 2

Ingredients:
- 4 (3-oz.) boneless Pork top-loin chops, fat trimmed
- 8 tsp. herb pesto
- ½ cup breadcrumbs
- 1 tbsp. olive oil

Directions:
1. Preheat the oven to 450°F.
2. Line a baking sheet with foil. Set aside.
3. Rub 1 teaspoon of pesto evenly over both sides of each pork chop.
4. Lightly dredge each pork chop in the breadcrumbs.
5. Heat the oil in a skillet.
6. Brown the pork chops on each side for 5 minutes.
7. Place the pork chops on the baking sheet.
8. Bake for 10 minutes or until pork reaches 145°F in the center.

Nutrition:
Calories: 210 Fat: 7g, Carb: 10g, Phosphorus: 179mg, Potassium: 220mg, Sodium: 148mg, Protein: 24g

78. Vegetable Curry

Preparation Time: 15 minutes
Cooking Time: 45 minutes
Servings: 2

Ingredients:
- 2 tsp. olive oil
- ½ sweet onion, diced
- 2 tsp. minced garlic
- 2 tsp. grated fresh ginger
- ½ eggplant, peeled and diced
- 1 carrot, peeled and diced
- 1 red bell pepper, diced
- 1 tbsp. hot curry powder
- 1 tsp. ground cumin
- ½ tsp. coriander
- Pinch of cayenne pepper
- 1 ½ cups homemade vegetable stock
- 1 tbsp. cornstarch
- ¼ cupwater

Directions:
1. Heat the oil in a stockpot.
2. Sauté the ginger, garlic, and onion for 3 minutes or until they are softened.
3. Add the red pepper, carrots, eggplant, and stir often for 6 minutes.
4. Stir in the cumin, curry powder, coriander, cayenne pepper, and vegetable stock.
5. Bring the curry to a boil and then lower the heat to low.
6. Simmer the curry for 30 minutes or until the vegetables are tender.

7. In a bowl, stir together the cornstarch and water.
8. Stir in the cornstarch mixture into the curry and simmer for 5 minutes or until the sauce has thickened.

Nutrition:
Calories: 100, Fat: 3g, Carb: 9g, Phosphorus: 28mg, Potassium: 180mg, Sodium: 218mg, Protein: 1g

79. Grilled Steak with Salsa

Preparation Time: 20 minutes
Cooking Time: 15 minutes
Servings: 2
Ingredients:
For the salsa:
- 1 cup chopped English cucumber
- ¼ cup boiled and diced red bell pepper
- 1 scallion, both green and white parts, chopped
- 2 tbsp. chopped fresh cilantro
- Juice of 1 lime

For the steak:
- 4 (3-oz.) beef tenderloin steaks, room temperature
- Olive oil
- Freshly ground black pepper

Directions:
1. In a bowl, to make the salsa, combine the lime juice, cilantro, scallion, bell pepper, and cucumber. Set aside.

To Make the Steak:
1. Preheat a barbecue to medium heat.
2. Rub the steaks all over with oil and season with pepper.
3. Grill the steaks for about 5 minutes per side for medium-rare, or until the desired doneness.
4. Serve the steaks topped with salsa.

Nutrition:
Calories: 130, Fat: 6g, Carb: 1g, Phosphorus: 186mg, Potassium: 272mg, Sodium: 39mg, Protein: 19g

80. Buffalo Chicken Lettuce Wraps

Preparation Time: 10 minutes
Cooking Time: 0 minutes
Servings: 2
Ingredients:
For the Buffalo Chicken Filling:
- 1 lb. chicken tenderloin, cut into ½-inch cubes
- 3 tbsp. vegetable oil
- ⅔ cup crumbled blue cheese
- ¼ cup light blue cheese dressing
- ¼ cup sour cream
- Hot pepper sauce
- 2 stalks finely chopped celery, trimmed

- 2 tbsp. chopped fresh cilantro.

For the Lettuce Wraps:
- 8 butter head lettuce leaves
- 4 celery sticks, cut into smaller pieces

Directions:
To Make the Buffalo Chicken Filling:
1. In a bowl, combine the chicken, celery, hot pepper sauce, blue cheese, and sour cream.
2. Mix the ingredients with a spoon until well combined.
3. Cover the bowl and store in the refrigerator until ready to use.

To Make the Lettuce Wraps:
1. Place the lettuce leaves on a platter or plate.
2. Divide the chicken mixture over the leaves and garnish with the celery sticks.
3. Serve the lettuce wraps cold or at room temperature.

Nutrition:
Calories: 106, Fat: 6g, Net Carbohydrates: 2g, Protein: 5g, Phosphorus: 216mg, Potassium: 285mg, Sodium: 281mg, Protein: 16g

81. Crazy Japanese Potato and Beef Croquettes

Preparation Time: 10 minutes
Cooking Time: 20 minutes
Servings: 2
Ingredients:
- 3 medium russet potatoes, peeled and chopped
- 1 tbsp. almond butter
- 1 tbsp. vegetable oil
- 3 onions, diced
- ¾ lb. ground beef
- 4 tsp. light coconut aminos
- All-purpose flour for coating
- 2 eggs, beaten
- Panko bread crumbs for coating
- ½ cup oil, frying

Directions:
1. Take a saucepan and place it over medium-high heat; add potatoes and sunflower seeds water, boil for 16 minutes.
2. Remove water and put potatoes in another bowl, add almond butter and mash the potatoes.
3. Take a frying pan and place it over medium heat, add 1 tablespoon oil and let it heat up.
4. Add onions and stir fry until tender.
5. Add coconut aminos to beef to onions.
6. Keep frying until beef is browned.
7. Mix the beef with the potatoes evenly.
8. Take another frying pan and place it over medium heat; add ½ cup of oil.

9. Form croquettes using the mashed potato mixture and coat them with flour, then eggs and finally breadcrumbs.
10. Fry patties until golden on all sides.

Nutrition:
Calories: 239, Fat: 4g, Carbohydrates: 20g, Protein: 10g, Phosphorus: 116mg, Potassium: 225mg, Sodium: 181mg

82. Saucy Garlic Greens

Preparation Time: 5 minutes
Cooking Time: 20 minutes
Servings: 2

Ingredients:
- 1 bunch of leafy greens
- Sauce
- ½ cup cashews soaked in water for 10 minutes
- ¼ cup water
- 1 tbsp. lemon juice
- 1 tsp. coconut aminos
- 1 clove whole peeled
- ⅛ tsp. of flavored vinegar

Directions:
1. Make the sauce by draining and discarding the soaking water from your cashews and add the cashews to a blender.
2. Add fresh water, lemon juice, flavored vinegar, coconut aminos, and garlic.
3. Blitz until you have a smooth cream and transfer to a bowl.
4. Add ½ cup of water to the pot.
5. Place the steamer basket to the pot and add the greens to the basket.
6. Lock the lid and steam for 1 minute.
7. Quick-release the pressure.
8. Transfer the steamed greens to the strainer and extract excess water.
9. Place the greens into a mixing bowl.
10. Add lemon garlic sauce and toss.

Nutrition:
Calories: 77, Fat: 5g, Carbohydrates: 0g, Protein: 2g, Phosphorus: 126mg, Potassium: 255mg, Sodium: 281mg

83. Garden Salad

Preparation Time: 5 minutes
Cooking Time: 20 minutes
Servings: 2

Ingredients:
- 1-lb. raw peanuts in the shell
- 1 bay leaf
- 2 medium-sized chopped up tomatoes
- ½ cup diced up green pepper
- ½ cup diced up sweet onion
- ¼ cup finely diced hot pepper
- ¼ cup diced up celery
- 2 tbsp. olive oil
- ¾ tsp. flavored vinegar
- ¼ tsp. freshly ground black pepper

Directions:
1. Boil your peanuts for 1 minute and rinse them.
2. The skin will be soft, so discard the skin.
3. Add 2 cups of water to the Instant Pot.
4. Add bay leaf and peanuts.
5. Lock the lid and cook on High pressure for 20 minutes.
6. Drain the water.
7. Take a large bowl and add the peanuts, diced up vegetables.
8. Whisk in olive oil, lemon juice, pepper in another bowl.
9. Pour the mixture over the salad and mix.

Nutrition:
Calories: 140, Fat: 4g, Carbohydrates: 24g, Protein: 5g Phosphorus: 216mg Potassium: 185mg Sodium: 141mg

84. Spicy Cabbage Dish

Preparation Time: 10 minutes
Cooking Time: 4 hours
Servings: 2

Ingredients:
- 2 yellow onions, chopped
- 10 cups red cabbage, shredded
- 1 cup plums, pitted and chopped
- 1 tsp. cinnamon powder
- 1 garlic clove, minced
- 1 tsp. cumin seeds
- ¼ tsp. cloves, ground
- 2 tbsp. red wine vinegar
- 1 tsp. coriander seeds
- ½ cup water

Directions:
1. Add cabbage, onion, plums, garlic, cumin, cinnamon, cloves, vinegar, coriander, and water to your Slow Cooker.
2. Stir well.
3. Place lid and cook on Low for 4 hours.
4. Divide between serving platters.

Nutrition:
Calories: 197, Fat: 1g, Carbohydrates: 14g, Protein: 3g, Phosphorus: 216mg, Potassium: 285mg, Sodium: 281mg

85. Extreme Balsamic Chicken

Preparation Time: 10 minutes
Cooking Time: 35 minutes
Servings: 2

Ingredients:

- 3 boneless chicken breasts, skinless
- Sunflower seeds to taste
- ¼ cup almond flour
- ⅔ cups low-fat chicken broth
- 1 ½ tsp. arrowroot
- ½ cup low sugar raspberry preserve
- 1 ½ tbsp. balsamic vinegar

Directions:

1. Cut chicken breast into bite-sized pieces and season them with seeds.
2. Dredge the chicken pieces in flour and shake off any excess.
3. Take a non-stick skillet and place it over medium heat.
4. Add chicken to the skillet and cook for 15 minutes, making sure to turn them halfway through.
5. Remove chicken and transfer to a platter.
6. Add arrowroot, broth, raspberry preserve to the skillet and stir.
7. Stir in balsamic vinegar and reduce heat to low, stir-cook for a few minutes.
8. Transfer the chicken back to the sauce and cook for 15 minutes more.
9. Serve and enjoy!

Nutrition: Calories: 546, Fat: 35g, Carbohydrates: 11g, Protein: 44g, Phosphorus: 136mg, Potassium: 195mg, Sodium: 81mg

86. Enjoyable Spinach and Bean Medley

Preparation Time: 10 minutes
Cooking Time: 4 hours
Servings: 2

Ingredients:

- 5 carrots, sliced
- 1 ½ cups great northern beans, dried
- 2 garlic cloves, minced
- 1 yellow onion, chopped
- Pepper to taste
- ½ tsp. oregano, dried
- 5 oz. baby spinach
- 4 ½ cups low sodium veggie stock
- 2 tsp. lemon peel, grated
- 3 tbsp. lemon juice

Directions:

1. Add beans, onion, carrots, garlic, oregano, and stock to your Slow Cooker.

2. Stir well.
3. Place lid and cook on High for 4 hours.
4. Add spinach, lemon juice, and lemon peel.
5. Stir and let it sit for 5 minutes.
6. Divide between serving platters and enjoy!

Nutrition: Calories: 219, Fat: 8g, Carbohydrates: 14g, Protein: 8g, Phosphorus: 216mg, Potassium: 285mg, Sodium: 131mg

87. Tantalizing Cauliflower and Dill Mash

Preparation Time: 10 minutes
Cooking Time: 6 hours
Servings: 2

Ingredients:

- 1 cauliflower head, florets separated
- ⅓ cup dill, chopped
- 6 garlic cloves
- 2 tbsp. olive oil
- Pinch of black pepper

Directions:

1. Add cauliflower to Slow Cooker.
2. Add dill, garlic, and water to cover them.
3. Place lid and cook on High for 5 hours.
4. Drain the flowers.
5. Season with pepper and add oil, mash using a potato masher.
6. Whisk and serve.

Nutrition:
Calories: 207, Fat: 4g, Carbohydrates: 14g, Protein: 3g, Phosphorus: 226mg, Potassium: 285mg, Sodium: 134mg

88. Secret Asian Green Beans

Preparation Time: 10 minutes
Cooking Time: 2 hours
Servings: 2

Ingredients:

- 16 cups green beans, halved
- 3 tbsp. olive oil
- ¼ cup tomato sauce, salt-free
- ½ cup coconut sugar
- ¾ tsp. low sodium soy sauce
- Pinch of pepper

Directions:

1. Add green beans, coconut sugar, pepper tomato sauce, soy sauce, and oil to your Slow Cooker.
2. Stir well.
3. Place lid and cook on Low for 3 hours.
4. Divide between serving platters and serve.
5. Enjoy!

Nutrition:

Calories: 200, Fat: 4g, Carbohydrates: 12g, Protein: 3g, Phosphorus: 216mg, Potassium: 285mg, Sodium: 131mg

89. Excellent Acorn Mix

Preparation Time: 10 minutes
Cooking Time: 7 hours
Servings: 2

Ingredients:

- 2 acorn squashes, peeled and cut into wedges
- 16 oz. cranberry sauce, unsweetened
- ¼ tsp. cinnamon powder
- Pepper to taste

Directions:

1. Add acorn wedges to your Slow Cooker.
2. Add cranberry sauce, cinnamon, raisins, and pepper.
3. Stir.
4. Place lid and cook on Low for 7 hours.
5. Serve and enjoy!

Nutrition:

Calories: 200, Fat: 3g, Carbohydrates: 15g, Protein: 2g, Phosphorus: 211mg, Potassium: 243mg, Sodium: 203mg

90. Crunchy Almond Chocolate Bars

Preparation Time: 10 minutes
Cooking Time: 2 hours 30 minutes
Servings: 2

Ingredients:

- 1 egg white
- ¼ cup coconut oil, melted
- 1 cup coconut sugar
- ½ tsp. vanilla extract
- 1 tsp. baking powder
- 1 ½ cups almond meal
- ½ cup dark chocolate chips

Directions:

1. Take a bowl and add sugar, oil, vanilla extract, egg white, almond flour, baking powder and mix it well.
2. Fold in chocolate chips and stir.
3. Line Slow Cooker with parchment paper.
4. Grease.
5. Add the cookie mix and press on the bottom.
6. Place lid and cook on Low for 2 hours 30 minutes.
7. Take the cookie sheet out and let it cool.
8. Cut in bars and enjoy!

Nutrition: Calories: 200, Fat: 2g, Carbohydrates: 13g, Protein: 6g, Phosphorus: 136mg, Potassium: 285mg, Sodium: 281mg

91. Golden Eggplant Fries

Preparation Time: 10 minutes
Cooking Time: 15 minutes
Servings: 2

Ingredients:

- 2 eggs
- 2 cups almond flour
- 2 tbsp. coconut oil, spray
- 2 eggplants, peeled and cut thinly
- Sunflower seeds and pepper

Directions:

1. Preheat your oven to 400°F.
2. Take a bowl and mix with sunflower seeds and black pepper.
3. Take another bowl and beat eggs until frothy.
4. Dip the eggplant pieces into the eggs.
5. Then coat them with the flour mixture.
6. Add another layer of flour and egg.
7. Then, take a baking sheet and grease with coconut oil on top.
8. Bake for about 15 minutes.
9. Serve and enjoy!

Nutrition:

Calories: 212, Fat: 15.8g, Carbohydrates: 12.1g, Protein: 8.6g, Phosphorus: 116mg, Potassium: 185mg, Sodium: 121mg

92. Lettuce and Chicken Platter

Preparation Time: 10 minutes
Cooking Time: Nil
Servings: 2

Ingredients:

- 2 cups chicken, cooked and coarsely chopped
- ½ head iceberg lettuce, sliced and chopped
- 1 celery rib, chopped
- 1 medium apple, cut
- ½ red bell pepper, deseeded and chopped
- 6-7 green olives, pitted and halved
- 1 red onion, chopped

For dressing:

- 1 tbsp. raw honey
- 2 tbsp. lemon juice
- Salt and pepper to taste

Directions:

1. Cut the vegetables and transfer them to your Salad Bowl.
2. Add olives.
3. Chop the cooked chicken and transfer it to your Salad bowl.
4. Prepare the dressing by mixing the ingredients listed under the dressing.

5. Pour the dressing into the Salad bowl. Toss and enjoy!

Nutrition: Calories: 296, Fat: 21g, Carbohydrates: 9g, Protein: 18g, Phosphorus: 146mg, Potassium: 205mg, Sodium: 221mg

93. Greek Lemon Chicken Bowl

Preparation Time: 10 minutes
Cooking Time: 15 minutes
Servings: 2

Ingredients:

- 2 cups chicken, cooked and chopped
- 2 cans chicken broth, fat-free
- 2 medium carrots, chopped
- ¼ tsp. pepper
- 2 tbsp. parsley, snipped
- ¼ cup lemon juice
- 1 can cream chicken soup, fat-free, low sodium
- ½ cup onion, chopped
- 1 garlic clove, minced

Directions:

1. Take a pot and add all the ingredients except parsley into it.
2. Season with salt and pepper.
3. Bring the mix to a boil over medium-high heat.
4. Reduce the heat and simmer for 15 minutes.
5. Garnish with parsley.
6. Serve hot and enjoy!

Nutrition:
Calories: 520, Fat: 33g, Carbohydrates: 31g, Protein: 30g, Phosphorus: 216mg, Potassium: 285mg, Sodium: 281mg

94. Spicy Chili Crackers

Preparation Time: 15 minutes
Cooking Time: 60 minutes
Servings: 2

Ingredients:

- ¾ cup almond flour
- ¼ cup coconut four
- ¼ cup coconut flour
- ½ tsp. paprika
- ½ tsp. cumin
- 1 ½ tsp. chili pepper spice
- 1 tsp. onion powder
- ½ tsp. sunflower seeds
- 1 whole egg
- ¼ cup unsalted almond butter

Directions:

1. Preheat your oven to 350°F.
2. Line a baking sheet with parchment paper and keep it on the side.
3. Add ingredients to your food processor and pulse until you have a nice dough.
4. Divide dough into two equal parts.
5. Place one ball on a sheet of parchment paper and cover with another sheet; roll it out.
6. Cut into crackers and repeat with the other ball.
7. Transfer the prepped dough to a baking tray and bake for 8-10 minutes.
8. Remove from oven and serve.
9. Enjoy!

Nutrition:
Total Carbs: 2.8g, Fiber: 1g, Protein: 1.6g, Fat: 4.1g, Phosphorus: 216mg, Potassium: 285mg, Sodium: 191mg

95. Dolmas Wrap

Preparation Time: 10 minutes
Cooking Time: 0 minutes
Servings: 2

Ingredients:

- 2 whole-wheat wraps
- 6 dolmas (stuffed grape leaves)
- 1 tomato, chopped
- 1 cucumber, chopped
- 2 oz. Greek yogurt
- ½ tsp. minced garlic
- ¼ cup lettuce, chopped
- 2 oz. feta, crumbled

Directions:

1. In the mixing bowl combine together chopped tomato, cucumber, Greek yogurt, minced garlic, lettuce, and Feta.
2. When the mixture is homogenous transfer it to the center of every wheat wrap.
3. Arrange dolma over the vegetable mixture.
4. Carefully wrap the wheat wraps.

Nutrition:
Calories 341, Fat 12.9, Fiber 9.2, Carbs 52.4, Protein 13.2, Phosphorus: 206mg, Potassium: 125mg, Sodium: 181mg

96. Green Palak Paneer

Preparation Time: 5 minutes
Cooking Time: 10 minutes
Servings: 2

Ingredients:

- 1-lb. spinach
- 2 cups cubed Paneer (vegan)
- 2 tbsp. coconut oil
- 1 tsp. cumin
- 1 chopped up onion

- 1-2 tsp. hot green chili minced up
- 1 tsp. minced garlic
- 15 cashews
- 4 tbsp. almond milk
- 1 tsp. Garam masala
- Flavored vinegar as needed

Directions:
1. Add cashews and milk to a blender and blend well.
2. Set your pot to Sauté mode and add coconut oil; allow the oil to heat up.
3. Add cumin seeds, garlic, green chilies, ginger, and sauté for 1 minute.
4. Add onion and sauté for 2 minutes.
5. Add chopped spinach, flavored vinegar, and a cup of water.
6. Lock up the lid and cook on High pressure for 10 minutes.
7. Quick-release the pressure.
8. Add ½ cup of water and blend to a paste.
9. Add cashew paste, Paneer, and Garam Masala and stir thoroughly.
10. Serve over hot rice!

Nutrition:
Calories: 367, Fat: 26g, Carbohydrates: 21g, Protein: 16g, Phosphorus: 236mg, Potassium: 385mg, Sodium: 128mg

97. Sporty Baby Carrots

Preparation Time: 5 minutes
Cooking Time: 5 minutes
Servings: 2
Ingredients:
- 1-lb. baby carrots
- 1 cup water
- 1 tbsp. clarified ghee
- 1 tbsp. chopped up fresh mint leaves
- Sea flavored vinegar as needed

Directions:
1. Place a steamer rack on top of your pot and add the carrots.
2. Add water.
3. Lock the lid and cook at High pressure for 2 minutes.
4. Do a quick release.
5. Pass the carrots through a strainer and drain them.
6. Wipe the insert clean.
7. Return the insert to the pot and set the pot to Sauté mode.
8. Add clarified butter and allow it to melt.
9. Add mint and sauté for 30 seconds.
10. Add carrots to the insert and sauté well.
11. Remove them and sprinkle with a bit of flavored vinegar on top.

Nutrition: Calories: 131, Fat: 10g, Carbohydrates: 11g, Protein: 1g, Phosphorus: 116mg, Potassium: 185mg, Sodium: 81mg

98. Traditional Black Bean Chili

Preparation Time: 10 minutes
Cooking Time: 4 hours
Servings: 2
Ingredients:
- 1 ½ cups red bell pepper, chopped
- 1 cup yellow onion, chopped
- 1 ½ cups mushrooms, sliced
- 1 tbsp. olive oil
- 1 tbsp. chili powder
- 2 garlic cloves, minced
- 1 tsp. chipotle chili pepper, chopped
- ½ tsp. cumin, ground
- 16 oz. canned black beans, drained and rinsed
- 2 tbsp. cilantro, chopped
- 1 cup tomatoes, chopped

Directions:
1. Add red bell peppers, onion, dill, mushrooms, chili powder, garlic, chili pepper, cumin, black beans, and tomatoes to your Slow Cooker.
2. Stir well.
3. Place lid and cook on High for 4 hours.
4. Sprinkle cilantro on top. Serve and enjoy!

Nutrition: Calories: 211, Fat: 3g, Carbohydrates: 22g, Protein: 5g, Phosphorus: 216mg, Potassium: 245mg, Sodium: 201mg

Chapter 6: Dinner

99. Lemon Sprouts

Preparation Time: 10 minutes
Cooking Time: Nil
Servings: 4
Ingredients:

- 1-lb. Brussels sprouts, trimmed and shredded
- 8 tbsp. olive oil
- 1 lemon, juiced, and zested
- Salt and pepper to taste
- ¾ cup spicy almond and seed mix

Directions:

1. Take a bowl and mix in lemon juice, salt, pepper, and olive oil
2. Mix well
3. Stir in shredded Brussels sprouts and toss
4. Let it sit for 10 minutes
5. Add nuts and toss
6. Serve and enjoy!

Nutrition:
Calories: 382 Fat: 36g Carbohydrates: 9g Protein: 7g

100. Lemon and Broccoli Platter

Preparation Time: 10 minutes
Cooking Time: 15 minutes
Servings: 6
Ingredients:

- 2 heads of broccoli, separated into florets
- 2 tsp. extra virgin olive oil
- 1 tsp. salt
- ½ tsp. black pepper
- 1 garlic clove, minced
- ½ tsp. lemon juice

Directions:

1. Preheat your oven to 400°F
2. Take a large-sized bowl and add broccoli florets
3. Drizzle olive oil and season with pepper, salt, and garlic
4. Spread the broccoli out in a single even layer on a baking sheet
5. Bake for 15-20 minutes until fork tender
6. Squeeze lemon juice on top
7. Serve and enjoy!

Nutrition:
Calories: 49 Fat: 1.9g Carbohydrates: 7g Protein: 3g

101. Chicken Liver Stew

Preparation Time: 10 minutes
Cooking Time: 20 minutes
Servings: 2
Ingredients:

- 10 oz. chicken livers
- 1-oz. onion, chopped
- 2 oz. sour cream
- 1 tbsp. olive oil
- Salt to taste

Directions:

1. Take a pan and place it over medium heat
2. Add oil and let it heat up
3. Add onions and fry until just browned
4. Add livers and season with salt
5. Cook until livers are half cooked
6. Transfer the mix to a stew pot
7. Add sour cream and cook for 20 minutes
8. Serve and enjoy!

Nutrition:
Calories: 146 Fat: 9g Carbohydrates: 2g Protein: 15g

102. Mushroom Cream Soup

Preparation Time: 5 minutes
Cooking Time: 30 minutes
Servings: 4
Ingredients:

- 1 tbsp. olive oil
- ½ large onion, diced
- 20 oz. mushrooms, sliced
- 6 garlic cloves, minced
- 2 cups vegetable broth
- 1 cup coconut cream
- ¾ tsp. salt
- ¼ tsp. black pepper

Directions:

1. Take a large-sized pot and place it over medium heat
2. Add onion and mushrooms in olive oil and Sauté for 10-15 minutes
3. Make sure to keep stirring it from time to time until browned evenly
4. Add garlic and Sauté for 10 minutes more
5. Add vegetable broth, coconut cream, coconut milk, black pepper, and salt
6. Bring it to a boil and reduce the temperature to low
7. Simmer for 15 minutes

8. Use an immersion blender to puree the mixture
9. Enjoy!

Nutrition: Calories: 200 Fat: 17g Carbohydrates: 5g Protein: 4g

103. Garlic Soup

Preparation Time: 10 minutes
Cooking Time: 60 minutes
Servings: 10

Ingredients:

- 1 tbsp. olive oil
- 2 bulbs garlic, peeled
- 3 shallots, chopped
- 1 large head cauliflower, chopped
- 6 cups vegetable broth
- Salt and pepper to taste

Directions:

1. Preheat your oven to 400°F
2. Slice ¼ inch top off the garlic bulb and place it in aluminum foil
3. Grease with olive oil and roast in the oven for 35 minutes
4. Squeeze the flesh out of the roasted garlic
5. Heat the oil in a saucepan and add shallots, Sauté for 6 minutes
6. Add the garlic and remaining ingredients
7. Cover the pan and reduce the heat to low
8. Let it cook for 15-20 minutes
9. Use an immersion blender to puree the mixture
10. Season soup with salt and pepper
11. Serve and enjoy!

Nutrition: Calories: 142 Fat: 8g Carbohydrates: 3.4g Protein: 4g

104. Simple Lamb Chops

Preparation Time: 35 minutes
Cooking Time: 5 minutes
Servings: 3

Ingredients:

- ¼ cup olive oil
- ¼ cup mint, fresh and chopped
- 8 lamb rib chops
- 1 tbsp. garlic, minced
- 1 tbsp. rosemary, fresh and chopped

Directions:

1. Add rosemary, garlic, mint, olive oil into a bowl and mix well
2. Keep a tablespoon of the mixture on the side for later use
3. Toss lamb chops into the marinade, letting them marinate for 30 minutes

4. Take a cast-iron skillet and place it over medium-high heat
5. Add lamb and cook for 2 minutes per side for medium-rare
6. Let the lamb rest for a few minutes and drizzle the remaining marinade
7. Serve and enjoy!

Nutrition:
Calories: 566 Fat: 40g Carbohydrates: 2g Protein: 47g

105. Garlic and Butter-Flavored Cod

Preparation Time: 5 minutes
Cooking Time: 20 minutes
Servings: 3

Ingredients:

- 3 Cod fillets, 8 oz. each
- ¾ lb. baby bok Choy halved
- ⅓ cup almond butter, thinly sliced
- 1 ½ tbsp. garlic, minced
- Salt and pepper to taste

Directions:

1. Preheat your oven to 400°F
2. Cut 3 sheets of aluminum foil (large enough to fit fillet)
3. Place cod fillet on each sheet and add butter and garlic on top
4. Fold packet and enclose them in pouches
5. Arrange on baking sheet
6. Bake for 20 minutes
7. Transfer to a cooling rack and let them cool
8. Enjoy!

Nutrition:
Calories: 355 Fat: 21g Carbohydrates: 3g Protein: 37g

106. Tilapia Broccoli Platter

Preparation Time: 4 minutes
Cooking Time: 14 minutes
Servings: 2

Ingredients:

- 6 oz. tilapia, frozen
- 1 tbsp. almond butter
- 1 tbsp. garlic, minced
- 1 tsp. lemon pepper seasoning
- 1 cup broccoli florets, fresh

Directions:

1. Preheat your oven to 350°F
2. Add fish in aluminum foil packets
3. Arrange the broccoli around fish
4. Sprinkle lemon pepper on top
5. Close the packets and seal
6. Bake for 14 minutes

7. Take a bowl and add garlic and butter, mix well and keep the mixture on the side
8. Remove the packet from the oven and transfer it to a platter
9. Place butter on top of the fish and broccoli, serve and enjoy!

Nutrition:
Calories: 362 Fat: 25g Carbohydrates: 2g Protein: 29g

107. Parsley Scallops

Preparation Time: 5 minutes
Cooking Time: 25 minutes
Servings: 4
Ingredients:
- 8 tbsp. almond butter
- 2 garlic cloves, minced
- 16 large sea scallops
- Salt and pepper to taste 1 ½ tbsp. olive oil

Directions:
1. Seasons scallops with salt and pepper
2. Take a skillet and place it over medium heat, add oil and let it heat up
3. Sauté scallops for 2 minutes per side, repeat until all scallops are cooked
4. Add butter to the skillet and let it melt
5. Stir in garlic and cook for 15 minutes
6. Return scallops to skillet and stir to coat Serve and enjoy!

Nutrition:
Calories: 417 Fat: 31g Net Carbohydrates: 5g Protein: 29g

108. Blackened Chicken

Preparation Time: 10 minutes
Cooking Time: 10 minutes
Servings: 4
Ingredients:
- ½ tsp. paprika
- ⅛ tsp. salt
- ¼ tsp. cayenne pepper
- ¼ tsp. ground cumin
- ¼ tsp. dried thyme
- ⅛ tsp. ground white pepper
- ⅛ tsp. onion powder
- 2 chicken breasts, boneless and skinless

Directions:
1. Preheat your oven to 350°F
2. Grease baking sheet
3. Take a cast-iron skillet and place it over high heat
4. Add oil and heat it up for 5 minutes until smoking hot

5. Take a small bowl and mix salt, paprika, cumin, white pepper, cayenne, thyme, onion powder
6. Oil the chicken breast on both sides and coat the breast with the spice mix
7. Transfer to your hot pan and cook for 1 minute per side
8. Transfer to your prepared baking sheet and bake for 5 minutes
9. Serve and enjoy!

Nutrition: Calories: 136 Fat: 3g Carbohydrates: 1g Protein: 24g

109. Spicy Paprika Lamb Chops

Preparation Time: 10 minutes
Cooking Time: 15 minutes
Servings: 4
Ingredients:
- 2 lamb racks, cut into chops
- Salt and pepper to taste
- 3 tbsp. paprika
- ¾ cup cumin powder
- 1 tsp. chili powder

Directions:
1. Take a bowl and add the paprika, cumin, chili, salt, pepper, and stir
2. Add lamb chops and rub the mixture
3. Heat grill over medium-temperature and add lamb chops, cook for 5 minutes
4. Flip and cook for 5 minutes more, flip again
5. Cook for 2 minutes, flip and cook for 2 minutes more
6. Serve and enjoy!

Nutrition:
Calories: 200 Fat: 5g Carbohydrates: 4g Protein: 8g

110. Steamed Fish

Preparation Time: 10 minutes
Cooking Time: 25 minutes
Servings: 4
Ingredients:
- ½ cup olive oil
- 4 fillets tilapia
- ½ cup onion, sliced
- ¾ cup red and green peppers, sliced
- 1 tsp. hot pepper sauce
- ¼ tsp. black pepper
- 1 tbsp. Ketchup
- 1 large sprig thyme
- 1 cup hot water
- 1 tbsp. lime juice

Directions:

1. In a frying pan, heat the oil on medium.
2. Sauté bell peppers and onion.
3. Add ½ cup of hot water, lime juice, ketchup, thyme, hot pepper sauce, and black pepper. Stir.
4. Put fish in a pan. Add ½ cup of hot water. Spoon veggies and sauce over fish.
5. Cover pan and cook for 5 minutes.
6. Turn fish. Cook covered until done

Nutrition: Calories: 376 Fat: 31g Net Carbohydrates: 6g Protein: 21g

111. Mushroom and Olive Sirloin Steak

Preparation Time: 10 minutes
Cooking Time: 14 minutes
Servings: 4

Ingredients:

- 1-lb. boneless beef sirloin steak, ¾ inch thick, cut into 4 pieces
- 1 large red onion, chopped
- 1 cup mushrooms
- 4 garlic cloves, thinly sliced
- 4 tbsp. olive oil
- 1 cup parsley leaves, finely cut

Directions:

1. Take a large-sized skillet and place it over medium-high heat
2. Add oil and let it heat up
3. Add beef and cook until both sides are browned, remove beef and drain fat
4. Add the rest of the oil to the skillet and heat it up
5. Add onions, garlic and cook for 2-3 minutes
6. Stir well
7. Add mushrooms olives and cook until mushrooms are thoroughly done
8. Return beef to skillet and lower heat to medium
9. Cook for 3-4 minutes (covered)
10. Stir in parsley
11. Serve and enjoy!

Nutrition: Calories: 386 Fat: 30g Carbohydrates: 11g Protein: 21g

112. Kale and Garlic Platter

Preparation Time: 5 minutes
Cooking Time: 10 minutes
Servings: 4

Ingredients:

- 1 bunch kale
- 2 tbsp. olive oil
- 4 garlic cloves, minced

Directions:

1. Carefully tear the kale into bite-sized portions, making sure to remove the stem
2. Discard the stems
3. Take a large-sized pot and place it over medium heat
4. Add olive oil and let the oil heat up
5. Add garlic and stir for 2 minutes
6. Add kale and cook for 5-10 minutes
7. Serve!

Nutrition:
Calories: 121 Fat: 8g Carbohydrates: 5g Protein: 4g

113. Blistered Beans and Almond

Preparation Time: 10 minutes
Cooking Time: 20 minutes
Servings: 4

Ingredients:

- 1-lb. fresh green beans, ends trimmed
- 1 ½ tbsp. olive oil
- ¼ tsp. salt
- 1 ½ tbsp. fresh dill, minced
- Juice of 1 lemon
- ¼ cup crushed almonds
- Salt as needed

Directions:

1. Preheat your oven to 400°F
2. Add in the green beans with your olive oil and also the salt
3. Then spread them in one single layer on a large-sized sheet pan
4. Roast for 10 minutes and stir nicely, then roast for another 8-10 minutes
5. Remove it from the oven and keep stirring in the lemon juice alongside the dill
6. Top it with crushed almonds, some flaky sea salt, and serve

Nutrition:
Calories: 347 Fat: 16g Carbohydrates: 6g Protein: 45g

114. Eggplant Crunchy Fries

Preparation Time: 10 minutes
Cooking Time: 10 minutes
Servings: 2

Ingredients:

- 1 eggplant – medium size
- 2 eggs
- 5 tbsp. cornstarch
- 5 tbsp. bread crumbs
- 1 tsp. garlic powder
- ½ cup oil – canola or olive oil

Directions:

1. Clean and peel the eggplant and cut it in French fries-like sticks. Make sure that you dry the sticks not to be too moisty.
2. In the meanwhile, beat the eggs until foamy and combine cornstarch, garlic powder, and bread crumbs in another bowl.
3. Heat the oil in a skillet.
4. Once the oil is hot, start dipping eggplant dip into the egg mixture, then coat the sticks with the cornstarch and bread crumbs mixture.
5. Fry the coated sticks for around 3 minutes, flipping them over to brown them on all sides
6. Serve hot.

Nutrition:

Potassium 215 mg Sodium 212 mg Phosphorus 86 mg Calories 233

115. Oregano Salmon with Crunchy Crust

Preparation Time: 10 minutes
Cooking Time: 2 hours
Servings: 2

Ingredients:

- 8 oz. salmon fillet
- 2 tbsp. panko bread crumbs
- 1 oz. Parmesan, grated
- 1 tsp. dried oregano
- 1 tsp. sunflower oil

Directions:

1. In the mixing bowl combine together panko bread crumbs, Parmesan, and dried oregano.
2. Sprinkle the salmon with olive oil and coat in the breadcrumb's mixture.
3. After this, line the baking tray with baking paper.
4. Place the salmon in the tray and transfer it to the preheated to the 385°F oven.
5. Bake the salmon for 25 minutes.

Nutrition:

Calories 245, Fat 12.8, Fiber 0.6, Carbs 5.9, Protein 27.5

116. Broiled Shrimp

Preparation Time: 0 minutes
Cooking Time: 5 minutes
Servings: 2

Ingredients:

- 1 lb. shrimp in shell
- ½ cup unsalted butter, melted
- 2 tsp. lemon juice
- 2 tbsp. chopped onion
- 1 clove garlic, minced
- ⅛ tsp. pepper

Directions:

1. Toss the shrimp with butter, lemon juice, onion, garlic, and pepper in a bowl.
2. Spread the seasoned shrimp in a baking tray.
3. Broil for 5 minutes in an oven on a broiler setting.
4. Serve warm.

Nutrition:

Calories 167, Fat 12.8, Fiber 0.1, Carbs 0.6, Protein 14.6

117. Shrimp Spaghetti

Preparation Time: 10 minutes
Cooking Time: 40 minutes
Servings: 2

Ingredients:

- ⅓ cup extra virgin olive oil
- ½ lb. spaghetti or spaghetti
- 2 cloves garlic, crushed
- ⅓ cup dry white wine
- 1 red pepper, diced
- ¼ tsp. crushed red chilies
- ⅓ cup toasted fresh bread crumbs
- 1 lb. raw shrimp
- Chopped fresh parsley (optional)
- Freshly ground pepper, to taste

Directions:

1. Cook pasta.
2. Heat the oil in a large skillet over medium-low.
3. Add crushed the red chilies and garlic. Cook, stirring, for 1 minute.
4. Add peppers, cooking for 5 minutes.
5. Add the shrimp. Cook for 1 minute.
6. Add the wine.
7. Turn the heat up to medium. Simmer until the shrimp start to curl and turn opaque.
8. Drain pasta. Put it in a large serving dish.
9. Pour sauce over pasta. Toss together with breadcrumbs.
10. Serve with parsley and freshly ground pepper.

Nutrition:

Calories 716, Fat 55, Fiber 0, Carbs 25, Protein 25

118. Teriyaki Tuna

Preparation Time: 10 minutes
Cooking Time: 6 minutes
Servings: 3

Ingredients:

- 3 tuna fillets
- 3 tsp. teriyaki sauce
- ½ tsp. minced garlic
- 1 tsp. olive oil

Directions:
1. Whisk together teriyaki sauce, minced garlic, and olive oil.
2. Brush every tuna fillet with teriyaki mixture.
3. Preheat grill to 390°F.
4. Grill the fish for 3 minutes from each side.

Nutrition:
Calories 382, Fat 32.6, Fiber 0, Carbs 1.1, Protein 21.4

119. Very Wild Mushroom Pilaf

Preparation Time: 10 minutes
Cooking Time: 3 hours
Servings: 2
Ingredients:
- 1 cup wild rice
- 2 garlic cloves, minced
- 6 green onions, chopped
- 2 tbsp. olive oil
- ½ lb. baby Bella mushrooms
- 2 cups water

Directions:
1. Add rice, garlic, onion, oil, mushrooms, and water to your Slow Cooker.
2. Stir well until mixed.
3. Place lid and cook on Low for 3 hours.
4. Stir pilaf and divide between serving platters.
5. Enjoy!

Nutrition:
Calories: 210, Fat: 7g, Carbohydrates: 16g, Protein: 4g, Phosphorus: 266mg, Potassium: 232mg, Sodium: 176mg

120. Lemon Pepper Trout

Preparation Time: 5 minutes
Cooking Time: 15 minutes
Servings: 2
Ingredients:
- 1 lb. trout fillets
- 1 lb. asparagus
- 3 tbsp. olive oil
- 5 garlic cloves, minced
- ½ tsp. black pepper
- ½ lemon, sliced

Directions:
1. Prepare and preheat the gas oven at 350°F.
2. Rub the washed and dried fillets with oil then place them in a baking tray.
3. Top the fish with lemon slices, black pepper, and garlic cloves.
4. Spread the asparagus around the fish.
5. Bake the fish for 15 minutes approximately in the preheated oven.

6. Serve warm.

Nutrition:
Calories 336, Total Fat 20.3g, Saturated Fat 3.2g, Cholesterol 84mg, Sodium 370mg, Protein 33g, Calcium 100mg, Phosphorous 107mg, Potassium 383mg

121. Salmon Stuffed Pasta

Preparation Time: 10 minutes
Cooking Time: 35 minutes
Servings: 1-2
Ingredients:
- 2-4 jumbo pasta shells, boiled
- ½ cup coffee creamer

Filling:
- 1 egg, beaten
- ½ cups creamed cottage cheese
- ¼ cup chopped onion
- ¼ red bell pepper, diced
- ½ tsp. dried parsley
- ¼ tsp. lemon peel
- ¼ can salmon, drained

Dill Sauce:
- ½ tsp. butter
- ½ tsp. flour
- Pinch of pepper
- ¼ tbsp. lemon juice
- ½ cup coffee creamer
- ¼ tsp. dried dill weed

Directions:
1. Beat the egg with the cream cheese and all the other filling ingredients in a bowl.
2. Divide the filling in the pasta shells and place the bodies in a 9x13 baking dish.
3. Pour the coffee creamer around the stuffed shells then cover with a foil.
4. Bake the shells for 30 minutes at 350°F.
5. Meanwhile, whisk all the ingredients for dill sauce in a saucepan.
6. Stir for 5 minutes until it thickens.
7. Pour this sauce over the baked pasta shells.
8. Serve warm.

Nutrition:
Calories 268, Total Fat 4.8g, Saturated Fat 2g, Cholesterol 27mg, Sodium 86mg, Protein 11.5g, Calcium 27mg, Phosphorous 314mg, Potassium 181mg

122. Tuna Casserole

Preparation Time: 15 minutes
Cooking Time: 35 minutes
Servings: 2

Ingredients:

- ½ cup Cheddar cheese, shredded
- 2 tomatoes, chopped
- 7 oz. tuna filet, chopped
- 1 tsp. ground coriander
- ½ tsp. salt
- 1 tsp. olive oil
- ½ tsp. dried oregano

Directions:

1. Brush the casserole mold with olive oil.
2. Mix up together chopped tuna fillet with dried oregano and ground coriander.
3. Place the fish in the mold and flatten well to get the layer.
4. Then add chopped tomatoes and shredded cheese.
5. Cover the casserole with foil and secure the edges.
6. Bake the meal for 35 minutes at 355°F.

Nutrition:
Calories 260, Fat 21.5, Fiber 0.8, Carbs 2.7, Protein 14.6, Sodium 80mg, Calcium 58mg, Phosphorous 220mg, Potassium 241mg

123. Cauliflower Bhajees

Preparation Time: 5 minutes
Cooking Time: 20 minutes
Servings: 2

Ingredients:

- 2 large eggs
- 2 egg whites
- ½ cup onion, finely diced
- 2 cups cauliflower, frozen
- 2 tbsp. all-purpose white flour
- 1 tsp. black pepper
- 1 tbsp. coconut oil
- 1 tsp. curry powder
- 1 tbsp. fresh cilantro

Directions:

1. Soak vegetables in warm water before cooking.
2. Steam cauliflower over a pan of boiling water for 10 minutes.
3. Blend eggs and onion in a food processor before adding cooked cauliflower, spices, cilantro, flour, and pepper, and blast in the processor for 30 seconds.
4. Heat a skillet on high heat and add oil.

5. Pour tablespoon portions of the cauliflower mixture into the pan and brown on each side for 3-4 minutes or until crispy.
6. Enjoy hot with a crunchy side salad or seasonal greens.

Nutrition: Protein: 2.1 g, Potassium: 145.7 mg, Sodium: 128.9 mg

124. Vegetable Barley Stew

Preparation Time: 5 minutes
Cooking Time: 6 hours
Servings: 1

Ingredients:

- ¼ cup pearl barley
- ⅓ cup red bell pepper, chopped
- 1 cup chicken broth, no salt
- ¼ cup water
- ¼ cup onion, chopped
- ½ tsp. garlic, minced
- ¼ tsp. oregano
- ½ tbsp. lime juice
- ½ tbsp. chili powder
- ½ tsp. ground cumin
- ½ tsp. ground black pepper
- Fresh cilantro, chopped, for garnish

Directions:

1. Pour chicken broth, barley, onion, water, chili powder, red bell pepper, lime juice, oregano, cumin, and black pepper into the slow cooker. Mix well.
2. Cover the pot and cook for 6 hours on low. Secure the lid.
3. After the 6-hour cooking cycle, turn off the heat.
4. To serve, ladle into bowls. Garnish with cilantro on top.

Nutrition: Protein: 2.1 g, Potassium: 145.7 mg, Sodium: 128.9 mg

125. Cajun Catfish

Preparation Time: 10 minutes
Cooking Time: 10 minutes
Servings: 2

Ingredients:

- 16 oz. catfish steaks (4-oz. each fish steak)
- 1 tbsp. Cajun spices
- 1 egg, beaten
- 1 tbsp. sunflower oil

Directions:

1. Pour sunflower oil into the skillet and preheat it until shimmering.

2. Meanwhile, dip every catfish steak in the beaten egg and coat in Cajun spices.
3. Place the fish steaks in the hot oil and roast them for 4 minutes from each side.
4. The cooked catfish steaks should have a light brown crust.

Nutrition:
Calories 263, Fat 16.7, Fiber 0, Carbs 0.1, Protein 26.3, Sodium 60mg, Calcium 78mg, Phosphorous 250mg, Potassium 231mg

126. Sausage and Bean Casserole

Preparation Time: 5 minutes
Cooking Time: 8 hours
Servings: 1

Ingredients:
- 1 ½ cups dried navy beans
- 1 lb. Italian sausage
- 1 cup red wine
- 1 ½ cups vegetable broth, no salt
- 1 cup onion, chopped
- ½ cup tomatoes, chopped – limit this
- ½ cup celery, sliced
- 1/ tsp dried rosemary

Directions:
1. Pour navy beans into a bowl of water. Let soak for 12 hours.
2. Drain beans. Transfer to a pot. Pour water until completely covered. Allow beans to simmer for 20 minutes. Drain thoroughly. Transfer to a slow cooker.
3. Cook Italian sausage in a non-stick skillet until browned on all sides. Sauté onion and celery for 3 minutes or until tender. Transfer to the slow cooker.
4. Pour vegetable broth, red wine, tomatoes, and rosemary. Stir well.
5. Cover the pot and cook for 8 hours on low. Secure the lid.
6. After the 8-hour cooking cycle, turn off the heat. Adjust seasoning according to your preferred taste. Serve immediately.

Nutrition: Protein: 22 g, Potassium: 1mg, Sodium: 1 mg

127. Herbed Vegetable Trout

Preparation Time: 10 minutes
Cooking Time: 15 minutes
Servings: 2

Ingredients:
- 14 oz. trout fillets
- ½ tsp. herb seasoning blend
- 1 lemon, sliced

- 2 green onions, sliced
- 1 stalk celery, chopped
- 1 medium carrot, julienne

Directions:
1. Prepare and preheat a charcoal grill over moderate heat.
2. Place the trout fillets over a large piece of foil and drizzle herb seasoning on top.
3. Spread the lemon slices, carrots, celery, and green onions over the fish.
4. Cover the dish with foil and pack it.
5. Place the packed fish in the grill and cook for 15 minutes.
6. Once done, remove the foil from the fish.
7. Serve.

Nutrition:
Calories 202, Total Fat 8.5g, Saturated Fat 1.5g, Cholesterol 73mg, Sodium 82mg, Protein 26.9g, Calcium 70mg, Phosphorous 287mg, Potassium 560mg

128. Citrus Glazed Salmon

Preparation Time: 10 minutes
Cooking Time: 17 minutes
Servings: 2

Ingredients:
- 2 garlic cloves, crushed
- 1 ½ tbsp. lemon juice
- 2 tbsp. olive oil and 1 tbsp. butter
- 1 tbsp. Dijon mustard
- 2 dashes of cayenne pepper
- 1 tsp. dried basil leaves
- 1 tsp. dried dill
- 24 oz. salmon filet

Directions:
1. Place a 1-quart saucepan over moderate heat and add the oil, butter, garlic, lemon juice, mustard, cayenne pepper, dill, and basil to the pan.
2. Stir this mixture for 5 minutes after it has boiled.
3. Prepare and preheat a charcoal grill over moderate heat.
4. Place the fish on a foil sheet and fold the edges to make a foil tray.
5. Pour the prepared sauce over the fish.
6. Place the fish in the foil in the preheated grill and cook for 12 minutes.
7. Slice and serve.

Nutrition: Calories 401, Total Fat 20.5g, Saturated Fat 5.3g, Cholesterol 144mg, Sodium 256mg, Protein 48.4g, Calcium 549mg, Phosphorous 214mg, Potassium 446mg

129. Broiled Salmon Fillets

Preparation Time: 10 minutes
Cooking Time: 13 minutes
Servings: 2

Ingredients:

- 1 tbsp. ginger root, grated
- 1 clove garlic, minced
- ¼ cup maple syrup
- 1 tbsp. hot pepper sauce
- 4 salmon fillets, skinless

Directions:

1. Grease a pan with cooking spray and place it over moderate heat.
2. Add the ginger and garlic and sauté for 3 minutes then transfer to a bowl.
3. Add the hot pepper sauce and maple syrup to the ginger-garlic.
4. Mix well and keep this mixture aside.
5. Place the salmon fillet in a suitable baking tray, greased with cooking oil.
6. Brush the maple sauce over the fillets liberally
7. Broil them for 10 minutes in the oven at broiler settings.
8. Serve warm.

Nutrition:
Calories 289, Total Fat 11.1g, Saturated Fat 1.6g, Cholesterol 78mg, Sodium 80mg, Protein 34.6g, Calcium 78mg, Phosphorous 230mg, Potassium 331mg

130. Eggplant and Red Pepper Soup

Preparation Time: 20 minutes
Cooking Time: 40 minutes
Servings: 2

Ingredients:

- 1 small sweet onion, cut into quarters
- 2 small red bell peppers, halved
- 2 cups cubed eggplant
- 2 cloves garlic, crushed
- 1 tbsp. olive oil
- 1 cup chicken stock
- Water
- ¼ cup chopped fresh basil
- Ground black pepper

Directions:

1. Preheat the oven to 350°F.
2. Put the onions, red peppers, eggplant, and garlic in a baking dish.
3. Drizzle the vegetables with olive oil.
4. Roast the vegetables for 30 minutes or until they are slightly charred and soft.

5. Cool the vegetables slightly and remove the skin from the peppers.
6. Puree the vegetables with a hand mixer (with the chicken stock).
7. Transfer the soup to a medium pot and add enough water to reach the desired thickness.
8. Heat the soup to a simmer and add the basil.
9. Season with pepper and serve.

Nutrition:
Calories: 61, Fat: 2g, Carb: 9g, Phosphorus: 33mg, Potassium: 198mg, Sodium: 98mg, Protein: 2g

131. Seafood Casserole

Preparation Time: 20 minutes
Cooking Time: 45 minutes
Servings: 2

Ingredients:

- 2 cups eggplant peeled and diced into 1-inch pieces
- Butter, for greasing the baking dish
- 1 tbsp. olive oil
- ½ sweet onion, chopped
- 1 tsp. minced garlic
- 1 celery stalk, chopped
- ½ red bell pepper, boiled and chopped
- 3 tbsp. freshly squeezed lemon juice
- 1 tsp. hot sauce
- ¼ tsp. creole seasoning mix
- ½ cup white rice, uncooked
- 1 large egg
- 4 oz. cooked shrimp
- 6 oz. Queen crab meat

Directions:

1. Preheat the oven to 350°F. Boil the eggplant in a saucepan for 5 minutes. Drain and set aside.
2. Grease a 9-by-13-inch baking dish with butter and set aside. Heat the olive oil in a large skillet over medium heat.
3. Sauté the garlic, onion, celery, and bell pepper for 4 minutes or until tender
4. Add the sautéed vegetables to the eggplant, along with the lemon juice, hot sauce, seasoning, rice, and egg. Stir to combine. Fold in the shrimp and crab meat.
5. Spoon the casserole mixture into the casserole dish, patting down the top.
6. Bake for 25 to 30 minutes or until casserole is heated through and rice is tender.
7. Serve warm.

Nutrition:
Calories: 61, Fat: 2g, Carb: 9g, Phosphorus: 23mg, Potassium: 178mg, Sodium: 98mg, Protein: 2g

132. Ground Beef and Rice Soup

Preparation Time: 15 minutes
Cooking Time: 40 minutes
Servings: 2

Ingredients:

- ½ lb. extra-lean ground beef
- ½ small sweet onion, chopped
- 1 tsp. minced garlic
- 2 cups water and 1 cup low-sodium beef broth
- ½ cup long-grain white rice, uncooked
- 1 celery stalk, chopped
- ½ cup fresh green beans, cut into – 1-inch pieces
- 1 tsp. chopped fresh thyme
- Ground black pepper

Directions:

1. Sauté the ground beef in a saucepan for 6 minutes or until the beef is completely browned. Drain off the excess fat and add the onion and garlic to the saucepan. Sauté the vegetables for about 3 minutes, or until they are softened
2. Add the celery, rice, beef broth, and water. Bring the soup to a boil, reduce the heat to low, and simmer for 30 minutes or until the rice is tender.
3. Add the green beans and thyme and simmer for 3 minutes. Remove the soup from the heat and season with pepper.

Nutrition: Calories: 51, Fat: 2g, Carb: 9g, Phosphorus: 63mg, Potassium: 198mg, Sodium: 128mg, Protein: 2g

133. Couscous Burgers

Preparation Time: 20 minutes
Cooking Time: 10 minutes
Servings: 2

Ingredients:

- ½ cup canned chickpeas, rinsed and drained
- 2 tbsp. chopped fresh cilantro
- Chopped fresh parsley
- 1 tbsp. lemon juice
- 2 tsp. lemon zest
- 1 tsp. minced garlic
- 2 ½ cups cooked couscous
- 2 lightly beaten eggs
- 2 tbsp. olive oil

Directions:

1. Put the cilantro, chickpeas, parsley, lemon juice, lemon zest, and garlic in a food processor and pulse until a paste form.
2. Transfer the chickpea mixture to a bowl and add the eggs and couscous. Mix well.
3. Chill the mixture in the refrigerator for 1 hour.
4. Form the couscous mixture into 4 patties.

5. Heat olive oil in a skillet.
6. Place the patties in the skillet, 2 at a time, gently pressing them down with a spatula.
7. Cook for 5 minutes or until golden and flip the patties over.
8. Cook the other side for 5 minutes and transfer the cooked burgers to a plate covered with a paper towel. Repeat with the remaining 2 burgers.

Nutrition:
Calories: 61, Fat: 2g, Carb: 9g, Phosphorus: 133mg, Potassium: 168mg, Sodium: 108mg, Protein: 2g

134. Baked Flounder

Preparation Time: 20 minutes
Cooking Time: 5 minutes
Servings: 2

Ingredients:

- ¼ cup homemade mayonnaise
- Juice of 1 lime
- Zest of 1 lime
- ½ cup chopped fresh cilantro
- 4 (3-oz.) flounder fillets
- Ground black pepper

Directions:

1. Preheat the oven to 400°F. In a bowl, stir together the cilantro, lime juice, lime zest, and mayonnaise.
2. Place 4 pieces of foil, about 8 by 8 inches square, on a clean work surface.
3. Place a flounder fillet in the center of each square.
4. Top the fillets evenly with the mayonnaise mixture.
5. Season the flounder with pepper.
6. Fold the foil's sides over the fish, create a snug packet, and place the foil packets on a baking sheet.
7. Bake the fish for 4 to 5 minutes.
8. Unfold the packets and serve.

Nutrition: Calories: 51, Fat: 2g, Carb: 9g, Phosphorus: 33mg, Potassium: 98mg, Sodium: 78mg Protein: 2g

135. Persian Chicken

Preparation Time: 10 minutes
Cooking Time: 20 minutes
Servings: 3

Ingredients:

- ½ sweet onion, chopped
- ¼ cup lemon juice
- 1 tbsp. dried oregano
- 1 tsp. minced garlic
- 1 tsp. sweet paprika
- ½ tsp. ground cumin
- ½ cup olive oil
- 5 boneless, skinless chicken thighs

Directions:

1. Put the cumin, paprika, garlic, oregano, lemon juice, and onion in a food processor and pulse to mix the ingredients.
2. Keep the motor running and add the olive oil until the mixture is smooth.
3. Place the chicken thighs in a large sealable freezer bag and pour the marinade into the bag.
4. Seal the bag and place it in the refrigerator, turning the bag twice, for 2 hours.
5. Remove the thighs from the marinade and discard the extra marinade.
6. Preheat the barbecue to medium. Grill the chicken for about 20 minutes, turning once, until it reaches 165°F.

Nutrition: Calories: 321, Fat: 21g, Carb: 3g, Phosphorus: 131mg, Potassium: 220mg, Sodium: 86mg, Protein: 22g

136. Pork Souvlaki

Preparation Time: 20 minutes
Cooking Time: 12 minutes
Servings: 2

Ingredients:

- 3 tbsp. olive oil
- 2 tbsp. lemon juice
- 1 tsp. minced garlic
- 1 tbsp. chopped fresh oregano
- ¼ tsp. ground black pepper
- 1 lb. Pork leg, cut into 2-inch cubes

Directions:

1. In a bowl, stir together the lemon juice, olive oil, garlic, oregano, and pepper. Add the pork cubes and toss to coat. Place the bowl in the refrigerator, covered, for 2 hours to marinate. Thread the pork chunks onto 8 wooden skewers that have been soaked in water.
2. Preheat the barbecue to medium-high heat. Grill the pork skewers for about 12 minutes, turning once, until just cooked through but still juicy.

Nutrition:
Calories: 61, Fat: 2g, Carb: 9g, Phosphorus: 33mg, Potassium: 198mg, Sodium: 98mg, Protein: 2g

137. Pork Meatloaf

Preparation Time: 10 minutes
Cooking Time: 50 minutes
Servings: 2

Ingredients:

- 1 lb. 95% lean ground beef
- ½ cup breadcrumbs
- ½ cup chopped sweet onion
- 1 egg
- 2 tbsp. chopped fresh basil
- 1 tsp. chopped fresh thyme
- 1 tsp. chopped fresh parsley
- ¼ tsp. ground black pepper
- 1 tbsp. brown sugar
- 1 tsp. white vinegar
- ¼ tsp. garlic powder

Directions:

1. Preheat the oven to 350°F. Mix together the breadcrumbs, beef, onion, basil, egg, thyme, parsley, and pepper until well combined.
2. Press the meat mixture into a 9-by-5-inch loaf pan. In a small bowl, stir together the brown sugar, vinegar, and garlic powder.
3. Spread the brown sugar mixture evenly over the meat. Bake the meatloaf for about 50 minutes or until it is cooked through.
4. Let the meatloaf stand for 10 minutes, and then pour out any accumulated grease.

Nutrition:
Calories: 51, Fat: 2g, Carb: 9g, Phosphorus: 23mg, Potassium: 190mg, Sodium: 98mg, Protein: 2g

138. Chicken Stew

Preparation Time: 20 minutes
Cooking Time: 50 minutes
Servings: 2

Ingredients:

- 1 tbsp. olive oil
- 1 lb. boneless, skinless chicken thighs, cut into 1-inch cubes
- ½ sweet onion, chopped
- 1 tbsp. minced garlic
- 2 cups chicken stock
- 1 cup plus 2 tbsp. water
- 1 carrot, sliced
- 2 stalks celery, sliced
- 1 turnip, sliced thin
- 1 tbsp. chopped fresh thyme
- 1 tsp. chopped fresh rosemary
- 2 tsp. cornstarch
- Ground black pepper to taste

Directions:

1. Place a large saucepan on medium heat and add the olive oil.
2. Sauté the chicken for 6 minutes or until it is lightly browned, stirring often.
3. Add the onion, garlic, and sauté for 3 minutes. Add 1-cup water, chicken stock, carrot, celery, and turnip, and bring the stew to a boil.
4. Reduce the heat to low and simmer for 30 minutes or until the chicken is cooked through and tender.

Add the thyme and rosemary and simmer for 3 minutes more.

5. In a small bowl, stir together the 2 tablespoons of water and the cornstarch; add the mixture to the stew.
6. Stir to incorporate the cornstarch mixture and cook for 3 to 4 minutes or until the stew thickens.
7. Remove from the heat and season with pepper.

Nutrition:
Calories: 141, Fat: 8g, Carb: 5g, Phosphorus: 53mg, Potassium: 192mg, Sodium: 214mg, Protein: 9g

139. Beef Chili

Preparation Time: 10 minutes
Cooking Time: 30 minutes
Servings: 2

Ingredients:
- 1 onion, diced
- 1 red bell pepper, diced
- 2 cloves garlic, minced
- 6 oz. lean ground beef
- 1 tsp. chili powder
- 1 tsp. oregano
- 2 tbsp. extra virgin olive oil
- 1 cup water
- 1 cup brown rice
- 1 tbsp. fresh cilantro to serve

Directions:
1. Soak vegetables in warm water.
2. Bring a pan of water to a boil and add rice for 20 minutes.
3. Meanwhile, add the oil to a pan and heat it on medium-high heat.
4. Add the pepper, onions, and garlic and sauté for 5 minutes until soft.
5. Remove and set aside.
6. Add the beef to the pan and stir until browned.
7. Add the vegetables back into the pan and stir.
8. Now add the chili powder and herbs and the water, cover, and turn the heat down a little to simmer for 15 minutes.
9. Meanwhile, drain the water from the rice and the lid and steam while the chili is cooking.
10. Serve hot with the fresh cilantro sprinkled over the top.

Nutrition:
Calories: 61, Fat: 2g, Carb: 9g, Phosphorus: 33mg, Potassium: 198mg, Sodium: 98mg, Protein: 2g

140. Shrimp Paella

Preparation Time: 5 minutes
Cooking Time: 10 minutes

Servings: 2

Ingredients:
- 1 cup cooked brown rice
- 1 chopped red onion
- 1 tsp. paprika
- 1 chopped garlic clove
- 1 tbsp. olive oil
- 6 oz. frozen cooked shrimp
- 1 deseeded and sliced chili pepper
- 1 tbsp. oregano

Directions:
1. Heat the olive oil in a large pan on medium-high heat. Add the onion, garlic, and sauté for 2-3 minutes until soft.
2. Now add the shrimp and sauté for a further 5 minutes or until hot through. Now add the herbs, spices, chili, and rice with ½ cup boiling water. Stir until everything is warm and the water has been absorbed.
3. Plate up and serve.

Nutrition:
Calories: 221, Protein: 17g, Carbs: 31g, Fat: 8g, Sodium (Na): 235mg, Potassium (K): 176mg, Phosphorus: 189 mg

141. Salmon & Pesto Salad

Preparation Time: 5 minutes
Cooking Time: 15 minutes
Servings: 2

Ingredients:
For the pesto:
- 1 minced garlic clove
- ½ cup fresh arugula
- ¼ cup extra virgin olive oil
- ½ cup fresh basil
- 1 tsp. black pepper

For the salmon:
- 4 oz. skinless salmon fillet
- 1 tbsp. coconut oil

For the salad:
- ½ juiced lemon
- 2 sliced radishes
- ½ cup iceberg lettuce
- 1 tsp. black pepper

Directions:
1. Prepare the pesto by blending all the ingredients for the pesto in a food processor or by grinding with a pestle and mortar. Set aside.
2. Add a skillet to the stove on medium-high heat and melt the coconut oil.
3. Add the salmon to the pan.
4. Cook for 7-8 minutes and turn over.

5. Cook for a further 3-4 minutes or until cooked through.
6. Remove fillets from the skillet and allow to rest.
7. Mix the lettuce and the radishes and squeeze over the juice of ½ lemon.
8. Flake the salmon with a fork and mix through the salad.
9. Toss to coat and sprinkle with a little black pepper to serve.

Nutrition:
Calories: 221, Protein: 13 g, Carbs: 1 g, Fat: 34 g, Sodium (Na): 80 mg, Potassium (K): 119 mg, Phosphorus: 158 mg

142. Baked Fennel & Garlic Sea Bass

Preparation Time: 5 minutes
Cooking Time: 15 minutes
Servings: 2

Ingredients:

- 1 lemon
- ½ sliced fennel bulb
- 6 oz. sea bass fillets
- 1 tsp. black pepper
- 2 garlic cloves

Directions:

1. Preheat the oven to 375°F/Gas Mark 5.
2. Sprinkle black pepper over the Sea Bass.
3. Slice the fennel bulb and garlic cloves.
4. Add 1 salmon fillet and half the fennel and garlic to one sheet of baking paper or tin foil.
5. Squeeze in ½ lemon juices.
6. Repeat for the other fillet.
7. Fold and add to the oven for 12-15 minutes or until fish is thoroughly cooked through.
8. Meanwhile, add boiling water to your couscous, cover, and allow to steam.
9. Serve with your choice of rice or salad.

Nutrition: Calories: 221, Protein: 14 g, Carbs: 3 g, Fat: 2 g, Sodium (Na): 119 mg, Potassium (K): 398 mg, Phosphorus: 149 mg

143. Lemon, Garlic & Cilantro Tuna and Rice

Preparation Time: 5 minutes
Cooking Time: 0 minutes
Servings: 2

Ingredients:

- ½ cup arugula
- 1 tbsp. extra virgin olive oil
- 1 cup cooked rice
- 1 tsp. black pepper
- ¼ finely diced red onion
- 1 juiced lemon
- 3 oz. canned tuna

- 2 tbsp. chopped fresh cilantro

Directions:

1. Mix the olive oil, pepper, cilantro, and red onion in a bowl.
2. Stir in the tuna, cover, and leave in the fridge for as long as possible (if you can) or serve immediately.
3. When ready to eat, serve up with the cooked rice and arugula!

Nutrition:
Calories: 221, Protein: 11 g, Carbs: 26 g, Fat: 7 g, Sodium (Na): 143 mg, Potassium (K): 197 mg, Phosphorus: 182 mg

144. Shore Lunch–Style Sole

Preparation Time: 20 minutes
Cooking Time: 10 minutes
Servings: 2

Ingredients:

- ¼ cup all-purpose flour
- ¼ tsp. freshly ground black pepper
- 12 oz. sole fillets, deboned and skinned
- 2 tbsp. olive oil
- 1 scallion, both green and white parts, chopped
- Lemon wedges, for garnish

Directions:

1. In a large plastic freezer bag, shake together the flour and pepper to combine.
2. Add the fish fillets to the flour and shake to coat.
3. In a large skillet over medium-high heat, heat the olive oil.
4. When the oil is hot, add the fish fillets and fry for about 10 minutes, turning once, or until they are golden and cooked through.
5. Remove the fish from the oil onto paper towels to drain.
6. Serve topped with chopped scallions and a squeeze of lemon.

Nutrition:
Calories: 148 Potassium: 148mg Phosphorous: 223mg Protein: 11g Sodium: 242mg, Fat: 8g

145. Sardine Fish Cakes

Preparation Time: 10 minutes
Cooking Time: 10 minutes
Servings: 2

Ingredients:

- 11 oz. sardines, canned, drained
- ⅓ cup shallot, chopped
- 1 tsp. chili flakes
- ½ tsp. salt
- 2 tbsp. wheat flour, whole grain

- 1 egg, beaten
- 1 tbsp. chives, chopped
- 1 tsp. olive oil
- 1 tsp. butter

Directions:
1. Put the butter in the skillet and melt it.
2. Add shallot and cook it until translucent.
3. After this, transfer the shallot to the mixing bowl.
4. Add sardines, chili flakes, salt, flour, egg, chives, and mix up until smooth with the help of the fork.
5. Make the medium size cakes and place them in the skillet.
6. Add olive oil.
7. Roast the fish cakes for 3 minutes from each side over medium heat.
8. Dry the cooked fish cakes with a paper towel if needed and transfer them to the serving plates.

Nutrition:
Calories: 221g, Fat: 12.2g, Fiber: 0.1g, Carbs: 5.4g, Protein: 21.3g

146. Shrimp Szechuan

Preparation Time: 10 minutes
Cooking Time: 9 minutes
Servings: 2
Ingredients:

- 1 tbsp. canola oil
- ½ cup bean sprouts
- ½ cup green bell pepper, chopped
- ½ cup onion, chopped
- ½ cup raw mushroom pieces
- 1 tsp. ginger root, grated
- ½ tsp. garlic powder
- 1 tbsp. sesame oil
- 1 tsp. red pepper flakes
- ⅓ cup low-sodium chicken broth
- 4 tbsp. sherry wine
- 1 tsp. cornstarch
- 4 oz. shrimp, frozen

Directions:
1. Start by heating oil in the Instant pot on Sauté mode.
2. Toss in onions, ginger, mushrooms, bell pepper, and bean sprouts.
3. Sauté for 2 minutes then toss in all the ingredients except cornstarch.
4. Seal the lid and cook for 2 minutes on Manual mode at High pressure.
5. Then, release the pressure completely then remove the pot's lid.
6. Mix the cornstarch with 2 tablespoons of water in a bowl.

7. Combine the mixture into the Instant pot and cook for 5 minutes on sauté mode.
8. Serve warm.

Nutrition:
Calories 274, Total Fats 10 g, Saturated Fat 5.1 g, Cholesterol 115 mg, Sodium 261 mg, Total Carbs 30 g, Fiber 1.6 g, Sugar 0.3 g

147. 4-Ingredients Salmon Fillet

Preparation Time: 5 minutes
Cooking Time: 25 minutes
Servings: 1
Ingredients:

- 4 oz. salmon fillet
- ½ tsp. salt
- 1 tsp. sesame oil
- ½ tsp. sage

Directions:
1. Rub the fillet with salt and sage. Place the fish in the tray and sprinkle it with sesame oil.
2. Cook the fish for 25 minutes at 365°F. Flip the fish carefully onto another side after 12 minutes of cooking.

Nutrition:
Calories: 191g, Fat: 11.6g, Fiber: 0.1g, Carbs: 0.2g, Protein: 22g

148. Spanish Cod in Sauce

Preparation Time: 10 minutes
Cooking Time: 5 hours and 30 minutes
Servings: 2
Ingredients:

- 1 tsp. tomato paste
- 1 tsp. garlic, diced
- 1 white onion, sliced
- 1 jalapeno pepper, chopped
- ⅓ cup chicken stock
- 7 oz. Spanish cod fillet
- 1 tsp. paprika
- 1 tsp. salt

Directions:
1. Pour chicken stock into the saucepan.
2. Add tomato paste and mix up the liquid until homogenous.
3. Add garlic, onion, jalapeno pepper, paprika, and salt.
4. Bring the liquid to a boil and then simmer it.
5. Chop the cod fillet and add it to the tomato liquid.
6. Close the lid and simmer the fish for 10 minutes over low heat.
7. Serve the fish in the bowls with tomato sauce.

Nutrition:
Calories: 113g, Fat: 1.2g, Fiber: 1.9g, Carbs 7.2g, Protein: 18.9g

149. Fish Shakshuka

Preparation Time: 5 minutes
Cooking Time: 15 minutes
Servings: 3
Ingredients:
- 5 eggs
- 1 cup tomatoes, chopped
- 3 bell peppers, chopped
- 1 tbsp. butter
- 1 tsp. tomato paste
- 1 tsp. chili pepper
- 1 tsp. salt
- 1 tbsp. fresh dill
- 5 oz. cod fillet, chopped
- 1 tbsp. scallions, chopped

Directions:
1. Melt butter in the skillet and add chili pepper, bell peppers, and tomatoes.
2. Sprinkle the vegetables with scallions, dill, salt, and chili pepper. Simmer them for 5 minutes.
3. After this, add chopped cod fillet and mix up well.
4. Close the lid and simmer the ingredients for 5 minutes over medium heat.
5. Then crack the eggs over the fish and close the lid.
6. Cook Shakshuka with the closed lid for 5 minutes.

Nutrition: Calories 143g, Fat 7.3g, Fiber 1.6g, Carbs 7.9g, Protein 12.8g

Chapter 7: Sides and Snacks Recipes

150. Cinnamon Apple Chips

Preparation Time: 5 minutes
Cooking Time: 2 to 3 hours
Servings: 2

Ingredients:

- 4 apples
- 1 tsp. ground cinnamon

Directions:

1. Preheat the oven to 200°F. Line a baking sheet with parchment paper.
2. Core the apples and cut them into ⅛-inch slices.
3. In a medium bowl, toss the apple slices with the cinnamon. Spread the apples in a single layer on the prepared baking sheet.
4. Cook for 2 to 3 hours, until the apples are dry. They will still be soft while hot, but will crisp once completely cooled. Store in an airtight container for up to four days.
5. Cooking Tip: If you don't have parchment paper, use cooking spray to prevent sticking.

Nutrition:
Calories: 96; Total Fat: 0g; Saturated Fat: 0g; Cholesterol: 0mg; Carbohydrates: 26g; Fiber: 5g; Protein: 1g; Phosphorus: 0mg; Potassium: 198mg; Sodium: 2mg

151. Savory Collard Chips

Preparation Time: 5 minutes
Cooking Time: 20 minutes
Servings: 2

Ingredients:

- 1 bunch collard greens
- 1 tsp. extra-virgin olive oil
- Juice of ½ lemon
- ½ tsp. garlic powder
- ¼ tsp. freshly ground black pepper

Directions:

1. Preheat the oven to 350°F. Line a baking sheet with parchment paper.
2. Cut the collards into 2-by-2-inch squares and pat dry with paper towels. In a large bowl, toss the greens with olive oil, lemon juice, garlic powder, and pepper. Use your hands to mix well, massaging the dressing into the greens until evenly coated.
3. Arrange the collards in a single layer on the baking sheet, and cook for 8 minutes. Flip the pieces and cook for an additional 8 minutes, until crisp. Remove from the oven, let cool, and store in an airtight container in a cool location for up to three days.

4. Substitution Tip: If you prefer, use fresh garlic instead of dried. Mince 2 or 3 cloves, toss with the collards, and proceed as directed.

Nutrition:
Calories: 24; Total Fat: 1g; Saturated Fat: 0g; Cholesterol: 0mg; Carbohydrates: 3g; Fiber: 1g; Protein: 1g; Phosphorus: 6mg; Potassium: 72mg; Sodium: 8mg

152. Roasted Red Pepper Hummus

Preparation Time: 10 minutes
Cooking Time: 10 minutes
Servings: 2

Ingredients:

- 1 red bell pepper
- 1 (15-oz.) can chickpeas, drained and rinsed
- Juice of 1 lemon
- 2 tbsp. tahini and 2 garlic cloves
- 2 tbsp. extra-virgin olive oil

Directions:

1. Move an oven rack to the highest position. Heat the broiler to high.
2. Core the pepper and cut it into three or four large pieces. Arrange them on a baking sheet, skin-side up.
3. Broil the peppers for 5 to 10 minutes, until the skins are charred. Remove from the oven and transfer the peppers to a small bowl. Cover with plastic wrap and let them steam for 10 to 15 minutes, until cool enough to handle.
4. Peel the charred skin off the peppers, and place the peppers in a blender.
5. Add the chickpeas, lemon juice, tahini, garlic, and olive oil. Process until smooth, adding up to 1 tablespoon of water to adjust consistency as desired.
6. Substitution Tip: This hummus can also be made without the red pepper if desired. To do this, simply follow Step 5. This will cut the potassium to 59mg per serving.

Nutrition: Calories: 103; Total Fat: 6g; Saturated Fat: 1g; Cholesterol: 0mg; Carbohydrates: 10g; Fiber: 3g; Protein: 3g; Phosphorus: 58mg; Potassium: 91mg; Sodium: 72mg

153. Thai-Style Eggplant Dip

Preparation Time: 10 minutes
Cooking Time: 30 minutes
Servings: 2
Ingredients:

- 1 lb. Thai eggplant (or Japanese or Chinese eggplant)
- 2 tbsp. rice vinegar
- 2 tsp. sugar
- 1 tsp. low-sodium soy sauce
- 1 jalapeño pepper
- 2 garlic cloves
- ¼ cup chopped basil
- Cut vegetables or crackers, for serving

Directions:

1. Preheat the oven to 425°F.
2. Pierce the eggplant in several places with a skewer or knife. Place on a rimmed baking sheet and cook until soft, about 30 minutes. Let cool, cut in half, and scoop out the flesh of the eggplant into a blender.
3. Add the rice vinegar, sugar, soy sauce, jalapeño, garlic, and basil to the blender. Process until smooth. Serve with cut vegetables or crackers.
4. Lower sodium Tip: If you need to lower your sodium further, omit the soy sauce to lower the sodium to 3 mg.

Nutrition: Calories: 40; Total Fat: 0g; Saturated Fat: 0g; Cholesterol: 0mg; Carbohydrates: 10g; Fiber: 4g; Protein: 2g; Phosphorus: 34mg; Potassium: 284mg; Sodium: 47mg

154. Collard Salad Rolls with Peanut Dipping Sauce

Preparation Time: 20 minutes
Cooking Time: 15 minutes
Servings: 2

Ingredients:

For the Dipping Sauce:
- ¼ cup peanut butter
- 2 tbsp. honey
- Juice of 1 lime
- ¼ tsp. red chili flakes

For the Salad Rolls:
- 4 oz. extra-firm tofu
- 1 bunch collard greens
- 1 cup thinly sliced purple cabbage
- 1 cup bean sprouts
- 2 carrots, cut into matchsticks
- ½ cup cilantro leaves and stems

Directions:

To Make the Dipping Sauce

1. In a blender, combine the peanut butter, honey, lime juice, and chili flakes, and process until smooth. Add 1 to 2 tablespoons of water as desired for consistency.

To Make the Salad Rolls

1. Using paper towels, press the excess moisture from the tofu. Cut into ½-inch-thick matchsticks.
2. Remove any tough stems from the collard greens and set aside.
3. Arrange all of the ingredients within reach. Cup one collard green leaf in your hand, and add a couple of pieces of the tofu and a small amount each of the cabbage, bean sprouts, and carrots. Top with a couple of cilantro sprigs, and roll into a cylinder. Place each roll, seam-side down, on a serving platter while you assemble the rest of the rolls. Serve with the dipping sauce.
4. Substitution Tip: To lower the potassium, omit the cabbage and use only 1 carrot, which will drop the potassium to 208 mg.

Nutrition:
Calories: 174; Total Fat: 9g; Saturated Fat: 2g; Cholesterol: 0mg; Carbohydrates: 20g; Fiber: 5g; Protein: 8g; Phosphorus: 56mg; Potassium: 284mg; Sodium: 42mg

155. Simple Roasted Broccoli

Preparation Time: 5 minutes
Cooking Time: 20 minutes
Servings: 2
Ingredients:

- 2 small heads of broccoli, cut into florets
- 1 tbsp. extra-virgin olive oil
- 3 garlic cloves, minced

Directions:

1. Preheat the oven to 425°F.
2. In a medium bowl, toss the broccoli with olive oil and garlic. Arrange in a single layer on a baking sheet.
3. Roast for 10 minutes, then flip the broccoli and roast an additional 10 minutes. Serve.

Cooking Tip: Roasted broccoli makes for great leftovers—throw them in a quick salad for added flavor and bulk. To save leftovers, refrigerate in an airtight container for three to five days.

Nutrition:
Calories: 38; Total Fat: 2g; Saturated Fat: 0g; Cholesterol: 0mg; Carbohydrates: 4g; Fiber: 1g; Protein: 1g; Phosphorus: 32mg; Potassium: 150mg; Sodium: 15mg

156. Roasted Mint Carrots

Preparation Time: 5 minutes
Cooking Time: 20 minutes
Servings: 2

Ingredients:

- 1-lb. carrots, trimmed
- 1 tbsp. extra-virgin olive oil
- Freshly ground black pepper
- ¼ cup thinly sliced mint

Directions:

1. Preheat the oven to 425°F.
2. Arrange the carrots in a single layer on a rimmed baking sheet. Drizzle with the olive oil, and shake the carrots on the sheet to coat. Season with pepper.
3. Roast for 20 minutes, or until tender and browned, stirring twice while cooking. Sprinkle with the mint and serve.

Substitution Tip: To lower the potassium in this dish, use 8 ounces of carrots and 8 ounces of turnips cut into cubes. This will cut the potassium to 193mg.

Nutrition:
Calories: 51; Total Fat: 2g; Saturated Fat: 0g; Cholesterol: 0mg; Carbohydrates: 7g; Fiber: 2g; Protein: 1g; Phosphorus: 26mg; Potassium: 242mg; Sodium: 52mg

157. Roasted Root Vegetables

Preparation Time: 10 minutes
Cooking Time: 25 minutes
Servings: 2

Ingredients:

- 1 cup chopped turnips
- 1 cup chopped rutabaga
- 1 cup chopped parsnips
- 1 tbsp. extra-virgin olive oil
- 1 tsp. fresh chopped rosemary
- Freshly ground black pepper

Directions:

1. Preheat the oven to 400°F.
2. In a large bowl, toss the turnips, rutabaga, and parsnips with olive oil and rosemary. Arrange in a single layer on a baking sheet, and season with pepper.
3. Bake until the vegetables are tender and browned, 20 to 25 minutes, stirring once.

Substitution Tip: Experiment with other fresh herbs in this dish to suit your own tastes. Thyme, tarragon, oregano, and minced garlic all add unique flavors to these root vegetables.

Nutrition:
Calories: 52; Total Fat: 2g; Saturated Fat: 0g; Cholesterol: 0mg; Carbohydrates: 7g; Fiber: 2g; Protein: 1g; Phosphorus: 35mg; Potassium: 205mg; Sodium: 22mg

158. Vegetable Couscous

Preparation Time: 10 minutes
Cooking Time: 15 minutes
Servings: 2

Ingredients:

- 1 tbsp. extra-virgin olive oil
- ½ sweet onion, diced
- 1 carrot, diced
- 1 celery stalk, diced
- ½ cup diced red or yellow bell pepper
- 1 small zucchini, diced
- 1 cup couscous
- 1 ½ cups Simple Chicken Broth or low-sodium store-bought chicken stock
- ½ tsp. garlic powder
- Freshly ground black pepper

Directions:

1. In a large skillet, heat the olive oil over medium heat. Add the onion, carrot, celery, and bell pepper, and cook, stirring occasionally, until the vegetables are just becoming tender, about 5 to 7 minutes.
2. Add the zucchini, couscous, broth, and garlic powder. Stir to blend, and bring to a boil. Cover and remove from the heat. Let stand for 5 to 8 minutes. Fluff with a fork, season with pepper and serve.

Substitution Tip: Swap out vegetables to make this couscous your own creation. Yellow summer squash or patty pan squash can be substituted for the zucchini. Other vegetables, like asparagus, broccoli, or cauliflower, can be added instead of carrots and bell peppers.

Nutrition:
Calories: 154; Total Fat: 3g; Saturated Fat: 1g; Cholesterol: 0mg; Carbohydrates: 27g; Fiber: 2g; Protein: 5g; Phosphorus: 83mg; Potassium: 197mg; Sodium: 36mg

159. Garlic Cauliflower Rice

Preparation Time: 5 minutes
Cooking Time: 10 minutes
Servings: 2

Ingredients:

- 1 medium head cauliflower
- 1 tbsp. extra-virgin olive oil
- 4 garlic cloves, minced
- Freshly ground black pepper

Directions:

1. Using a sharp knife, remove the core of the cauliflower, and separate the cauliflower into florets.
2. In a food processor, pulse the florets until they are the size of rice, being careful not to over-process them to the point of becoming mushy.
3. In a large skillet over medium heat, heat the olive oil. Add the garlic, and stir until just fragrant.
4. Add the cauliflower, stirring to coat. Add 1 tablespoon of water to the pan, cover, and reduce the heat to low. Steam for 7 to 10 minutes, until the cauliflower is tender. Season with pepper and serve.

Cooking Tip: Cauliflower rice tastes great both when fresh and after resting in the refrigerator for a day or two. Make a batch and use it throughout the week as a side dish, heating it in the microwave before serving. In an airtight container, it will keep refrigerated for three to five days.

Nutrition: Calories: 37; Total Fat: 2g; Saturated Fat: 0g; Cholesterol: 0mg; Carbohydrates: 4g; Fiber: 2g; Protein: 2g; Phosphorus: 35mg; Potassium: 226mg; Sodium: 22mg

160. Citrus Sesame Cookies

Preparation Time: 15 minutes
Cooking Time: 10 minutes
Servings: 15

Ingredients:

- ¾ cup unsalted butter, at room temperature
- ½ cup sugar
- 1 egg
- 1 tsp. vanilla extract
- 2 cups all-purpose flour
- 2 tbsp. toasted sesame seeds
- ½ tsp. baking soda
- 1 tsp. freshly grated lemon zest
- 1 tsp. freshly grated orange zest

Directions:

1. In a large bowl and using a mixer, beat together the butter and sugar on high speed until thick and fluffy, about 3 minutes.
2. Add the egg and vanilla and beat to mix thoroughly, scraping down the sides of the bowl.
3. In a small bowl, stir together the flour, sesame seeds, baking soda, lemon zest, and orange zest.
4. Add the flour mixture to the butter mixture, and stir until well blended.
5. Roll the dough into a long cylinder about 2 inches in diameter, and wrap in plastic wrap. Refrigerate for 1 hour.
6. Preheat the oven to 350°F.
7. Line a baking sheet with parchment paper.
8. Cut the firm cookie dough into ½-inch-thick rounds, and place them on the prepared baking sheet.
9. Bake for 10 to 12 minutes until lightly golden. Cool completely on wire racks.
10. Store in a sealed container in the refrigerator for up to 1 week, or in the freezer for up to 2 months.

Nutrition:
Calories: 150 Potassium: 25mg Phosphorus: 29mg Protein 2g Sodium: 5mg, Fat: 9g

161. Mexican Steak Tacos

Preparation Time: 5 minutes
Cooking Time: 10 minutes
Servings: 2

Ingredients:

- 1 red bell pepper
- 1 (15-oz.) can chickpeas, drained and rinsed
- Juice of 1 lemon
- 2 tbsp. tahini
- 2 garlic cloves
- 2 tbsp. extra-virgin olive oil

Directions:

1. Move the rack of the oven to the highest position. Heat the broiler to high. Core the pepper and cut it into three or four large pieces. Arrange them on a baking sheet, skin-side up. Broil the peppers for 5 to 10 minutes, until the skins are charred. Remove from the oven then transfer the peppers to a small bowl. Cover with plastic wrap and let them steam for 10 to 15 minutes, until cool enough to handle. Peel the charred skin off the peppers, and place the peppers in a blender. Add the chickpeas, lemon juice, tahini, garlic, and olive oil. Wait until smooth, then add up to 1 tablespoon of water to adjust consistency as desired.

Substitution Tip: This hummus can also be made without the red pepper if desired. To do this, simply follow Step 5. This will cut the potassium to 59mg per serving.

Nutrition: Calories: 103, Total Fat: 6g, Saturated Fat: 1g, Cholesterol: 0mg, Carbohydrates: 10g, Fiber: 3g, Protein: 3g, Phosphorus: 58mg, Potassium: 91mg, Sodium: 72mg

162. Traditional Spritz Cookies

Preparation Time: 15 minutes
Cooking Time: 5 minutes
Servings: 24

Ingredients:

- 1 cup unsalted butter, at room temperature
- ½ cup sugar
- 1 egg
- 2 tsp. vanilla extract

- 2 ½ cups all-purpose flour

Directions:

1. Preheat the oven to 400°F.
2. Line a baking sheet with parchment paper.
3. Beat in the egg and vanilla, scraping down the sides of the bowl.
4. Beat in the flour on low speed until blended.
5. Drop the cookies by the spoonful onto the prepared baking sheet.
6. Bake until firm and lightly golden, 5 to 7 minutes. Cool completely on a rack.
7. Store in a sealed container in a cool, dry place for up to 1 week.

Nutrition:

Calories: 271 Potassium: 39mg Phosphorus: 40mg Protein: 3g Sodium: 11mg, Fat: 16g

163. Coconut Pancakes

Preparation Time: 5 minutes
Cooking Time: 10 minutes
Servings: 2

Ingredients:

- 2 free-range egg whites
- 2 tbsp. all-purpose white flour
- 3 tbsp. coconut shavings
- 2 tbsp. coconut milk (optional)
- 1 tbsp. coconut oil

Directions:

1. Get a bowl and combine all the ingredients. Mix well until you get a thick batter. Heat a skillet on medium heat and heat the coconut oil. Pour half the mixture to the center of the pan, forming a pancake, and cook through for 3-4 minutes on each side. Serve with your choice of berries on the top.

Tip: Check with your doctor or dietitian as to whether you can still have coconut milk. Alternatively, use non-dairy milk, such as almond.

Nutrition:

Calories: 177, Fat: 13g, Carbohydrates: 12g, Phosphorus: 37mg, Potassium: 133mg, Sodium: 133mg, Protein: 5g

164. Spiced Peaches

Preparation Time: 5 minutes
Cooking Time: 10 minutes
Servings: 2

Ingredients:

- 1 cup canned peaches in their own juices
- ½ tsp. cornstarch
- 1 tsp. ground cloves
- 1 tsp. ground cinnamon

- 1 tsp. ground nutmeg
- ½ lemon zest
- ½ cup water

Directions:

1. Drain peaches. Combine water, cornstarch, cinnamon, nutmeg, ground cloves, and lemon zest in a pan on the stove. Heat on medium heat and add peaches. Bring to a boil, reduce the heat and simmer for 10 minutes. Serve warm.

Nutrition:

Calories: 70, Fat: 1g, Carbohydrates: 18g, Phosphorus: 26mg, Potassium: 184mg, Sodium: 9mg, Protein: 1g

165. Pumpkin Cheesecake Bar

Preparation Time: 5 minutes
Cooking Time: 10 minutes
Servings: 2

Ingredients:

- 2 ½ tbsp. unsalted butter
- 4 oz. cream cheese
- ½ cup all-purpose white flour
- 3 tbsp. golden-brown sugar
- ¼ cup granulated sugar
- ½ cup puréed pumpkin
- 2 egg whites
- 1 tsp. ground cinnamon
- 1 tsp. ground nutmeg
- 1 tsp. vanilla extract

Directions:

1. Set the oven 350°F/170°C/Gas Mark 4 for Preheating. Mix the flour and brown sugar in a mixing bowl. Mix in the butter with your fingertips to form 'breadcrumbs.'
2. Place ¾ of this mixture into the bottom of an ovenproof dish. Bake in the oven for 15 minutes and remove to cool. Lightly whisk the egg and fold in the cream cheese, sugar (or substitute stevia), pumpkin, cinnamon, nutmeg, and vanilla until smooth.
3. Pour this mixture over the oven-baked base and sprinkle with the rest of the breadcrumbs from earlier. Place back in the oven and bake for a further 30–35 minutes. Allow to cool and slice to Serve.

Nutrition:

Calories: 296, Fat: 17g, Carbohydrates: 30g, Phosphorus: 62mg, Potassium: 164g, Sodium: 159mg, Protein: 5g

166. Blueberry and Vanilla Mini Muffins

Preparation Time: 5 minutes
Cooking Time: 10 minutes

Servings: 2

Ingredients:

- 3 egg whites
- ¼ cup all-purpose white flour
- 1 tbsp. coconut flour
- 1 tsp. baking soda
- 1 tbsp. nutmeg, grated
- 1 tsp. vanilla extract
- 1 tsp. stevia
- ¼ cup fresh blueberries

Directions:

1. Set the oven 325°F/170°C/Gas Mark 3 for Preheating. Add all the ingredients to a bowl. Divide the batter into 4 and spoon into a lightly oiled muffin tin. Bake in the oven for 15–20 minutes or until cooked through. Your knife should pull out clean from the middle of the muffin once done. Allow to cool on a wired rack before serving.

Nutrition:

Calories: 48, Fat: 1g, Carbohydrates: 8g, Phosphorus: 14mg, Potassium: 44mg, Sodium: 298mg, Protein: 2g

167. Puffy French toast

Preparation Time: 5 minutes
Cooking Time: 10 minutes
Servings: 2

Ingredients:

- 4 slices white bread, cut in ½ diagonally
- 3 whole eggs and 1 egg white
- 1 cup plain almond milk
- 2 tbsp. canola oil
- 1 tsp. cinnamon

Directions:

1. Preheat your oven to 400°F/180°C Beat the eggs and the almond milk. Heat the oil in a pan. Dip each bread slice/triangle into the egg and almond milk mixture. Fry in the pan until golden brown on each side. Place the toasts in a baking sheet and let cook in the oven for another 5 minutes. Serve warm and drizzle with some honey, icing sugar, or cinnamon on top.

Nutrition:

Calories: 293.75, Carbohydrate: 25.3g, Protein: 9.27g, Sodium: 211g, Potassium: 97mg, Phosphorus: 165mg, Dietary Fiber: 12.3g, Fat: 16.50g

168. Puff Oven Pancakes

Preparation Time: 5 minutes
Cooking Time: 10 minutes

Servings: 2

Ingredients:

- 2 large eggs.
- ½ cup rice flour
- ½ cup rice milk
- 2 tbsp. unsalted butter
- ⅛ tsp. salt

Directions:

1. Preheat the oven at 400°F/190°C. Grease a 10-inch skillet or Pyrex with the butter and heat in the oven until it melts. Beat the eggs and whisk in the rice milk, flour and salt in a mixing bowl until smooth. Take off the skillet or pie dish from the oven. Transfer the batter directly into the skillet and put it back in the oven for 25–30 minutes. Place in a serving dish and cut into 4 portions. Serve hot with honey or icing sugar on top.

Nutrition:

Calories: 159.75 Carbohydrate: 17g Protein: 5g Sodium 120g Potassium: 52mg Phosphorus: 66.25mg Dietary Fiber 0.5g Fat: 9g

169. Savory Muffins with Protein

Preparation Time: 5 minutes
Cooking Time: 10 minutes
Servings: 2

Ingredients:

- 2 cups corn flakes
- ½ cup unfortified almond milk
- 4 large eggs
- 2 tbsp. olive oil
- ½ cup almond milk
- 1 medium white onion, sliced
- 1 cup plain Greek yogurt
- ¼ cup pecans, chopped
- 1 tbsp. mixed seasoning blend, e.g., Mrs. Dash

Directions:

1. Preheat the oven at 350°F/180°C. Heat the olive oil in the pan. Sauté the onions with the pecans and seasoning blend for a couple of minutes. Add the rest of the ingredients and toss well. Split the mixture into 12 small muffin cups (lightly greased) and bake for 30–35 minutes or until an inserted knife or toothpick is coming out clean. Serve warm or keep at room temperature for a couple of days.

Nutrition:

Calories: 106.58, Carbohydrate: 8.20g, Protein: 4.77g, Sodium: 51.91mg, Potassium: 87.83 mg, Phosphorus: 49.41 mg, Dietary Fiber: 0.58 g, Fat: 5 g

Chapter 8: Fish and Seafood Recipes

170. Grilled Shrimp with Cucumber Lime Salsa

Preparation Time: 15 minutes
Cooking Time: 10 minutes
Servings: 2

Ingredients:

- 2 tbsp. olive oil
- 6 oz. large shrimp (16 to 20 count), peeled and deveined, tails left on
- 1 tsp. minced garlic
- ½ cup chopped English cucumber
- ½ cup chopped mango
- Zest of 1 lime
- Juice of 1 lime
- Freshly ground black pepper
- Lime wedges for garnish

Directions:

1. Soak 4 wooden skewers in water for 30 minutes.
2. Preheat the barbecue to medium-high heat.
3. In a large bowl, toss together the olive oil, shrimp, and garlic.
4. Thread the shrimp onto the skewers, about 4 shrimp per skewer.
5. In a small bowl, stir together the cucumber, mango, lime zest, and lime juice, and season the salsa lightly with pepper. Set aside.
6. Grill the shrimp for about 10 minutes, turning once or until the shrimp is opaque and cooked through.
7. Season the shrimp lightly with pepper.
8. Serve the shrimp on the cucumber salsa with lime wedges on the side.

Nutrition:
Calories: 120 Potassium: 129mg Phosphorus: 91mg Protein: 9g Sodium: 60mg, Fat: 8g

171. Salmon and Pesto Salad

Preparation Time: 5 minutes
Cooking Time: 15 minutes
Servings: 2

Ingredients:
For the pesto:

- 1 minced garlic clove
- ½ cup fresh arugula
- ¼ cup extra virgin olive oil
- ½ cup fresh basil
- 1 tsp. black pepper

For the salmon:

- 4 oz. skinless salmon fillet
- 1 tbsp. coconut oil

For the salad:

- ½ juiced lemon
- 2 sliced radishes
- ½ cup iceberg lettuce
- 1 tsp. black pepper

Directions:

1. Prepare the pesto by blending all the pesto ingredients in a kitchen appliance or by grinding with a pestle and mortar. Set aside.
2. Add a skillet to the stove on medium-high heat and melt the copra oil.
3. Add the salmon to the pan.
4. Cook for 7-8 minutes and switch over.
5. Cook for an extra 3-4 minutes or until cooked through.
6. Remove fillets from the skillet and permit to rest.
7. Mix the lettuce and therefore the radishes and squeeze over the juice of ½ lemon.
8. Flake the salmon with a fork and blend through the salad.
9. Toss to coat and sprinkle with a little black pepper to serve.

Nutrition:
Calories 221, Protein 13 g, Carbohydrates 1 g, Fat 34 g, Sodium (Na) 80 mg, Potassium (K) 119 mg, Phosphorus 158 mg

172. Baked Fennel and Garlic Sea Bass

Preparation Time: 5 minutes
Cooking Time: 15 minutes
Servings: 2

Ingredients:

- 1 lemon
- ½ sliced fennel bulb
- 6 oz. sea bass fillets
- 1 tsp. black pepper
- 2 garlic cloves

Directions:

1. Preheat the oven to 375°F/Gas Mark 5.
2. Sprinkle black pepper over the ocean Bass.
3. Slice the fennel bulb and garlic cloves.
4. Add 1 salmon fillet and half the fennel and garlic to at least one sheet of baking paper or tin foil.
5. Squeeze in ½ lemon juices. Repeat for the opposite fillet.

6. Fold and increase the oven for 12-15 minutes or until the fish is thoroughly cooked through.
7. Meanwhile, add boiling water to your couscous, cover, and permit to steam.
8. Serve together with your choice of rice or salad.

Nutrition: Calories 221, Protein 14 g, Carbohydrates 3 g, Fat 2 g, Sodium (Na) 119 mg, Potassium (K) 398 mg, Phosphorus 149 mg

173. Herb-Crusted Baked Haddock

Preparation Time: 10 minutes
Cooking Time: 20 minutes
Servings: 2
Ingredients:

- ½ cup bread crumbs
- 3 tbsp. chopped fresh parsley
- 1 tbsp. lemon zest
- 1 tsp. chopped fresh thyme
- ¼ tsp. freshly ground black pepper
- 1 tbsp. melted unsalted butter
- 12-oz. haddock fillets, deboned and skinned

Directions:

1. Preheat the oven to 350°F.
2. In a small bowl, stir together the bread crumbs, parsley, lemon zest, thyme, and pepper until well combined.
3. Add the melted butter and toss until the mixture resembles coarse crumbs
4. Place the haddock on a baking sheet and spoon the bread crumb mixture on top, pressing down firmly.
5. Bake the haddock in the oven for about 20 minutes or until the fish is just cooked through and flakes off in chunks when pressed.

Nutrition:
Calories: 143 Potassium: 285mg Phosphorus: 216mg Protein: 16g Sodium: 281mg, Fat: 4g

174. Cod & Green Bean Risotto

Preparation Time: 4 minutes
Cooking Time: 40 minutes
Servings: 2
Ingredients:

- ½ cup arugula
- 1 finely diced white onion
- 4 oz. cod fillet
- 1 cup white rice
- 2 lemon wedges
- 1 cup boiling water
- ¼ tsp. black pepper
- 1 cup of low sodium chicken broth
- 1 tbsp. extra-virgin olive oil
- ½ cup green beans

Directions:

1. Heat the oil in a large pan on medium heat.
2. Sauté the chopped onion for 5 minutes until soft before adding in the rice and stirring for 1-2 minutes.
3. Combine the broth with boiling water.
4. Add half the liquid to the pan and stir slowly.
5. Slowly add the juice's remainder while continuously stirring for up to 20-30 minutes.
6. Stir in the green beans to the risotto.
7. Place the fish on top of the rice, cover, and steam for 10 minutes.
8. Ensure the water doesn't dry out and keep topping up until the rice is cooked thoroughly.
9. Use your fork to interrupt up the fish fillets and stir into the rice.
10. Sprinkle with freshly ground pepper and a squeeze of fresh lemon to serve.
11. Garnish with lemon wedges and serve with the arugula.

Nutrition:
Calories 221, Protein 12 g, Carbohydrates 29 g, Fat 8 g, Sodium (Na) 398 mg, Potassium (K) 347 mg, Phosphorus 241 mg

175. Mixed Pepper Stuffed River Trout

Preparation Time: 5 minutes
Cooking Time: 20 minutes
Servings: 2
Ingredients:

- 1 whole river trout
- 1 tsp. thyme
- ¼ diced yellow pepper
- 1 cup baby spinach leaves
- ¼ diced green pepper
- 1 juiced lime
- ¼ diced red pepper
- 1 tsp. oregano
- 1 tsp. extra virgin olive oil
- 1 tsp. black pepper

Directions:

1. Preheat the broiler /grill on high heat.
2. Lightly oil a baking tray.
3. Mix all the ingredients aside from the trout and lime.
4. Slice the trout lengthways (there should be a gap here from where it had been gutted) and stuff the mixed ingredients inside.
5. Squeeze the juice over the fish, then place the lime wedges on the tray.

6. Place under the broiler on the baking tray and broil for 15-20 minutes or until fish is thoroughly cooked through and flakes easily.
7. Enjoy the dish because it is, or with a side helping of rice or salad.

Nutrition:
Calories 290, Protein 15 g, Carbohydrates 0 g, Fat 7 g, Sodium (Na) 43 mg, Potassium (K) 315 mg, Phosphorus 189 mg

176. Haddock & Buttered Leeks

Preparation Time: 5 minutes
Cooking Time: 15 minutes
Servings: 2

Ingredients:
- 1 tbsp. unsalted butter
- 1 sliced leek
- ¼ tsp. black pepper
- 2 tsp. chopped parsley
- 6 oz. haddock fillets
- ½ juiced lemon

Directions:
1. Preheat the oven to 375°F/Gas Mark 5.
2. Add the haddock fillets to baking or parchment paper and sprinkle with the black pepper.
3. Squeeze over the juice and wrap it into a parcel.
4. Bake the parcel on a baking tray for 10-15 minutes or until the fish is thoroughly cooked through.
5. Meanwhile, heat the butter over medium-low heat in a small pan.
6. Add the leeks and parsley and sauté for 5-7 minutes until soft.
7. Serve the haddock fillets on a bed of buttered leeks and enjoy!

Nutrition:
Calories 124, Protein 15 g, Carbohydrates 0 g, Fat 7 g, Sodium (Na) 161 mg, Potassium (K) 251 mg, Phosphorus 220 mg

177. Thai Spiced Halibut

Preparation Time: 5 minutes
Cooking Time: 20 minutes
Servings: 2

Ingredients:
- 2 tbsp. coconut oil
- 1 cup white rice
- ¼ tsp. black pepper
- ½ diced red chili
- 1 tbsp. fresh basil
- 2 pressed garlic cloves
- 4 oz. halibut fillet
- 1 halved lime
- 2 sliced green onions
- 1 lime leaf

Directions:
1. Preheat oven to 400°F/Gas Mark 5.
2. Add half the ingredients into baking paper and fold into a parcel.
3. Repeat for your second parcel.
4. Increase the oven for 15-20 minutes or until the fish is thoroughly cooked through.
5. Serve with cooked rice.

Nutrition:
Calories 311, Protein 16 g, Carbohydrates 17 g, Fat 15 g, Sodium (Na) 31 mg, Potassium (K) 418 mg, Phosphorus 257 mg

178. Homemade Tuna Niçoise

Preparation Time: 5 minutes
Cooking Time: 10 minutes
Servings: 2

Ingredients:
- 1 egg
- ½ cup green beans
- ¼ sliced cucumber
- 1 juiced lemon
- 1 tsp. black pepper
- ¼ sliced red onion
- 1 tbsp. olive oil
- 1 tbsp. capers
- 4 oz. drained canned tuna
- 4 iceberg lettuce leaves
- 1 tsp. chopped fresh cilantro

Directions:
1. Prepare the salad by washing and slicing the lettuce, cucumber, and onion.
2. Increase a salad bowl.
3. Mix one tablespoon oil with the juice, cilantro, and capers for a dressing. Set aside.
4. Boil a pan of water on high heat, then lower to simmer and add the egg for six minutes. (Steam the green beans over an equivalent pan in a steamer/colander for 6 minutes).
5. Remove the egg and rinse under cold water.
6. Peel before slicing in half.
7. Mix the tuna, salad, and dressing together in a salad bowl.
8. Toss to coat.
9. Top with the egg and serve with a sprinkle of black pepper.

Nutrition:
Calories 199, Protein 19 g, Carbohydrates 7 g, Fat 8 g, Sodium (Na) 466 mg, Potassium (K) 251 mg, Phosphorus 211 mg

179. Monk-Fish Curry

Preparation Time: 5 minutes
Cooking Time: 20 minutes
Servings: 2

Ingredients:

- 1 garlic clove
- 3 finely chopped green onions
- 1 tsp. grated ginger 1 cup water.
- 2 tsp. chopped fresh basil
- 1 cup cooked rice noodles
- 1 tbsp. coconut oil
- ½ sliced red chili
- 4 oz. Monkfish fillet
- ½ finely sliced stick lemongrass
- 2 tbsp. chopped shallots

Directions:

1. Slice the Monkfish into bite-size pieces.
2. Employing a pestle and mortar or kitchen appliance, crush the basil, garlic, ginger, chili, and lemongrass to make a paste.
3. Heat the oil in a large wok or pan over medium-high heat and add the shallots.
4. Now add the water to the pan and convey to a boil.
5. Add the Monkfish, lower the warmth, and Canopy to simmer for 10 minutes or until cooked through.
6. Enjoy with rice noodles and scatter with green onions to serve.

Nutrition:
Calories 249, Protein 12 g, Carbohydrates 30 g, Fat 10 g, Sodium (Na) 32 mg, Potassium (K) 398 mg, Phosphorus 190 mg

180. Sweet Glazed Salmon

Preparation Time: 10 minutes
Cooking Time: 10 minutes
Servings: 2

Ingredients:

- 2 tbsp. honey
- 1 tsp. lemon zest
- ½ tsp. ground black pepper
- 4 (3-oz.) each salmon fillets
- 1 tbsp. olive oil
- ½ scallion, white and green parts, chopped

Directions:

1. In a bowl, stir together the lemon zest, honey, and pepper.
2. Wash the salmon and pat dry with paper towels.
3. Rub the honey mixture all over each fillet. In a large skillet, heat the olive oil. Add the salmon fillets and cook the salmon for 10 minutes, turning once, or until it is lightly browned and just cooked through.
4. Serve topped with chopped scallion.

Nutrition:
Calories: 240 / Sodium: 51mg / Phosphorus: 3mg Potassium: 26mg / Carbohydrates: 9g / Protein: 17g

181. Fish Packets

Preparation Time: 15 minutes
Cooking Time: 20 minutes
Servings: 3

Ingredients:

- 3 tilapia fillets (4-oz. each fish fillet)
- 3 tsp. olive oil
- 1 red onion, sliced
- 3 lemon slices
- 1 zucchini, chopped

Directions:

1. Make the medium packets from the foil and brush them with olive oil from inside.
2. Then arrange tilapia fillets in the foil packets.
3. Add sliced lemon to the top of the fish.
4. Then add sliced onion and zucchini.
5. Bake the fish packets for 20 minutes at 360°F or until vegetables are tender.

Nutrition:
Calories: 161 / Sodium: 92mg / Phosphorus: 206mg Potassium: 427mg / Carbohydrates: 6.4g / Protein: 22.3g

182. Salmon Baked in Foil with Fresh Thyme

Preparation Time: 10 minutes
Cooking Time: 30 minutes
Servings: 2

Ingredients:

- 4 fresh thyme sprigs
- 4 garlic cloves, peeled, roughly chopped
- 16 oz. salmon fillets (4-oz. each fillet)
- ½ tsp. ground black pepper
- 4 tbsp. cream
- 2 tsp. olive oil
- ¼ tsp. cumin seeds

Directions:

1. Line the baking tray with foil.
2. Sprinkle the fish fillets with ground black pepper, cumin seeds, and arrange them in the tray with oil.
3. Add thyme sprig on the top of every fillet.
4. Then add cream and garlic.

5. Bake the fish for 30 minutes at 345°F.

Nutrition:
Calories: 198 / Sodium: 77mg / Phosphorus: 385mg / Potassium: 426mg / Carbohydrates: 1.8g / Protein: 22.4g

183. Grilled Salmon

Preparation Time: 15 minutes
Cooking Time: 15 minutes
Servings: 2

Ingredients:
*   1 lb. salmon fillets
*   1 tbsp. olive oil
*   1 tsp. salt-free lemon pepper
*   ½ tsp. paprika

Directions:
1. Preheat grill on high heat.
2. Spray or brush the fillet side of the salmon fillets lightly with oil. Combine seasonings in a small bowl. Sprinkle evenly over fillets.
3. Place salmon directly on the grill, fillet side down. Cook for 4 minutes. Spray or brush skin lightly with oil. Turn fillets over and cook until fish flakes easily with a fork, about 3 to 5 minutes.

Nutrition:
Calories: 114 / Sodium: 2mg / Phosphorus: 67mg / Potassium: 80mg / Carbohydrates: 432g / Protein: 11.9g

184. Baked Cod

Preparation Time: 10 minutes
Cooking Time: 25 minutes
Servings: 3

Ingredients:
*   ½ cup coconut oil
*   1 tsp. ground black pepper
*   ½ tsp. dried basil
*   3 cloves garlic, minced
*   6 (4-oz.) cod fillets
*   2 tbsp. lemon pepper

Directions:
1. Preheat oven to 350°F.
2. Melt the coconut oil in a medium saucepan over medium heat.
3. Arrange cod fillets in a single layer on a medium baking sheet. Cover with ½ coconut oil mixture, and sprinkle with lemon pepper and dried basil. Cover with foil.
4. Bake 15 to 20 minutes in the preheated oven, until fish, is easily flaked with a fork. Pour the remaining coconut oil mixture over the fish to serve.

Nutrition:
Calories: 168 / Sodium: 210mg / Phosphorus: 16mg / Potassium: 29mg / Carbohydrates: 15g / Protein: 6.7g

185. Baked Cod with Cucumber-Dill Salsa

Preparation Time: 20 minutes
Cooking Time: 10 minutes
Servings: 2

Ingredients:
For the Cucumber Salsa:
*   ½ English cucumber, chopped
*   2 tbsp. chopped fresh dill
*   Juice of 1 lime
*   Zest of 1 lime
*   ¼ cup boiled and minced red bell pepper
*   ½ tsp. granulated sugar

For the Fish:
*   12 oz. cod fillets, deboned and cut into 4 servings
*   Juice of 1 lemon
*   ½ tsp. freshly ground black pepper
*   1 tsp. olive oil

Directions:
To Make the Cucumber Salsa:
1. In a small bowl, mix together the cucumber, dill, lime juice, lime zest, red pepper, and sugar; set aside.

To Make the Fish
1. Preheat the oven to 350°F.
2. Place the fish on a pie plate and squeeze the lemon juice evenly over the fillets.
3. Sprinkle with pepper and drizzle the olive oil evenly over the fillets.
4. Bake the fish for about 6 minutes or until it flakes easily with a fork.
5. Transfer the fish to 4 plates and serve topped with cucumber salsa.

Nutrition:
Calories: 110 Potassium: 275mg Phosphorus: 120mg Protein: 20g Sodium: 67mg, Fat: 2g

186. Shrimp Scampi Linguine

Preparation Time: 15 minutes
Cooking Time: 15 minutes
Servings: 2

Ingredients:
*   4 oz. uncooked linguine
*   1 tsp. olive oil
*   2 tsp. minced garlic
*   4 oz. shrimp, peeled, deveined, and chopped
*   ½ cup dry white wine and Juice of 1 lemon
*   1 tbsp. chopped fresh basil

- ½ cup heavy (whipping) cream
- Freshly ground black pepper

Directions:

1. Cook the linguine according to the package instructions; drain and set aside.
2. In a large skillet over medium heat, heat the olive oil
3. Sauté the garlic and shrimp for about 6 minutes or until the shrimp is opaque and just cooked through.
4. Add the wine, lemon juice, and basil, and cook for 5 minutes.
5. Stir in the cream and simmer for 2 minutes more.
6. Add the linguine to the skillet and toss to coat.
7. Divide the pasta onto 4 plates to serve.

Nutrition: Calories: 219 Potassium: 155mg Phosphorous: 119mg Protein: 12g Sodium: 42mg, Fat: 7g

187. Crab Cakes with Lime Salsa

Preparation Time: 20 minutes plus 1-hour chilling time
Cooking Time: 20 minutes
Servings: 2

Ingredients:
For the Salsa:

- ½ English cucumber, diced
- 1 lime, chopped
- ½ cup boiled and chopped red bell pepper
- 1 tsp. chopped fresh cilantro
- Freshly ground black pepper

For the Crab Cakes:

- 8 oz. queen crab meat
- ¼ cup bread crumbs
- 1 small egg
- ¼ cup boiled and chopped red bell pepper
- 1 scallion, both green and white parts, minced
- 1 tbsp. chopped fresh parsley
- Splash hot sauce
- Olive oil spray, for the pan

Directions:
To Make the Salsa:

1. In a small bowl, stir together the cucumber, lime, red pepper, and cilantro.
2. Season with pepper; set aside.

To Make the Crab Cakes

1. In a medium bowl, mix together the crab, bread crumbs, egg, red pepper, scallion, parsley, and hot sauce until it holds together. Add more bread crumbs, if necessary.
2. Form the crab mixture into 4 patties and place them on a plate.
3. Refrigerate the crab cakes for 1 hour to firm them.

4. Spray a large skillet generously with olive oil spray and place it over medium-high heat.
5. Cook the crab cakes in batches, turning, for about 5 minutes per side or until golden brown.
6. Serve the crab cakes with the salsa.

Nutrition:
Calories: 115 Potassium: 200mg Phosphorus: 110mg Protein: 16g Sodium: 421mg, Fat: 2g

188. Cilantro-Lime Flounder

Preparation Time: 20 minutes
Cooking Time: 5 minutes
Servings: 2

Ingredients:

- ¼ cup Homemade Mayonnaise (here)
- Juice of 1 lime
- Zest of 1 lime
- ½ cup chopped fresh cilantro
- 4 (3-oz.) flounder fillets
- Freshly ground black pepper

Directions:

1. Preheat the oven to 400°F.
2. In a small bowl, stir together the mayonnaise, lime juice, lime zest, and cilantro.
3. Place 4 pieces of foil, about 8 by 8 inches square, on a clean work surface.
4. Place a flounder fillet in the center of each square.
5. Top the fillets evenly with the mayonnaise mixture.
6. Season the flounder with pepper.
7. Bake the fish for 4 to 5 minutes.
8. Unfold the packets and serve.

Nutrition:
Calories: 92 Potassium: 137mg Phosphorus: 208mg Protein: 12g Sodium: 267mg, Fat: 4g

189. Haddock and Leeks

Preparation Time: 5 minutes
Cooking Time: 15 minutes
Servings: 2

Ingredients:

- 2 ¼ tsp. olive oil
- 1 sliced leek
- ¼ tsp. black pepper
- 2 tsp. chopped parsley
- 6 oz. haddock fillets
- ½ juiced lemon

Directions:

1. Preheat the oven to 375°F.
2. Add the haddock fillets to baking or parchment paper and sprinkle with the black pepper.

3. Squeeze over the lemon juice and wrap it into a parcel.
4. Bake the parcel on a baking tray for 10-15 minutes or until fish is thoroughly cooked through.
5. Meanwhile, heat the olive oil over medium-low heat in a small pan.
6. Add the leeks and parsley and sauté for 5-7 minutes until soft.
7. Serve the haddock fillets on a bed of leeks and enjoy!

Nutrition:
Calories: 124 / Sodium: 161mg / Phosphorus: 220mg / Potassium: 251mg / Carbohydrates: 71g / Protein: 15g

Chapter 9: Desserts Recipes

190. Cream Cheese Tarts

Preparation Time: 10 minutes
Cooking Time: 10 minutes
Servings: 2
Ingredients:

- 8 oz. cream cheese
- 2 eggs
- ¾ cup sugar
- 2 tsp. vanilla extract
- 2 dozen paper cupcake liners
- 2 dozen vanilla wafers
- 1 ½ cups apple pie filling

Directions:

1. Preheat oven to 350°F.
2. Beat cream cheese with sugar, vanilla extract, and eggs in a mixer until smooth.
3. Layer a muffin tray with muffin cups and place one vanilla wafer in each cup.
4. Divide the cream cheese mixture into the cups, then bake for 10 minutes.
5. Allow it to cool, then refrigerate for 2 hours.
6. Serve.

Nutrition: Calories: 136, Protein: 2 g, Carbohydrates: 14 g, Fat: 8 g, Cholesterol: 28 mg, Sodium: 78 mg, Potassium: 49 mg, Phosphorus: 27 mg, Calcium: 18 mg, Fiber: 0.2 g

191. Blueberry Cream Cheese Pie

Preparation Time: 10 minutes
Cooking Time: 15 minutes
Servings: 2
Ingredients:

- ¾ cup unsalted butter
- 1 ½ cups all-purpose flour
- 6 tbsp. granulated sugar
- 3 cups whipped topping
- 3 oz. cream cheese
- 21 oz. canned blueberry pie filling

Directions:

1. Preheat oven to 350°F.
2. Whisk butter with 2 tablespoons sugar and flour, then spread this mixture in a 9x12 baking dish.
3. Bake the crust for 15 minutes in the preheated oven.
4. Meanwhile, beat cream cheese in a mixer until fluffy, then stir in the remaining sugar.
5. Mix well, then spread half of the filling in the baked crust.

6. Top this filling with blueberry pie filling, then spread the remaining cream cheese mixture on top.
7. Garnish with blueberries.
8. Refrigerate for 4 hours, or overnight.
9. Slice and serve.

Nutrition: Calories: 405, Protein: 3 g, Carbohydrates: 59 g, Fat: 21 g, Cholesterol: 59 mg, Sodium: 42 mg, Potassium: 129 mg, Phosphorus: 55 mg, Calcium: 48 mg, Fiber: 2.0 g

192. Apple Cinnamon Farfel

Preparation Time: 10 minutes
Cooking Time: 45 minutes
Servings: 2
Ingredients:

- 1 cup hot water
- 1 cup Matzo farfel
- ¼ cup sugar
- 2 large apples; peeled, cored, and shredded
- 2 tsp. ground cinnamon
- 3 egg whites
- ½ cup pineapple chunks

Directions:

1. Mix hot water with farfel, sugar, apples, and cinnamon in a bowl.
2. Spread this farfel mixture in an 8x8 casserole dish, greased with cooking spray.
3. Whisk 3 egg whites in a mixer until they form peaks, then fold in pineapple chunks.
4. Spread this egg white mixture over the farfel-apples mixture.
5. Drizzle the cinnamon on top and bake for 45 minutes at 350°F.
6. Slice and serve.

Nutrition:
Calories: 170, Protein: 3 g, Carbohydrates: 40 g, Fat: 1 g, Cholesterol: 0 mg, Sodium: 2mg, Potassium: 118 mg, Phosphorus: 167 mg, Calcium: 16 mg, Fiber: 2.3 g

193. Orange Biscotti

Preparation Time: 10 minutes
Cooking Time: 25 minutes
Servings: 2
Ingredients:

- 2 ½ cups all-purpose flour
- 2 tsp. baking powder
- 2 tsp. anise seed
- 1 tsp. orange rind, grated
- ½ cup sugar

- 1 large egg
- 2 tbsp. canola oil
- 1 tsp. orange extract

Directions:
1. Layer a cookie sheet with a parchment sheet and keep it aside.
2. Preheat oven to 350°F.
3. Whisk flour, baking powder, anise seed, orange rind, and sugar in a bowl.
4. Beat egg with orange extract and oil in a mixer until frothy.
5. Add this egg-orange mixture to the flour mixture and mix well to form a biscotti dough.
6. Make 12-inch-long biscotti's out of the dough and place them on the cookie sheet.
7. Bake these biscotti for 20 minutes in the preheated oven.
8. Flip all the biscotti and bake for another 5 minutes. Serve.

Nutrition: Calories: 98, Protein: 2 g, Carbohydrates: 18 g, Fat: 2 g, Cholesterol: 12 mg, Sodium: 45 mg, Potassium: 26 mg, Phosphorus: 76 mg, Calcium: 43 mg, Fiber: 0.5 g

194. Strawberry Delight

Preparation Time: 10 minutes
Cooking Time: 45 minutes
Servings: 2

Ingredients:
- 1 package angel food cake mix
- 8 oz. whipped cream cheese
- ½ cup strawberry preserves
- 2 cups whipped topping

Directions:
1. Bake the cake using the cake mix as per the package's instructions.
2. Meanwhile, beat cream cheese with strawberry preserves in a mixer until smooth.
3. Fold in whipped topping and mix gently.
4. Slice the baked cake into three layers, horizontally.
5. Spread ⅓ of the cream cheese filling over one cake layer.
6. Place the second layer on top of it and spread the ⅓ cream cheese filling over this cake.
7. Lastly, place the third cake slice over it and top it with the remaining cream cheese filling.
8. Refrigerate the layered cake for 4 hours.
9. Slice and serve.

Nutrition:
Calories: 278, Protein: 5 g, Carbohydrates: 42 g, Fat: 10 g, Cholesterol: 33 mg, Sodium: 367 mg, Potassium: 125 mg, Phosphorus: 155 mg, Calcium: 81 mg, Fiber: 0 g

195. Florida Lime Pie

Preparation Time: 10 minutes
Cooking Time: 5 minutes
Servings: 2

Ingredients:
- 5 tbsp. unsalted margarine
- 1 ¼ cups graham cracker crumbs
- ¼ cup granulated sugar
- ⅓ cup lime juice
- 14 oz. canned condensed milk
- 1 cup heavy whipping cream

Directions:
1. Preheat oven to 350°F.
2. Toss cracker crumbs with sugar and melted margarine in a bowl.
3. Spread this cracker crust in a 9-inch pie shell and bake it for 5 minutes.
4. Meanwhile, mix condensed milk with lime juice in a bowl.
5. Beat heavy cream in a mixer until fluffy, then stir in condensed milk mixture.
6. Mix well, then spread this filling in the baked crust.
7. Refrigerate this pie for 4 hours.
8. Slice and serve.

Nutrition:
Calories: 428, Protein: 6 g, Carbohydrates: 47 g, Fat: 24 g, Cholesterol: 58 mg, Sodium: 149 mg, Potassium: 241 mg, Phosphorus: 162 mg, Calcium: 166 mg, Fiber: 0.5 g

196. Pumpkin Log

Preparation Time: 10 minutes
Cooking Time: 15 minutes
Servings: 2

Ingredients:
- 8 oz. cream cheese
- 4 tbsp. unsalted butter
- ⅔ cup carrots, cooked and pureed
- 3 large eggs
- 1 cup granulated sugar
- 1 tsp. lemon juice
- ¾ cup all-purpose flour
- 1 tsp. baking powder
- 1 tsp. cinnamon
- 1 tsp. ginger
- 1 tsp. nutmeg
- 1 cup powdered sugar
- 1 tsp. vanilla

Directions:
1. Preheat oven to 375°F.
2. Whisk eggs with granulated sugar in a bowl.

3. Stir in lemon juice, carrots, baking powder, ginger, nutmeg, cinnamon, and flour.
4. Spread this mixture in a baking pan lined with a parchment sheet.
5. Bake for 15 minutes then allow it to cool for 10 minutes.
6. Now place another parchment sheet on top and roll it.
7. Prepare the filling by beat cream cheese with butter, vanilla, and sugar in a mixer at low speed.
8. Unroll the baked cake and remove the parchment paper from the top.
9. Spread the cream cheese filling on its top and roll it again.
10. Garnish with powder sugar, then slice.
11. Serve.

Nutrition:
Calories: 264, Protein: 4 g, Carbohydrates: 35 g, Fat: 12 g, Cholesterol: 76 mg, Sodium: 220 mg, Potassium: 80 mg, Phosphorus: 67 mg, Calcium: 56 mg, Fiber: 0.6 g

197. Lemon Squares

Preparation Time: 10 minutes
Cooking Time: 35 minutes
Servings: 2

Ingredients:
- 1 cup powdered sugar
- 1 cup all-purpose white flour
- ½ cup unsalted butter
- 1 cup granulated sugar
- ½ tsp. baking powder
- 2 eggs, slightly beaten
- 4 tbsp. lemon juice
- 1 tbsp. unsalted butter, softened
- 1 tbsp. lemon rind, grated

Directions:
1. Start mixing ¼ cup confectioner's sugar, ½ cup butter, and flour in a bowl.
2. Spread this crust mixture in an 8-inch square pan and press it.
3. Bake this flour crust for 15 minutes at 350°F.
4. Meanwhile, prepare the filling by beating granulated sugar, 2 tablespoons lemon juice, lemon rind, eggs, and baking powder in a mixer.
5. Spread this filling in the baked crust and bake again for 20 minutes.
6. Prepare the icing meanwhile by beating 1 tablespoon butter with 2 tablespoons lemon juice and ¾ cup confectioners' sugar.
7. Once the lemon pie is baked, allow it to cool.
8. Drizzle the icing mixture on top of the lemon pie then cut it into 36 squares.
9. Serve.

Nutrition:
Calories: 146, Protein: 2 g, Carbohydrates: 22 g, Fat: 6 g, Cholesterol: 39 mg, Sodium: 45 mg, Potassium: 22 mg, Phosphorus: 32 mg, Calcium: 16 mg, Fiber: 0.2 g

198. Creamy Pineapple Dessert

Preparation Time: 10 minutes
Cooking Time: 0 minutes
Servings: 2

Ingredients:
- 16 oz. cottage cheese
- 15 oz. canned pineapple
- 8 oz. whipped topping
- ½ tsp. green food coloring

Directions:
1. Throw all the dessert ingredients into a suitably sized bowl.
2. Mix them well and refrigerate for 1 hour.
3. Serve.

Nutrition:
Calories: 204, Protein: 10 g, Carbohydrates: 23 g, Fat: 8 g, Cholesterol: 13 mg, Sodium: 303 mg, Potassium: 203 mg, Phosphorus: 152 mg, Calcium: 100 mg, Fiber: 0.6 g

199. Blackberry Mountain Pie

Preparation Time: 10 minutes
Cooking Time: 45 minutes
Servings: 2

Ingredients:
- ⅓ cup unsalted butter
- 4 cups blackberries
- 13 tbsp. sugar
- 1 cup all-purpose white flour
- ½ tsp. baking powder
- ¾ cup Rice Drink

Directions:
1. Preheat oven to 375°F.
2. Grease a 2-quart baking dish with melted butter.
3. Toss blackberries with 1 tablespoon sugar in a small bowl.
4. Whisk the remaining ingredients in a mixer until they form a smooth batter.
5. Spread this pie batter in the prepared baking dish and top it with blackberries.
6. Bake the blackberry pie for 45 minutes in the preheated oven.
7. Slice and serve once chilled.

Nutrition:
Calories: 320, Protein: 4 g, Carbohydrates: 49 g, Fat: 12 g, Cholesterol: 28 mg, Sodium: 222 mg, Potassium: 186 mg, Phosphorus: 91 mg, Calcium: 65 mg, Fiber: 5.6 g

200.   Dessert Cocktail

Preparation Time: 1 minute
Cooking Time: 0 minute
Servings: 2

Ingredients:

- 1 cup cranberry juice
- 1 cup fresh ripe strawberries, washed and hull removed
- 2 tbsp. lime juice
- ¼ cup white sugar
- 8 ice cubes

Directions:

1. Toss all ingredients in a blender until smooth and creamy.
2. Pour the liquid into chilled tall glasses and serve cold.

Nutrition:
Calories: 92 kcal Carbohydrate: 23.5 g Protein: 0.5 g Sodium: 3.62 mg Potassium: 103.78 mg Phosphorus: 17.86 mg Dietary Fiber: 0.84 g Fat: 0.17 g

201. Baked Egg Custard

Preparation Time: 15 minutes
Cooking Time: 30 minutes
Servings: 2

Ingredients:

- 2 medium eggs, at room temperature
- ¼ cup semi-skimmed milk
- 3 tbsp. white sugar
- ½ tsp. nutmeg
- 1 tsp. vanilla extract

Directions:

1. Preheat your oven at 375°F/180°C
2. Combine all the ingredients in a bowl then beat with a hand mixer for a few seconds until creamy and uniform.
3. Put the mixture into lightly greased muffin tins.
4. Bake for 25-30 minutes or until the knife, you place inside, comes out clean.

Nutrition:
Calories: 96.56 kcal Carbohydrate: 10.5 g Protein: 3.5 g Sodium: 37.75 mg Potassium: 58.19 mg Phosphorus: 58.76 mg Dietary Fiber: 0.06 g Fat: 2.91 g

202.   Gumdrop Cookies

Preparation Time: 15 minutes
Cooking Time: 12 minutes
Servings: 1-2

Ingredients:

- 1 tbsp. spreadable unsalted butter
- 1 medium egg
- 1 tbsp. brown sugar
- ½ all-purpose flour
- 1 tbsp. cup milk
- ¼ tsp. vanilla
- ¼ tsp. baking powder
- 5 large gumdrops, chopped finely

Directions:

1. Preheat the oven at 400°F/195°C.
2. Combine the sugar, butter, and egg until creamy.
3. Add the milk and vanilla and stir well.
4. Combine the flour with the baking powder in a different bowl. Incorporate to the sugar, butter mixture, and stir.
5. Add the gumdrops and place the mixture in the fridge for ½ hour.
6. Drop the dough with a tablespoonful into a lightly greased baking or cookie sheet.
7. Bake in the oven for about 10-12 minutes or until golden brown in color.

Nutrition: Calories: 102.17 kcal Carbohydrate: 16.5 g Protein: 0.86 g Sodium: 23.42 mg Potassium: 45 mg Phosphorus: 32.15 mg Dietary Fiber: 0.13 g Fat: 4 g

203.   Pound Cake with Pineapple

Preparation Time: 10 minutes
Cooking Time: 50 minutes
Servings: 1-2

Ingredients:

- 1 cup all-purpose flour, sifted
- 1 cup sugar
- ½ cup butter
- 1 whole egg and 1 egg whites
- ¼ tsp. vanilla extract
- ¼ cup pineapple chunks

For glaze:

- ¼ cup sugar
- ¼ stick unsalted butter or margarine
- ¼ cup reserved juice from the pineapple

Directions:

1. Preheat the oven at 350°F/180°C.
2. Beat the sugar and the butter with a hand mixer until creamy and smooth.
3. Slowly add the eggs (1 or 2 every time) and stir well after pouring each egg.
4. Add the vanilla extract, follow up with the flour and stir well.
5. Add the drained and chopped pineapple.
6. Transfer the mixture into a greased cake tin and bake for 45-50 minutes.
7. In a small saucepan, combine the sugar with the butter and pineapple juice. Stir every few seconds

and bring to boil. Cook until you get a creamy to thick glaze consistency.

8. Pour the glaze over the cake while still hot.
9. Let cook for at least 10 seconds and serve.

Nutrition:
Calories: 407.4 kcal Carbohydrate: 79 g Protein: 4.25 g Sodium: 118.97 mg Potassium: 180.32 mg Phosphorus: 66.37 mg Dietary Fiber: 2.25 g Fat: 16.48 g

204. Apple Crunch Pie

Preparation Time: 10 minutes
Cooking Time: 35 minutes
Servings: 2

Ingredients:
- 4 large tart apples, peeled, seeded, and sliced
- ½ cup white all-purpose flour
- ⅓ cup margarine
- 1 cup sugar
- ¾ cup rolled oat flakes
- ½ tsp. ground nutmeg

Directions:
1. Preheat the oven to 375°F/180°C.
2. Place the apples over a lightly greased square pan (around 7 inches).
3. Mix the rest of the ingredients in a medium bowl and spread the batter over the apples.
4. Bake for about 30-35 minutes, until the top crust has gotten golden brown.
5. Serve hot.

Nutrition:
Calories: 261.9 kcal Carbohydrate: 47.2 g Protein: 1.5 g Sodium: 81 mg Potassium: 123.74 mg Phosphorus: 35.27 mg Dietary Fiber: 2.81 g Fat: 7.99 g

205. Easy Turnip Puree

Preparation Time: 10 minutes
Cooking Time: 12 minutes
Servings: 2

Ingredients:
- 1 ½ lbs. turnips, peeled and chopped
- 1 tsp. dill
- 3 bacon slices, cooked and chopped
- 2 tbsp. fresh chives, chopped

Directions:
1. Add turnip into the boiling water and cook for 12 minutes. Drain well and place in a food processor.
2. Add dill and process until smooth.
3. Transfer turnip puree into the bowl and top with bacon and chives.
4. Serve and enjoy.

Nutrition:
Calories 127 Fat 6 g Carbohydrates 11.6 g Sugar 7 g Protein 6.8 g Cholesterol 16 mg

206. Tart Apple Granita

Preparation Time: 15 minutes, plus 4 hours freezing time
Cooking Time: 0
Servings: 2

Ingredients:
- ½ cup granulated sugar
- ½ cup water
- 2 cups unsweetened apple juice
- ¼ cup freshly squeezed lemon juice

Directions:
1. Heat the sugar and water.
2. Bring to a boil and then lessen the heat to low and simmer for about 15 minutes or until the liquid has reduced by half.
3. Take away the pan from the heat and pour the liquid into a large shallow metal pan.
4. Let the liquid cool for about 40 minutes and then stir in the apple juice and lemon juice.
5. Place the pan in the freezer.
6. After 1 hour, run a fork through the liquid to break up any ice crystals formed. Scrape down the sides as well.
7. Place the pan back in the freezer and repeat the stirring and scraping every 20 minutes, creating slush.
8. Serve when the mixture is completely frozen and looks like crushed ice, after about 3 hours.

Nutrition: Calories: 157; Fat: 0g; Carbohydrates: 0g Phosphorus: 10mg; Potassium: 141mg; Sodium: 5mg Protein: 0g

207. Lemon-lime Sherbet

Preparation Time: 5 minutes, plus 3 hours chilling time
Cooking Time: 15 minutes
Servings: 2

Ingredients:
- 2 cups water
- 1 cup granulated sugar
- 3 tbsp. lemon zest, divided
- ½ cup freshly squeezed lemon juice
- Zest of 1 lime
- Juice of 1 lime
- ½ cup heavy (whipping) cream

Directions:
1. Place a large saucepan and add the water, sugar and 2 tablespoons of the lemon zest.
2. Bring the mixture to a boil and then reduce the heat and simmer for 15 minutes.

3. Transfer the mixture to a large bowl and add the remaining 1 tablespoon lemon zest, the lemon juice, lime zest, and lime juice.
4. Whisk in the heavy cream and transfer the mixture to an ice cream maker.
5. Freeze according to the manufacturer's direction.

Nutrition:
Calories: 151; Fat: 6g; Carbohydrates: 26g; Phosphorus: 10mg; Potassium: 27mg; Sodium: 6mg; Protein: 0g

208. Pavlov with Peaches

Preparation Time: 30 minutes
Cooking Time: 1 hour, plus cooling time
Servings: 3
Ingredients:
- 4 large egg whites, at room temperature
- ½ tsp. cream of tartar
- 1 cup superfine sugar
- ½ tsp. pure vanilla extract
- 2 cups drained canned peaches in juice

Directions:
1. Preheat the oven to 225°F.
2. Line a baking sheet with parchment paper; set aside.
3. In a large bowl, beat the egg whites for about 1 minute or until soft peaks form.
4. Beat in the cream of tartar.
5. Add the sugar, 1 tablespoon at a time, until the egg whites are very stiff and glossy. Do not overbeat.
6. Beat in the vanilla.
7. Evenly spoon the meringue onto the baking sheet so that you have 8 rounds.
8. Use the back of the spoon to create an indentation in the middle of each round.
9. Bake the meringues for about 1 hour or until a light brown crust form.
10. Turn off the oven and let the meringues stand, still in the oven, overnight.
11. Remove the meringues from the sheet and place them on serving plates.
12. Spoon the peaches, dividing evenly, into the centers of the meringues, and serve.
13. Store any unused meringues in a sealed container at room temperature for up to 1 week.

Nutrition:
Calories: 132; Fat: 0g; Carbohydrates: 32g; Phosphorus: 7mg; Potassium: 95mg; Sodium: 30mg; Protein: 2g

209. Tropical Vanilla Snow Cone

Preparation Time: 15 minutes, plus freezing time
Cooking Time: 0
Servings: 2

Ingredients:
- 1 cup pineapple
- 1 cup frozen strawberries
- 6 tbsp. water
- 2 tbsp. granulated sugar
- 1 tbsp. vanilla extract

Directions:
1. In a large saucepan, mix the peaches, pineapple, strawberries, water, and sugar over medium-high heat and bring to a boil.
2. Lessen the heat to low and simmer the mixture, stirring occasionally, for 15 minutes.
3. Remove from the heat and let the mixture cool completely, for about 1 hour.
4. Stir in the vanilla and transfer the fruit mixture to a food processor or blender.
5. Purée until smooth, and pour the purée into a 9-by-13-inch glass baking dish.
6. Cover and place the dish in the freezer overnight.
7. When the fruit mixture is completely frozen, use a fork to scrape the sorbet until you have flaked flavored ice.
8. Scoop the ice flakes into 4 serving dishes.

Nutrition:
Calories: 92; Fat: 0g; Carbohydrates: 22g; Phosphorus: 17mg; Potassium: 145mg; Sodium: 4mg; Protein: 1g

210. Strawberry Pie

Preparation Time: 15 minutes
Cooking Time: 25 minutes
Servings: 2

Ingredients:
- 1 unbaked (9 inches) pie shell
- 4 cups strawberries, fresh
- 1 cup brown Swerve
- 3 tbsp. arrowroot powder
- 2 tbsp. lemon juice
- 8 tbsp. whipped cream topping

Directions:
1. Spread the pie shell in the pie pan and bake it until golden brown.
2. Now mash 2 cups of strawberries with the lemon juice, arrowroot powder, and Swerve in a bowl.
3. Add the mixture to a saucepan and cook on moderate heat until it thickens.
4. Allow the mixture to cool then spread it in the pie shell.
5. Slice the remaining strawberries and spread them over the pie filling.
6. Refrigerate for 1 hour then garnish with whipped cream.
7. Serve fresh and enjoy.

Nutrition:

Calories 236 Total Fat 11.1g Cholesterol 3mg Sodium 183mg Protein 2.2g Calcium 23mg Phosphorous 47.2mg Potassium 178mg

211. Baked Custard

Preparation Time: 15 minutes
Cooking Time: 30 minutes
Servings: 1

Ingredients:

- ½ cup milk
- 1 egg, beaten
- ⅛ tsp. nutmeg
- ⅛ tsp. vanilla
- Sweetener, to taste
- ½ cup water

Directions:

1. Lightly warm up the milk in a pan, then whisk in the egg, nutmeg, vanilla and sweetener.
2. Pour this custard mixture into a ramekin.
3. Transfer the ramekin to a baking pan and pour ½ cup water into the pan.
4. Bake the custard for 30 minutes at 325°F.
5. Serve fresh.

Nutrition:

Calories 127 Total Fat 7g Cholesterol 174mg Sodium 119mg Calcium 169mg Phosphorous 309mg Potassium 171mg

212. Raspberry Popsicle

Preparation Time: 2 hours
Cooking Time: 15 minutes
Servings: 2

Ingredients:

- 1 ½ cups raspberries
- 2 cups water

Directions:

1. Fill a pan with water.
2. Add raspberries
3. Put it under medium heat and let the water boil.
4. Reduce the heat and simmer for 15 minutes
5. Remove heat and pour the mix into Popsicle molds
6. Add a popsicle stick and let it chill for 2 hours
7. Serve and enjoy!

Nutrition:

Calories: 58 Fat: 0.4g Carbohydrates: 0g Protein: 1.4g

213. Jalapeno Crisp

Preparation Time: 10 minutes
Cooking Time: 1 hour and 15 minutes
Servings: 3-4

Ingredients:

- ½ cup sesame seeds
- ½ cup sunflower seeds
- ½ cup flaxseeds
- ¼ cup hulled hemp seeds
- 1 tbsp. Psyllium husk
- ¼ tsp. salt
- ¼ tsp. baking powder
- ½ cups water

Directions:

1. Preheat your oven to 350°F
2. Take your blender and add seeds, baking powder, salt, and Psyllium husk
3. Blend well until a sand-like texture appears
4. Stir in water and mix until a batter form
5. Allow the batter to rest for 10 minutes until a dough-like thick mixture forms
6. Transfer the dough onto a cookie sheet which is lined with parchment paper
7. Spread it evenly, making sure that it has a thickness of ¼ inch thick all around
8. Bake for 75 minutes in your oven
9. Remove and cut into 20 spices
10. Allow them to cool for 30 minutes and enjoy!

Nutrition: Calories: 156 Fat: 13g Carbohydrates: 2g Protein: 5g

214. Lemon Mousse

Preparation Time: 10 + chill time
Cooking Time: 10 minutes
Servings: 2

Ingredients:

- 1 cup coconut cream
- 8 oz. cream cheese, soft
- ¼ cup fresh lemon juice
- 3 pinches salt
- 1 tsp. lemon liquid stevia

Directions:

1. Preheat your oven to 350°F
2. Grease a ramekin with butter
3. Beat cream, cream cheese, fresh lemon juice, salt and lemon liquid stevia in a mixer
4. Pour batter into ramekin
5. Bake for 10 minutes, then transfer the mousse to a serving glass
6. Let it chill for 2 hours and serve
7. Enjoy!

Nutrition:

Calories: 395 Fat: 31g Carbohydrates: 3g Protein: 5g

215. Chocolate Chip Cookies

Preparation Time: 7 minutes
Cooking Time: 10 minutes
Servings: 2

Ingredients:

- ½ cup semi-sweet chocolate chips
- ½ tsp. baking soda
- ½ tsp. vanilla
- 1 egg
- 1 cup flour
- ½ cup margarine
- 4 tsp. stevia

Directions:

1. Sift the dry ingredients.
2. Cream the margarine, stevia, vanilla, and egg with a whisk.
3. Add flour mixture and beat well.
4. Stir in the chocolate chips, then drop teaspoonfuls of the mixture over a greased baking sheet.
5. Bake the cookies inside the oven for about 10 minutes at 375°F.
6. Cool and serve.

Nutrition:

Calories: 106.2 Fat: 7g Carb: 8.9g Phosphorus: 19mg Potassium: 28mg Sodium: 98mg Protein: 1.5g

216. Vanilla Custard

Preparation Time: 7 minutes
Cooking Time: 10 minutes
Servings: 2

Ingredients:

- 1 egg
- ⅛ tsp. vanilla
- ⅛ tsp. nutmeg
- ½ cup almond milk
- 2 tbsp. stevia

Directions:

1. Scald the milk then let it cool.
2. Crack the egg into a bowl and beat it with the nutmeg.
3. Add the scalded milk, the vanilla, and the sweetener to taste. Mix well.
4. Place the bowl in a baking pan filled with ½ deep of water.
5. Bake for 30 minutes at 325°F.
6. Serve.

Nutrition:

Calories: 167.3 Fat: 9g Carb: 11g Phosphorus: 205mg Potassium: 249mg Sodium: 124mg Protein: 10g

217. Blueberry Mini Muffins

Preparation Time: 10 minutes
Cooking Time: 35 minutes
Servings: 2

Ingredients:

- 3 egg whites
- ¼ cup all-purpose white flour
- 1 tbsp. coconut flour
- 1 tsp. baking soda
- 1 tbsp. nutmeg, grated
- 1 tsp. vanilla extract
- 1 tsp. stevia
- ¼ cup fresh blueberries

Directions:

- Preheat the oven to 325°F.
- Mix all the ingredients in a bowl.
- Divide the batter into 4 and spoon into a lightly oiled muffin tin.
- Bake in the oven for 15 to 20 minutes or until cooked through.
- Cool and serve.

Nutrition:

Calories: 62 Fat: 0g Carb: 9g Phosphorus: 103mg Potassium: 65mg Sodium: 62mg Protein: 4g

218. Old-fashioned Apple Kuchen

Preparation Time: 25 minutes
Cooking Time: 1 hour
Servings: 3-4

Ingredients:

- Unsalted butter, for greasing the baking dish
- ¼ cup unsalted butter, at room temperature
- ½ cups granulated sugar
- 1 egg, beaten
- ½ tsp. pure vanilla extract
- ½ cups all-purpose flour
- ¼ tsp. Ener-G baking soda substitute
- ½ tsp. ground cinnamon
- ¼ tsp. ground nutmeg
- Pinch ground allspice
- 1 large apple, peeled, cored, and diced

Directions:

1. Preheat the oven to 350°F.
2. Grease a 9-by-13-inch glass baking dish; set aside.
3. Cream together the butter and sugar with a hand mixer until light and fluffy, for about 3 minutes.
4. Add the eggs and vanilla and beat until combined, scraping down the sides of the bowl, about 1 minute.

5. mix together the flour, baking soda substitute, cinnamon, nutmeg, and allspice.
6. Add the dry ingredients to the wet ingredients and stir to combine.
7. Stir in the apple and spoon the batter into the baking dish.
8. Bake for about 1 hour or until the cake is golden.
9. Cool the cake on a wire rack.
10. Serve warm or chilled.

Nutrition:
Calories: 368; Fat: 16g; Carbohydrates: 53g; Phosphorus: 46mg; Potassium: 68mg; Sodium: 15mg; Protein: 3g

Chapter 10: Smoothies and Drinks Recipes

219. Distinctive Pineapple Smoothie

Preparation Time: 5 minutes
Cooking Time: 0 minutes
Servings: 2

Ingredients:

- 2 peaches, peeled, pitted, and chopped
- 1 large carrot, peeled and grated
- 1-inch piece peeled fresh ginger, lightly crushed
- 3 fresh thyme sprigs
- 10 cups water

Directions:

1. Place the peaches, carrot, ginger, and thyme in a large pitcher.
2. Pour in the water and stir the mixture.
3. Place the pitcher in the refrigerator and leave to infuse, overnight if possible.
4. Serve cold.

Nutrition:
Calories: 3; Total fat: 0g; Saturated fat: 0g; Cholesterol: 0g; Sodium: 0g; Carbohydrates: 0g; Fiber: 0g; Phosphorus: 0mg; Potassium: 4mg; Protein: 0g

220. Baby Spinach and Dill Smoothie

Preparation Time: 5 minutes
Cooking Time: 0 minutes
Servings: 2

Ingredients:

- 1 cup fresh baby spinach leaves
- 2 tbsp. fresh dill, chopped
- 1 ½ cup water
- 1 tbsp. chia seeds (optional)
- 2 tbsp. natural sweetener Stevia or Erythritol (optional)

Directions:

1. Place all ingredients into a fast-speed blender. Beat until smooth and all ingredients united well.
2. Serve and enjoy!

Nutrition:
Calories 136, Carbohydrates: 8g, Proteins: 7g, Fat: 10g, Fiber 9g

221. Papaya Mint Water

Preparation Time: 5 minutes
Cooking Time: 0 minutes
Servings: 2

Ingredients:

- 1 cup fresh papaya, peeled, seeded, and diced
- 2 tbsp. chopped fresh mint leaves
- 10 cups distilled or filtered water

Directions:

1. Place the papaya and mint in a large pitcher. Pour in the water.
2. Stir, and place the pitcher in the refrigerator to infuse, overnight if possible.
3. Serve cold.

Nutrition:
Calories: 2, Total fat: 0g, Saturated fat: 0g, Cholesterol: 0g, Sodium: 0g, Carbohydrates: 0g, Fiber: 0g, Phosphorus: 0mg, Potassium: 4mg, Protein: 0g

222. Blueberries and Coconut Smoothie

Preparation Time: 5 minutes
Cooking Time: 3 minutes
Servings: 3

Ingredients:

- 1 cup frozen blueberries, unsweetened
- 1 cup Stevia or Erythritol sweetener
- 2 cups coconut milk (canned)
- 1 cup fresh spinach leaves
- 2 tbsp. shredded coconut (unsweetened)
- ¾ cup water

Directions:

1. Place all ingredients from the list in the food processor or your strong blender.
2. Blend for 45–60 seconds or to taste.
3. Ready for the drink! Serve!

Nutrition:
Calories 190, Carbohydrates: 8g, Proteins: 3g, Fat: 18g, Fiber 2g

223. Collard Greens and Cucumber Smoothie

Preparation Time: 15 minutes
Cooking Time: 0 minutes
Servings: 2

Ingredients:

- 1 cup Collard greens
- A few fresh pepper mint leaves
- 1 big cucumber
- 1 lime, freshly juiced
- 1 ½ cup water
- 1 cup crushed ice

Optional:

- ¼ cup natural sweetener Erythritol or Stevia

Directions:

1. Rinse and clean your Collard greens from any dirt.
2. Mix all ingredients in a blender.
3. Blend until all ingredients in your smoothie are combined well.
4. Pour in a glass and drink. Enjoy!

Nutrition:

Calories 123, Carbohydrates 8g, Proteins 4g, Fat 11g, Fiber 6g

224. Creamy Dandelion Greens and Celery Smoothie

Preparation Time: 10 minutes
Cooking Time: 0 minutes
Servings: 2

Ingredients:

- 1 handful raw dandelion greens
- 2 celery sticks
- 2 tbsp. chia seeds
- 1 small piece ginger, minced
- ½ cup almond milk
- ½ cup water
- ½ cup plain yogurt

Directions:

1. Rinse and clean dandelion leaves from any dirt; add in a high-speed blender.
2. Clean the ginger; keep only the inner part and cut into small slices; add in a food processor.
3. Put in all remaining ingredients and blend until smooth.
4. Serve and enjoy!

Nutrition:

Calories 58, Carbohydrates 5g, Proteins 3g, Fat 6g, Fiber 3g

225. Dark Turnip Greens Smoothie

Preparation Time: 10 minutes
Cooking Time: 3 minutes
Servings: 2

Ingredients:

- 1 cup raw turnip greens
- 1 ½ cup almond milk
- 1 tbsp. almond butter
- ½ cup water
- ½ tsp. cocoa powder, unsweetened
- 1 tbsp. dark chocolate chips
- ¼ tsp. cinnamon
- A pinch salt
- ½ cup crushed ice

Directions:

1. Rinse and clean turnip greens from any dirt.
2. Place the turnip greens in your blender along with all other ingredients.
3. Blend it for 45–60 seconds or until done; smooth and creamy.
4. Serve with or without crushed ice.

Nutrition:

Calories 131, Carbohydrates 6g, Proteins 4g, Fat 10g, Fiber 2.5g

226. Butter Pecan and Coconut Smoothie

Preparation Time: 5 minutes
Cooking Time: 2 minutes
Servings: 2

Ingredients:

- 1 cup coconut milk, canned
- 1 scoop Butter Pecan powdered creamer
- 2 cups fresh spinach leaves, chopped
- 2 tbsp. stevia granulated sweetener to taste
- ½ cup water
- 1 cup ice cubes crushed

Directions:

1. Place ingredients from the list above in your high-speed blender.
2. Blend for 35–50 seconds or until all ingredients are combined well.
3. Add less or more crushed ice.
4. Drink and enjoy!

Nutrition:

Calories 268, Carbohydrates: 7g, Proteins: 6g, Fat: 26g, Fiber 1.5g

227. Fresh Cucumber, Kale and Raspberry Smoothie

Preparation Time: 10 minutes
Cooking Time: 3 minutes
Servings: 3

Ingredients:

- 1 ½ cups cucumber, peeled
- ½ cup raw kale leaves
- 1 ½ cups fresh raspberries
- 1 cup almond milk
- 1 cup water
- Ice cubes crushed (optional)
- 2 tbsp. natural sweetener (Stevia, Erythritol, etc.)

Directions:

1. Add the ingredients to a blender and pulse for 35 – 40 seconds.
2. Serve into chilled glasses.
3. Add more natural sweeter if you like. Enjoy!

Nutrition:
Calories 70, Carbohydrates 8g, Proteins 3g, Fat 6g, Fiber 5g

228. Fresh Lettuce and Cucumber-Lemon Smoothie

Preparation Time: 10 minutes
Cooking Time: 0 minutes
Servings: 2
Ingredients:

- 2 cups fresh lettuce leaves, chopped (any kind)
- 1 cup cucumber
- 1 lemon washed and sliced.
- 2 tbsp. chia seeds
- 1 ½ cup water or coconut water
- ¼ cup stevia granulate sweetener (or to taste)

Directions:

1. Add all ingredients from the list above to the high-speed blender; blend until completely smooth.
2. Pour your smoothie into chilled glasses and enjoy!

Nutrition:
Calories 51, Carbohydrates 4g, Proteins 2g, Fat 4g, Fiber 3.5g

229. Green Coconut Smoothie

Preparation Time: 10 minutes
Cooking Time: 0 minutes
Servings: 2
Ingredients:

- 1 ¼ cup coconut milk (canned)
- 2 tbsp. chia seeds
- 1 cup fresh kale leaves
- 1 cup spinach leaves
- 1 scoop vanilla protein powder
- 1 cup ice cubes
- Granulated stevia sweetener (to taste; optional)
- ½ cup water

Directions:

1. Rinse and clean kale and the spinach leaves from any dirt.
2. Add all ingredients to your blender.
3. Blend until you get a nice smoothie.
4. Serve into chilled glass.

Nutrition:
Calories 179, Carbohydrates 5g, Proteins 4g, Fat 18g, Fiber 2.5g

230. Instant Coffee Smoothie

Preparation Time: 20 minutes
Cooking Time: 7 minutes
Servings: 2

Ingredients:

- 2 cups instant coffee
- 1 cup almond milk (or coconut milk)
- ¼ cup heavy cream
- 2 tbsp. cocoa powder (unsweetened)
- 1–2 Handful fresh spinach leaves
- 10 drops liquid stevia

Directions:

1. Make a coffee; set aside.
2. Place all remaining ingredients in your fast-speed blender; blend for 45–60 seconds or until done.
3. Pour your instant coffee into a blender and continue to blend for a further 30–45 seconds.
4. Serve immediately.

Nutrition:
Calories 142, Carbohydrates 6g, Proteins 5g, Fat 14g, Fiber 3g

231. Keto Blood Sugar Adjuster Smoothie

Preparation Time: 10 minutes
Cooking Time: 0 minutes
Servings: 2
Ingredients:

- 2 cups green cabbage
- 1 tbsp. Apple cider vinegar
- Juice of 1 small lemon
- 1 cup water
- 1 cup crushed ice cubes for serving

Directions:

1. Place all ingredients in your high-speed blender or in a food processor and blend until smooth and soft.
2. Serve in chilled glasses with crushed ice.
3. Enjoy!

Nutrition:
Calories 74, Carbohydrates 7g, Proteins 2g, Fat 6g, Fiber 4g

232. Strengthening Smoothie Bowl

Preparation Time: 5 minutes
Cooking Time: 4 minutes
Servings: 2
Ingredients:

- ¼ cup fresh blueberries
- ¼ cup fat-free plain Greek yogurt
- ⅓ cup unsweetened almond milk
- 2 tbsps. Whey protein powder
- 2 cups frozen blueberries

Directions:

1. In a blender, add blueberries and pulse for about 1 minute.

2. Add almond milk, yogurt, and protein powder and pulse till desired consistency.
3. Transfer the mixture into 2 bowls evenly.
4. Serve with the topping of fresh blueberries.

Nutrition:
Calories 176, Fat 2.1g, Carbs 27g, Protein 15.1g, Potassium 242mg

233. Brilliant Berry Smoothie

Preparation Time: 5 minutes
Cooking Time: 0 minutes
Servings: 2

Ingredients:
- ¼ cup blackberries
- ¼ cup unenriched rice milk.
- ¼ cup sliced strawberries
- ¼ cup blueberries

Directions:
1. Add the ingredients to a blender and serve over ice if desired.
2. Enjoy!

Nutrition:
Calories 90, Fat 1g, Carbs 18g, Phosphorus 82mg, Potassium 70mg, Sodium 30mg

234. Pineapple Juice

Preparation Time: 5 minutes
Cooking Time: 0 minutes
Servings: 2

Ingredients:
- ½ cup canned pineapple
- 1 cup water

Directions:
1. Blend all ingredients and serve over ice.

Nutrition:
Calories 135, Protein 0g, Carbs 0g, Fat 0g, Sodium 0mg, Potassium 180mg, Phosphorus 8mg

235. Blueberry Burst

Preparation Time: 5 minutes
Cooking Time: 0 minutes
Servings: 2

Ingredients:
- 1 cup chopped collard greens
- 1 cup unsweetened rice milk
- 1 tbsp. almond butter
- 1 cup blueberries
- 3 ice cubes

Directions:
1. Combine all in a blender until smooth. Pour into 2 glasses and serve.

Nutrition:
Calories 131, Sodium 60mg, Protein 3g, Potassium 146mg Phosphorus 51mg, Carbs 4g, Fat 0g

236. Peach Iced-Tea

Preparation Time: 15 minutes
Cooking Time: 0 minutes
Servings: 2

Ingredients:
- 1 lemon
- 1 cup sliced canned peaches
- 1 tbsp. loose black

Directions:
1. Put the peach slices in a hot pot of water
2. Simmer for 10 minutes before turning off the heat
3. Put the loose tea leaves and let it steep for 5- minutes.
4. Pour liquid through a sieve or tea strainer.
5. Enjoy hot.

Nutrition:
Calories 74, Protein 0g, Carbs 15 g, Fat 0g, Sodium 5mg Potassium 15 mg, Phosphorus 14mg

237. Homemade Rice Milk

Preparation Time: 5 minutes plus 8 to 12 hours to soak
Cooking Time: 0 minutes
Servings: 2

Ingredients:
- 1 cup long-grain white rice
- 4 cups water
- ½ tsp. vanilla extract (optional)

Directions:
1. In a medium dry skillet over medium heat, toast the rice until lightly browned, about 5 minutes.
2. Transfer the rice to a jar or bowl, and add the water. Cover, refrigerate, and soak overnight.
3. In a blender, add the rice and water, along with the vanilla (if using), and process until smooth.
4. Place a fine-mesh strainer over a glass jar or bowl and pour the milk into it. Serve immediately, or cover, refrigerate and serve within three days Shake before using.
5. Substitution Tip: Rice milk can be substituted in most recipes calling for whole milk or another nut milk as a low-fat, low-phosphorus, and low-potassium alternative. Use an equal amount of rice milk in place of other milk products, and proceed as directed in the recipe.

Nutrition:
Calories: 112; Total Fat: 0g; Saturated Fat: 0g; Cholesterol: 0mg; Carbohydrates: 24g; Fiber: 0g; Protein: 0g; Phosphorus: 0mg; Potassium: 55mg; Sodium: 80mg

238.   Cinnamon Horchata

Preparation Time: 5 minutes plus 3 hours to soak
Cooking Time: 0 minutes
Servings: 2
Ingredients:

- 1 cup long-grain white rice
- 4 cups water
- 1 cinnamon stick, broken into pieces
- 1 cup Homemade Rice Milk or unsweetened store-bought rice milk
- 1 tsp. vanilla extract
- 1 tsp. ground cinnamon
- ⅓ cup granulated sugar

Directions:

1. In a blender, combine the rice, water, and cinnamon-stick pieces. Blend for about 1 minute, until the rice begins to break up. Let stand at room temperature for at least 3 hours or overnight.
2. Place a wire mesh strainer over a pitcher, and pour the liquid into it. Discard the rice.
3. Add the milk, vanilla, ground cinnamon, and sugar. Stir to combine. Serve over ice.

Variation Tip: For an even richer flavor, add 1 tablespoon of unsweetened cocoa powder to the Horchata with the ground cinnamon in Step 3.

Nutrition:
Calories: 123; Total Fat: 2g; Saturated Fat: 0g; Cholesterol: 0mg; Carbohydrates: 26g; Fiber: 0g; Protein: 1g; Phosphorus: 34mg; Potassium: 78mg; Sodium: 32mg

Chapter 11: Vegetables Recipes

239.   Egg White Frittata with Penne

Preparation Time: 15 minutes
Cooking Time: 30 minutes
Servings: 4

Ingredients:

- 6 egg whites
- ¼ cup rice milk
- 1 tbsp. chopped fresh parsley
- 1 tsp. chopped fresh thyme
- 1 tsp. chopped fresh chives
- Freshly ground black pepper
- 2 tsp. olive oil
- ¼ small sweet onion, chopped
- 1 tsp. minced garlic
- ½ cup boiled and chopped red bell pepper
- 2 cups cooked penne

Directions:

1. Heat the oven to 350°F.
2. In a container, whisk together the egg whites, rice milk, parsley, thyme, chives, and pepper.
3. Preheat the olive oil.
4. Sauté the onion, garlic, and red pepper for about 4 minutes or until they are softened.
5. Using a spatula, add the cooked penne to the skillet to evenly distribute the pasta.
6. Pour the egg mixture over the pasta and shake the pan to coat the pasta.
7. Leave the skillet on the heat for 1 minute to set the bottom of the frittata and then transfer the skillet to the oven.
8. Bake the frittata for about 25 minutes or until it is set and golden brown.
9. Remove from the oven and serve immediately.

Nutrition:
Calories: 170, Fat: 3g, Carbohydrates: 25g, Phosphorus: 62mg, Potassium: 144mg, Sodium: 90mg, Protein: 10g

240.   Vegetable Fried Rice

Preparation Time: 20 minutes
Cooking Time: 20 minutes
Servings: 6

Ingredients:

- 1 tbsp. olive oil
- ½ sweet onion, chopped
- 1 tbsp. grated fresh ginger
- 2 tsp. minced garlic
- 1 cup sliced carrots
- ½ cup chopped eggplant
- ½ cup peas
- ½ cup green beans, cut into 1-inch pieces
- 2 tbsp. chopped fresh cilantro
- 3 cups cooked rice

Directions:

1. Over medium-high heat, heat the olive oil.
2. Sauté the onion, ginger, and garlic for about 3 minutes or until softened.
3. Stir in the carrot, eggplant, peas, and green beans and sauté for 3 minutes more.
4. Add the cilantro and rice.
5. Sauté, stirring constantly, for about 10 minutes or until the rice is heated through.
6. Serve immediately.

Nutrition: Calories: 189, Fat: 7g, Carbohydrates: 28g, Phosphorus: 89mg, Potassium: 172mg, Sodium: 13mg, Protein: 6g

241. Bulgur-Stuffed Spaghetti Squash

Preparation Time: 20 minutes
Cooking Time: 50 minutes
Servings: 4

Ingredients:
For the Squash:

- 2 small spaghetti squash, halved
- 1 tsp. olive oil
- Freshly ground black pepper

For the Filling:

- 1 tsp. olive oil
- ½ small sweet onion, finely diced
- 1 tsp. minced garlic
- ½ cup chopped carrot
- ½ cup cranberries
- 1 tsp. chopped fresh thyme
- ½ tsp. ground cumin
- ½ tsp. ground coriander
- Juice of ½ lemon
- 1 cup cooked bulgur

Directions:
To Make the Squash:

1. Preheat the oven to 350°F.
2. Line a baking sheet with parchment paper.
3. Grease the cut sides of the squash, season with pepper, and place them cut-side down on the baking sheet.
4. Bake for 25 to 30 minutes until it become tender. Remove the squash from the oven and flip the squash halves over.

5. Scoop the flesh from each half, leaving about ½ inch around the edges and keeping the skin intact.
6. Place 2 cups of squash flesh in a large bowl and reserve the rest for another recipe.

To Make the Filling
1. Heat the olive oil.
2. Sauté the onion, garlic, carrot, and cranberries for 5 to 6 minutes or until softened.
3. Add the sautéed vegetables to the squash in the bowl.
4. Add the thyme, cumin, and coriander, stirring to combine.
5. Stir in the lemon juice and cooked bulgur until well mixed.
6. Spoon the filling evenly into the squash halves.
7. Bake for about 15 minutes or until heated through.
8. Serve warm.

Nutrition:
Calories: 111, Fat: 2g, Carbohydrates: 17g, Phosphorus: 38mg, Potassium: 182mg, Sodium: 22mg, Protein: 3g

242.   Red Pepper Strata

Preparation Time: 20 minutes, **Cooking Time:** 1 hour and 5 minutes
Servings: 8
Ingredients:
- Butter, for greasing the baking dish
- 8 slices fresh white bread, cut into cubes
- 1 tbsp. unsalted butter
- ½ sweet onion, chopped
- 1 tsp. minced garlic
- 1 red bell pepper, boiled and chopped
- 6 eggs
- ¼ cup tarragon vinegar
- 1 cup rice milk
- 1 tsp. Tabasco sauce
- ½ tsp. freshly ground black pepper
- 1 oz. Parmesan cheese, grated

Directions:
1. Preheat the oven to 250°F.
2. Grease a 9-by-9-inch baking dish with butter; set aside.
3. Layer the baking sheet with parchment paper and scatter the bread cubes on the sheet.
4. Bake the bread cubes until they are crisp.
5. Remove the bread cubes from the oven then set them aside.
6. Over medium-high heat, melt the butter.
7. Sauté the onion and garlic for about 3 minutes or until softened.
8. Add the red pepper and sauté for an additional 2 minutes.

9. Spread half of the bread cubes in a layer in the baking dish and top with half of the sautéed vegetables.
10. Repeat with the remaining half of the bread cubes and vegetables.
11. In a medium bowl, whisk together the eggs, vinegar, rice milk, hot sauce, and pepper.
12. Put the egg mixture evenly into the baking dish.
13. Cover the dish and place in the fridge to soak for at least 2 hours or overnight.
14. Let the strata come to room temperature.
15. Preheat the oven to 325°F.
16. Remove the plastic wrap and bake for about 45 minutes or until golden.
17. Sprinkle the top of the strata with cheese and bake for an additional 5 minutes.
18. Serve hot.

Nutrition:
Calories: 150, Fat: 6g, Carbohydrates: 10g, Phosphorus: 120mg, Potassium: 89mg, Sodium: 168mg, Protein: 7g

243.   Chicken and Broccoli Pan Bake

Preparation Time: 5 minutes
Cooking Time: 25 minutes
Servings: 2
Ingredients:
- 16 oz. boneless skinless chicken breasts, cubed
- 1½ cups frozen broccoli florets
- 2 cups frozen sliced carrots
- 4 tbsp. olive oil
- Juice of 1 lemon
- 1 tsp. dried oregano leaves

Directions:
1. Preheat the oven to 450°F.
2. Arrange the chicken, broccoli, and carrots on a baking sheet with a lip.
3. Drizzle with olive oil and lemon juice and sprinkle with the oregano. Toss to coat and arrange everything in a single layer.
4. Roast for 15 to 20 minutes until the chicken registers 165°F internal temperature and the vegetables are tender-crisp.
5. Serve.

Nutrition:
Calories: 282; Total fat: 17g; Saturated fat: 3g; Sodium: 85mg; Potassium: 578mg; Phosphorus: 276mg; Carbohydrates: 6g; Fiber: 2g; Protein: 27g; Sugar: 2g

244.   Marinated Tofu Stir-Fry

Preparation Time: 20 minutes
Cooking Time: 20 minutes
Servings: 4
Ingredients:
For the Tofu:

- 1 tbsp. freshly squeezed lemon juice
- 1 tsp. minced garlic
- 1 tsp. grated fresh ginger
- Pinch red pepper flakes
- 5 oz. extra-firm tofu, pressed well and cubed (see ingredient tip)

For the Stir-Fry:

- 1 tbsp. olive oil
- ½ cup cauliflower florets
- ½ cup thinly sliced carrots
- ½ cup julienned red pepper
- ½ cup fresh green beans
- 2 cups cooked white rice

Directions:
To Make the Tofu:

1. Combine together the lemon juice, garlic, ginger, and red pepper flakes.
2. Add the tofu and toss it around for coating.
3. Place the bowl in the refrigerator and marinate for 2 hours.

To Make the Stir Fry

1. Heat the oil.
2. Sauté the tofu for about 8 minutes or until it is lightly browned and heated through.
3. Add the cauliflower and carrots and sauté for 5 minutes, stirring and tossing constantly.
4. Add the red pepper and green beans; sauté for 3 additional minutes.
5. Serve over the white rice.

Ingredient Tip: Draining tofu is a crucial step to ensure this porous product absorbs all the flavor in the dish. Drench the oil of the tofu on a paper towel-lined plate and cover the block with more paper towels. Set something heavy such as a large can or a book on the tofu. Check the drainage every 30 minutes, changing the paper towels if needed, for two hours.
Dialysis Modification: Omit the red peppers from the dish to lower the amount of potassium in the recipe.

Nutrition:
Calories: 190, Fat: 6g, Carbohydrates: 30g, Phosphorus: 90mg, Potassium: 199mg, Sodium: 22mg, Protein: 6g

245.   Thai-Inspired Vegetable Curry

Preparation Time: 15 minutes
Cooking Time: 45 minutes
Servings: 4

Ingredients:

- 2 tsp. olive oil
- ½ sweet onion, diced
- 2 tsp. minced garlic
- 2 tsp. grated fresh ginger
- ½ eggplant, peeled and diced
- 1 carrot, peeled and diced
- 1 red bell pepper, diced
- 1 tbsp. Hot Curry Powder
- 1 tsp. ground cumin
- ½ tsp. coriander
- Pinch cayenne pepper
- 1 ½ cups homemade vegetable stock
- 1 tbsp. cornstarch
- ¼ cup water

Directions:

1. Over medium-high heat, heat the oil.
2. Sauté the onion, garlic, and ginger for 3 minutes or until they are softened.
3. Add the eggplant, carrots, and red pepper, and sauté, stirring often, for 6 additional minutes.
4. Stir in the curry powder, cumin, coriander, cayenne pepper, and vegetable stock.
5. Put the curry to a boil and then reduce the heat to low.
6. Simmer the curry for about 30 minutes or until the vegetables are tender.
7. Stir together the cornstarch and water.
8. Mix the cornstarch mixture into the curry and simmer for about 5 minutes or until the sauce is thickened.

Nutrition:
Calories: 100, Fat: 3g, Carbohydrates: 9g, Phosphorus: 28mg, Potassium: 180mg, Sodium: 218mg, Protein: 1g

246.   Linguine with Roasted Red Pepper–Basil Sauce

Preparation Time: 20 minutes
Cooking Time: 20 minutes
Servings: 4

Ingredients:

- 8 oz. uncooked linguine
- 1 tsp. olive oil
- ½ sweet onion, chopped and 2 tsp. minced garlic
- 1 cup chopped roasted red bell peppers
- 1 tsp. balsamic vinegar
- ¼ cup shredded fresh basil
- Pinch red pepper flakes and freshly ground black pepper
- 4 tsp. grated low-fat Parmesan cheese, for garnish

Directions:

1. Cook the pasta and following the package instructions.
2. While the pasta is cooking, place a large skillet over medium-high heat and add the olive oil.
3. Sauté the onions and garlic for about 3 minutes or until they are softened.
4. Add the red pepper, vinegar, basil, and red pepper flakes to the skillet and stir for about 5 minutes or until heated through.
5. Mix the cooked pasta with the sauce and season with pepper.
6. Serve topped with Parmesan cheese.

Nutrition: Calories: 246, Fat: 3g, Carbohydrates: 41g, Phosphorus: 117mg, Potassium: 187mg, Sodium: 450mg, Protein: 13g

247.   Baked Mac and Cheese

Preparation Time: 10 minutes
Cooking Time: 25 minutes
Servings: 4

Ingredients:

- 1 tsp. olive oil
- ½ sweet onion, chopped
- 1 tsp. minced garlic
- ¼ cup rice milk
- 1 cup cream cheese
- ½ tsp. dry mustard
- ½ tsp. freshly ground black pepper
- Pinch cayenne pepper
- 3 cups cooked macaroni

Directions:

1. Preheat the oven to 375°F.
2. Grease a 9-by-9-inch baking dish with butter; set aside.
3. In a medium saucepan over medium heat, heat the olive oil.
4. Sauté the onion and garlic for about 3 minutes or until softened.
5. Stir in the milk, cheese, mustard, black pepper, and cayenne pepper until the mixture is smooth and well blended.
6. Add the cooked macaroni, stirring to coat.
7. Transfer the mixture into a baking dish and place it in the oven.
8. Bake for about 15 minutes or until the macaroni is bubbly.
9. Dialysis modification: This dish is rich, so you can choose a smaller portion size to reduce your phosphorus and potassium intake.

Nutrition:
Calories: 386, Fat: 22g, Carbohydrates: 37g, Phosphorus: 120mg, Potassium: 146mg, Sodium: 219mg, Protein: 10g

248.   Grilled Kale and Fried Egg on Bread

Preparation Time: 10 minutes
Cooking Time: 20 minutes
Servings: 2

Ingredients:

- 2 medium kale leaves
- ½ tsp. olive oil
- Pinch red pepper flakes
- 4 tsp. unsalted butter, divided
- 2 slices white bread
- 2 tsp. cream cheese
- 2 small eggs
- Freshly ground black pepper

Directions:

1. Preheat the oven to 350°F.
2. Mix the kale leaves with olive oil until they are completely coated.
3. Sprinkle a pinch of red pepper flakes over the kale leaves.
4. Place the leaves in a pie plate and roast for about 10 minutes or until crispy.
5. Remove the kale from the oven; set aside.
6. Butter both sides of the bread with 1 teaspoon butter per slice.
7. Toast the bread on both sides for about 3 minutes or until it is golden brown.
8. Transfer the bread from the skillet and spread 1 teaspoon cream cheese on each slice.
9. Melt the remaining 2 teaspoons of butter in the skillet and fry the eggs sunny-side up, for about 4 minutes.
10. Place a piece of crispy kale and a fried egg on top of each slice of the cream cheese–topped bread.
11. Serve seasoned with pepper.

Nutrition:
Calories: 224, Fat: 15g, Carbohydrates: 14g, Phosphorus: 118mg, Potassium: 175mg, Sodium: 200mg, Protein: 8g

249.   Tofu and Eggplant Stir-Fry

Preparation Time: 20 minutes
Cooking Time: 20 minutes
Servings: 4

Ingredients:

- 1 tbsp. granulated sugar
- 1 tbsp. all-purpose flour
- 1 tsp. grated fresh ginger
- 1 tsp. minced garlic
- 1 tsp. minced jalapeño pepper
- Juice of 1 lime
- Water
- 2 tbsp. olive oil, divided

- 5 oz. extra-firm tofu, cut into ½-inch cubes
- 2 cups cubed eggplant
- 2 scallions
- 3 tbsp. chopped cilantro

Directions:
1. Combine together the sugar, flour, ginger, garlic, jalapeño, lime juice, and enough water to make ⅔ cup of sauce then set aside.
2. In a large skillet over medium-high heat, heat 1 tablespoon of the oil.
3. Sauté the tofu for about 6 minutes or until it is crisp and golden.
4. Remove the tofu; set it aside on a plate.
5. Add the remaining 1 tablespoon oil and sauté the eggplant cubes for about 10 minutes or until they look golden brown.
6. Add the tofu and scallions to the skillet and toss to combine.
7. Mix in the sauce and bring to a boil, stirring constantly, for about 2 minutes or until the sauce is thickened.
8. Add the cilantro before serving.

Nutrition:
Calories: 386, Fat: 22g, Carbohydrates: 37g, Phosphorus: 120mg, Potassium: 146mg, Sodium: 219mg, Protein: 10g

250. Mie Goreng with Broccoli

Preparation Time: 10 minutes, plus 30 minutes draining time
Cooking Time: 20 minutes
Servings: 4

Ingredients:
- ½ lb. rice noodles
- ¼ cup packed dark brown sugar
- 2 tsp. minced garlic
- 1 tsp. grated fresh ginger
- 1 tsp. low-sodium soy sauce
- ½ tsp. sambal oelek
- 4 oz. extra-firm tofu, cut into ½-inch cubes
- 1 tbsp. cornstarch
- 2 tbsp. olive oil, divided
- 2 cups broccoli, cut into small size
- 2 scallions, both green and white parts, sliced thin on the diagonal
- Lime wedges, for garnish

Directions:
1. Cook the noodles by following the package instructions; drain and set aside.
2. In a small bowl, whisk together the brown sugar, garlic, ginger, soy sauce, and sambal oelek; set aside.

3. Drain the tofu on paper towels for 30 minutes and pat the tofu dry.
4. Toss the tofu with the cornstarch and shake to remove the excess.
5. Heat 1 tablespoon of the olive oil over medium heat.
6. Add the tofu and sauté for about 10 minutes or until the tofu is browned on all sides and crispy.
7. Put the tofu on a plate with a slotted spoon.
8. Add the 1 tablespoon oil to the skillet.
9. Sauté the broccoli for about 4 minutes or until it is tender.
10. Add the sauce and tofu to the skillet and cook for about 2 minutes or until the sauce thickens.
11. Serve topped with scallions and garnish with lime wedges.

Nutrition:
Calories: 360, Fat: 11g, Carbohydrates: 62g, Phosphorus: 120mg, Potassium: 193mg, Sodium: 166mg, Protein: 4g

251. Spicy Veggie Pancakes

Preparation Time: 20 minutes
Cooking Time: 10 minutes
Servings: 4

Ingredients:
- 3 tbsp. olive oil, divided
- 2 small onions, finely chopped
- 1 jalapeño pepper, minced
- ¾ cup carrot, grated
- ¾ cup cabbage, finely chopped
- 1½ cups quick-cooking oats
- ¾ cup cooked brown rice
- ¾ cup water
- ½ cup whole-wheat flour
- 1 large egg
- 1 large egg white
- 1 tsp. baking soda
- ¼ tsp. cayenne pepper

Directions:
1. Heat 2 teaspoons oil over medium heat.
2. Sauté the onion, jalapeño, carrot, and cabbage for 4 minutes.
3. While the veggies are cooking, combine the oats, rice, water, flour, egg, egg white, baking soda, and pepper in a mixing bowl.
4. Add the cooked vegetables to the mixture and stir to combine.
5. Heat the remaining oil in a pan over medium heat.
6. Drop the mixture into the skillet, about ⅓ cup per pancake. Cook for 4 minutes until bubbles form on the surface of the pancakes and the edges look cooked, then carefully flip them over.

7. Cook the second side for 3 to 5 minutes or until the pancakes are hot and firm.
8. Repeat with the remaining mixture and serve.

Make It Easier Tip: To save on prep time, purchase pre-grated carrots and cabbage. Brown rice can also be bought frozen and then microwaved according to package directions when you're ready to use it.

Nutrition:
Calories: 323, Total fat 11g, Saturated fat 2g, Sodium: 366mg, Potassium: 381mg, Phosphorus: 263mg, Carbohydrates: 48g, Fiber: 7g, Protein: 10g

252. Egg and Veggie Fajitas

Preparation Time: 20 minutes
Cooking Time: 10 minutes
Servings: 4
Ingredients:

- 3 large eggs
- 3 egg whites
- 2 tsp. chili powder
- 1 tbsp. unsalted butter
- 1 onion, chopped
- 2 garlic cloves, minced
- 1 jalapeño pepper, minced
- 1 red bell pepper, chopped
- 1 cup frozen corn, thawed and drained
- 8 (6-inch) corn tortillas

Directions:

1. Whisk the eggs, egg whites, and chili powder in a small bowl until well combined. Set aside.
2. Melt the butter over medium heat.
3. Sauté the onion, garlic, jalapeño, bell pepper, and corn, until the vegetables are tender, 3 to 4 minutes.
4. Put in the beaten egg mixture to the skillet. Cook, stirring occasionally, until the eggs form large curds and are set, 3 to 5 minutes.
5. Meanwhile, soften the corn tortillas as directed on the package.
6. Divide the egg mixture evenly among the softened corn tortillas. Roll the tortillas up and serve.

Increase Protein Tip: To make this a medium-protein recipe, increase the egg whites to 6 and replace 1 cup frozen corn with 1 cup canned no-salt-added or low-sodium canned black beans. The protein will increase to 19 grams.

Nutrition:
Calories: 316, Total fat 14g, Saturated fat: 3g, Sodium: 167mg, Potassium: 408mg, Phosphorus: 287mg, Carbohydrates: 35g, Fiber: 5g, Protein: 14g, Sugar: 4g

253. Pesto Pasta Salad

Preparation Time: 15 minutes
Cooking Time: 15 minutes
Servings: 3
Ingredients:

- 1 cup fresh basil leaves
- ½ cup packed fresh flat-leaf parsley leaves
- ½ cup arugula, chopped
- 2 tbsp. Parmesan cheese, grated
- ¼ cup extra-virgin olive oil
- 3 tbsp. mayonnaise
- 2 tbsp. water
- 12 oz. whole-wheat rotini pasta
- 1 red bell pepper, chopped
- 1 medium yellow summer squash, sliced
- 1 cup frozen baby peas

Directions:

1. Bring a large pot of water to boil.
2. Meanwhile, combine the basil, parsley, arugula, cheese, and olive oil in a blender or food processor. Blend until the herbs are finely chopped. Add the mayonnaise and water, then process again. Set aside.
3. Put the pasta in the pot of boiling water; cook according to package directions, about 8 to 9 minutes. Drain well, reserving ¼ cup of the cooking liquid.
4. Combine the pesto, pasta, bell pepper, squash, and peas in a large bowl and toss gently, adding enough of the reserved pasta cooking liquid to make a sauce on the salad. Serve immediately or cover and chill, then serve.
5. Store in an airtight container and refrigerate for up to 3 days.

Ingredient Tip: Since you don't cook the extra-virgin olive oil in this recipe, a good quality brand will contribute to increased flavor and richness. Reserve the more expensive, higher-quality extra-virgin olive oil for recipes like this one and stick to using regular olive oil for sautéing.

Nutrition:
Calories: 378, Total fat 24g, Saturated fat: 4g, Sodium: 163mg, Potassium: 472mg, Phosphorus: 213mg, Carbohydrates: 35, Fiber: 6g, Protein: 9g, Sugar: 5g

254. Eggplant Casserole

Preparation Time: 10 minutes
Cooking Time: 20 minutes
Servings: 2
Ingredients:

- 3 cups eggplant
- 3 large eggs

- ½ cup liquid non-dairy creamer
- ½ tsp. black pepper
- ¼ tsp. sage
- ½ cup breadcrumbs
- 1 tbsp. margarine

Directions:
1. First, boil the eggplant in a saucepan filled with water until soft.
2. Drain and mash the eggplant in a bowl.
3. Now beat the eggs with black pepper, cream, sage, and eggplant mash.
4. Spread this mixture over the surface of the baking dish and top it with breadcrumbs and butter.
5. Pour 1.5 cups of water into the Instant pot and set the trivet over it.
6. Place the baking dish over the trivet.
7. Seal the lid and cook for 15 minutes on Manual mode at High pressure.
8. Then, release the pressure completely then remove the pot's lid.
9. Broil this casserole for 5 minutes in the oven at Broiler settings. Serve warm.

Nutrition: Calories 186, Total Fats 9 g, Saturated Fat 0.4 g, Cholesterol 124 mg, Sodium 246 mg, Total Carbs 19 g, Fiber 1.9 g, Sugar 1.2 g, Protein 7 g

255. Couscous with Vegetables

Preparation Time: 10 minutes
Cooking Time: 15 minutes
Servings: 2
Ingredients:
- 1 tbsp. margarine
- ½ cup frozen peas
- ½ cup onion and 1 garlic clove
- ¼ cup raw mushrooms
- 2 tbsp. dry white wine
- ½ tsp. dried basil
- 1 cup zucchini, diced
- ½ cup vegetable broth
- ⅛ tsp. black pepper
- ½ cup couscous, cooked

Directions:
1. Start by melting margarine in the Instant pot on sauté mode.
2. Add garlic, mushrooms, onion, and peas, to sauté for 5 minutes.
3. Stir in the remaining ingredients to the Instant Pot.
4. Close the lid and cook for 10 minutes on Manual mode at High pressure.
5. Then, release the pressure completely then remove the pot's lid.
6. Serve warm with cooked couscous.

Nutrition: Calories 104, Total Fats 2 g, Saturated Fat 3.4 g, Cholesterol 0 mg, Sodium 33 mg, Total Carbs 18 g, Fiber 2.1 g, Sugar 0.5 g, Protein 3 g

256. Crunchy Tofu Stir Fry

Preparation Time: 10 minutes
Cooking Time: 10 minutes
Servings: 2
Ingredients:
- 16 oz. extra firm tofu
- ½ red bell pepper
- 1 garlic clove
- 1 cup vegetable broth.
- 1-½ tbsp. lime juice
- 2 tsp. sugar
- 1-½ tbsp. canola oil
- 1 tbsp. sesame oil
- 1 cup fresh broccoli florets
- 1 tsp. salt-free herb seasoning blend
- ⅛ tsp. black pepper
- ⅛ tsp. cayenne pepper
- ½ tsp. sesame seeds

Directions:
1. Start by heating canola oil in the Instant pot on sauté mode.
2. Toss in tofu and sauté until golden brown.
3. Stir in all other ingredients and mix well.
4. Close the lid and cook for 5 minutes on Manual mode at High pressure.
5. After finishing, release the pressure completely then remove the pot's lid.
6. Serve warm with rice.

Nutrition:
Calories 400, Total Fats 16 g, Saturated Fat 1.2 g, Cholesterol 0 mg, Sodium 184 mg, Total Carbs 45 g, Fiber 2.7 g, Sugar 1.9 g, Protein 19 g

257. Creamy Rice Risotto

Preparation Time: 10 minutes
Cooking Time: 9 minutes
Servings: 2
Ingredients:
- ¾ cup onion, chopped
- 1 tbsp. fresh thyme leaves
- 4 cups low-sodium vegetable broth
- 2 tbsp. unsalted butter
- 1-½ cups Arborio rice
- ¼ cup dry white wine
- 1-½ cups sliced Cremini mushrooms
- ½ cup grated Parmigianino Reggiano cheese

Directions:

1. Start by melting butter in an Instant Pot on sauté mode.
2. Add onion and mushrooms then sauté for 4 minutes.
3. Stir in rice, broth, thyme, and white wine.
4. Close the lid tightly and cook for 5 minutes on manual mode at high pressure.
5. Then, release the pressure completely then remove the pot's lid.
6. Garnish with cheese and serve.

Nutrition:

Calories 262, Total Fats 6 g, Saturated Fat 2.4 g, Cholesterol 16 mg, Sodium 199 mg, Total Carbs 45 g, Fiber 3 g, Sugar 1.4 g, Protein 7 g

258.   Cauliflower Curry

Preparation Time: 10 minutes
Cooking Time: 12 minutes
Servings: 2

Ingredients:

- 1 medium head cauliflower
- 1 cup bell pepper chopped
- 1 cup carrots, chopped
- 1 one-inch ginger root cube
- 1 garlic clove
- 1 tsp. curry powder
- ½ tsp. chili powder
- ½ tsp. cumin powder
- 1 tsp. lemon juice
- 1 cup coconut milk

Directions:

1. Start by adding all the ingredients to the Instant Pot.
2. Seal the lid and cook for 12 minutes on Manual mode at High pressure.
3. After finishing, release the pressure completely then remove the pot's lid.
4. Serve warm.

Nutrition:

Calories 77, Total Fats 5 g, Saturated Fat 4.4 g, Cholesterol 0 mg, Sodium 23 mg, Total Carbs 6 g, Fiber 1.9 g, Sugar 1.9 g, Protein 2 g

Chapter 12: Poultry and Meat Recipes

259.   Chicken Fajita Bowls

Preparation Time: 5 minutes
Cooking Time: 15 minutes
Servings: 2
Ingredients:

- ¼ lb. chicken breast
- 1 ½ tbsp. olive oil
- 1 onion
- 1 bell pepper, green
- 1 bell pepper, red
- 4 cloves garlic, minced
- ¼ tsp. chili powder
- Pinch of cayenne pepper
- ¼ tsp. paprika
- ¼ tsp. cumin
- ¼ tsp. black pepper, ground
- 1 ½ cups white rice, cooked

Directions:

1. Combine the chili powder, cayenne pepper, paprika, cumin, and black pepper together to make your fajita seasonings, and then set the spices aside.
2. Slice the chicken breast into bite-sized cubes and then place it in a small bowl, massaging it with half of the prepared seasoning mix. Allow it to marinate for fifteen minutes.
3. In a large-sized cooking, pan warmed in a stove heat of medium with one tbsp. of the olive oil, cook the bell pepper and onion until soft, about five mins.
4. Add in the chicken and garlic, and continue to cook until the chicken is fully cooked through, reaching an internal 165°F. This should take about ten minutes. Don't forget to stir the chicken occasionally.
5. The skillet should then be removed away from the stove's heat. Serve the vegetables and chicken over the rice.

Nutrition:
Protein Grams: 17, Phosphorus Milligrams: 229, Potassium Milligrams: 510, Sodium Milligrams: 46, Fat Grams: 11, Total Carbohydrates Grams: 47, Net Carbohydrates Grams: 45

260.   BlackBerry Chicken Wings

Preparation Time: 35 minutes
Cooking Time: 50 minutes
Servings: 4

Ingredients:

- 3 lbs. chicken wings, about 20 pieces
- ½ cup blackberry chipotle jam
- Salt and pepper to taste
- ½ cup water

Directions:

1. Add water and jam to a bowl and mix well
2. Place chicken wings in a zip bag and add two-thirds of the marinade
3. Season with salt and pepper
4. Let it marinate for 30 minutes
5. Preheat your oven to 400°F
6. Prepare a baking sheet and wire rack, place chicken wings in a wire rack and bake for 15 minutes
7. Brush remaining marinade and bake for 30 minutes more
8. Enjoy!

Nutrition:
Calories: 502, Fat: 39g, Carbohydrates: 01.8g, Protein: 34g

261. Parsley and Chicken Breast

Preparation Time: 10 minutes
Cooking Time: 40 minutes
Servings: 4
Ingredients:

- 1 tbsp. dry parsley
- 1 tbsp. dry basil
- 4 chicken breast halves, boneless and skinless
- ½ tsp. salt
- ½ tsp. red pepper flakes, crushed

Directions:

1. Preheat your oven to 350°F
2. Take inch baking dish and grease it with cooking spray evenly
3. Sprinkle 1 tablespoon of parsley, 1 teaspoon of basil, and spread the mixture over your baking dish
4. Arrange the chicken breast halves over the dish and sprinkle garlic slices on top
5. Use a small mixing bowl and add 1 teaspoon parsley, 1 teaspoon of basil, salt, basil, red pepper and mix well. Pour the mixture over the chicken breast
6. Bake for 25 minutes.
7. Remove the cover and bake for 15 minutes.
8. Serve and enjoy!

Nutrition:
Calories: 150, Fat: 4g, Carbohydrates: 4g, Protein: 25g

262.   Easy Butternut Chicken

Preparation Time: 15 minutes
Cooking Time: 30 minutes
Servings: 4

Ingredients:

- ½ lb. Nitrate free bacon
- 6 chicken thighs, boneless and skinless
- 2-3 cups butternut squash, cubed
- Extra virgin olive oil
- Fresh chopped sage
- Salt and pepper as needed

Directions:

1. Prepare your oven by preheating it to 425°F.
2. Take a large skillet and place it over medium-high heat, add bacon and fry until crispy.
3. Take bacon and place it on the side, crumble the bacon.
4. Add cubed butternut squash in the bacon grease and Sauté, season with salt and pepper.
5. Remove the squash from the pan once tender then transfer to a plate.
6. Add coconut oil to the skillet and add chicken thighs, cook for 10 minutes.
7. Season with salt and pepper.
8. Remove the skillet from the stove and transfer it to the oven.
9. Bake for 12-15 minutes, top with crumbled bacon and sage. Enjoy!

Nutrition: Calories: 323, Fat: 19g, Carbohydrates: 8g, Protein: 12g

263.   Simple Mustard Chicken

Preparation Time: 10 minutes
Cooking Time: 40 minutes
Servings: 4

Ingredients:

- 4 chicken breasts
- ½ cup chicken broth
- 3-4 tbsp. mustard
- 3 tbsp. olive oil
- 1 tsp. paprika
- 1 tsp. chili powder
- 1 tsp. garlic powder

Directions:

1. Take a small bowl and mix mustard, olive oil, paprika, chicken broth, garlic powder, chicken broth, and chili
2. Add chicken breast and marinate for 30 minutes
3. Take a lined baking sheet and arrange the chicken
4. Bake for 35 minutes at 375°F
5. Serve and enjoy!

Nutrition:
Calories: 531, Fat: 23g, Carbohydrates: 10g, Protein: 64g

264.   Chicken Kebab Sandwich

Preparation Time: 15 minutes
Cooking Time: 15 minutes
Servings: 4

Ingredients:

- 12 oz. boneless, skinless chicken breast
- 2 tbsp. freshly squeezed lemon juice
- 1 tbsp. extra-virgin olive oil
- 4 garlic cloves, minced, divided
- Freshly ground black pepper
- ¼ cup plain, unsweetened yogurt
- 4 white flatbreads
- 1 cucumber, sliced
- 1 cup lettuce, shredded

Directions:

1. In a medium bowl, add the chicken breast, lemon juice, olive oil, and half the garlic, tossing to coat. Season with pepper. Let it sit to marinate then prepare the other ingredients.
2. In a small bowl, add the yogurt and remaining garlic. Season with pepper and mix well.
3. Over medium-high heat, and add the chicken and the marinade. Cook for 5 minutes, until the chicken, is well browned on the underside. Turn it over to cook the other until the chicken is golden brown and the juices run clear. Remove from the pan and let rest for 5 minutes. Cut the chicken into thin slices.
4. In each flatbread, add some chicken, cucumber, and lettuce. Top with the yogurt sauce, and serve.

Lower Sodium Tip: Reduce the amount of chicken breast to 8 ounces to lower this dish to 275mg and 15g of protein.

Nutrition:
Calories: 217, Total Fat: 6g, Saturated Fat: 1g, Cholesterol: 49mg, Carbohydrates: 21g, Fiber: 1g, Protein: 22g, Phosphorus: 80mg, Potassium: 231mg, Sodium: 339mg

265.   Aromatic Chicken and Cabbage Stir-Fry

Preparation Time: 10 minutes
Cooking Time: 10 minutes
Servings: 4

Ingredients:

- 1 tsp. canola oil
- 10 oz. boneless, skinless chicken breast, thinly sliced
- 3 cups green cabbage, thinly sliced
- 1 tbsp. cornstarch
- 1 tsp. ground ginger

- ½ tsp. garlic powder
- ¼ cup water
- Freshly ground black pepper

Directions:

- Over medium-high heat, heat the oil. Add the chicken and cook, stirring often, until browned and cooked through.
- Put the cabbage in the pan, and cook for another 2 to 3 minutes, until the cabbage is tender but still crisp.
- In a small bowl, mix the cornstarch, ginger, garlic, and water. Add the mixture to the pan, and continue cooking until the sauce has slightly thickened about 1 minute. Season with pepper.

Substitution Tip: Collards, turnip greens, or mustard greens can be used in this stir-fry in place of cabbage. Because the cooking time is short, remove any tough stems to ensure even cooking.

Nutrition:
Calories: 96; Total Fat: 2g; Saturated Fat: 0g; Cholesterol: 38mg; Carbohydrates: 5g; Fiber: 1g; Protein: 15g; Phosphorus: 15mg; Potassium: 140mg; Sodium: 156m

266. Chicken Chow Mein

Preparation Time: 10 minutes
Cooking Time: 15 minutes
Servings: 6

Ingredients:

- 2 tsp. cornstarch
- 1 tbsp. water
- 1 tsp. low-sodium soy sauce
- 1 tsp. rice wine
- 1 tsp. sugar
- 1 tsp. sesame oil
- 2 tsp. canola oil
- 3 garlic cloves
- 8 oz. boneless, skinless chicken thighs, thinly sliced
- 2 cups shredded green cabbage
- 1 carrot
- 4 scallions, cut into 2-inch pieces
- 10 oz. chow Mein noodles, cooked according to package directions
- 1 cup mung bean sprouts

Directions:

1. Combine the cornstarch, water, and soy sauce. Mix in the rice wine, sugar, and sesame oil, mixing well. Set aside.
2. In a large skillet or wok over medium-high heat, heat the canola oil.
3. Add the garlic, and cook until just fragrant, stirring constantly. Add the chicken, and cook for 1 minute, stirring, until the chicken is browned but not cooked through.
4. Add the cabbage, carrot, and scallions, and cook for 1 to 2 minutes, until the cabbage begins to wilt and the chicken is cooked through.
5. Add the noodles, and toss with the chicken and vegetables. Pour in the sauce, and stir to coat. Add the bean sprouts, and stir. Remove from the heat, and serve.

Serving Tip: Examine your chopsticks skills with this recipe.

Nutrition:
Calories: 342; Total Fat: 18g; Saturated Fat: 3g; Cholesterol: 31mg; Carbohydrates: 34g; Fiber: 3g; Protein: 13g; Phosphorus: 169mg; Potassium: 308mg; Sodium: 289mg

267. Baked Herbed Chicken

Preparation Time: 10 minutes
Cooking Time: 40 minutes
Servings: 6

Ingredients:

- 4 tbsp. butter, at room temperature
- 4 garlic cloves, minced
- 1 tbsp. chopped fresh oregano
- 1 tbsp. chopped fresh parsley
- 1 tsp. lemon zest and 6 bone-in chicken thighs
- ¼ tsp. freshly ground black pepper

Directions:

1. Preheat the oven to 425°F. Combine the butter, garlic, oregano, parsley, and lemon zest in a small bowl and mix well.
2. Arrange the thighs on a baking tray, and gently peel back the skin, leaving it attached. Brush the thigh meat with a couple of teaspoons of the butter mixture, and replace the skin to cover the meat. Season with pepper.
3. Bake for 40 minutes, until the skin, is crisp and the juices run clear. Let rest for 5 minutes before serving.

Cooking Tip: To reduce the total fat nutrition to just 9g, remove and discard the skin after cooking.

Nutrition: Calories: 226; Total Fat: 17g; Saturated Fat: 8g; Cholesterol: 78mg; Carbohydrates: 1g; Fiber: 0g; Protein: 16g; Phosphorus: 114mg; Potassium: 158mg; Sodium: 120mg

268. Thai- Style Chicken Curry

Preparation Time: 15 minutes
Cooking Time: 15 minutes
Servings: 4
Ingredients:
For the Curry Paste:
- 2 dried Thai red chilies
- 2 tsp. coriander seeds
- 1 lemongrass stalk, outer layer removed, ends trimmed, tender green and white parts minced
- 1 shallot
- 4 garlic cloves
- 2-inch piece ginger, thinly sliced
- ½ cup coarsely chopped fresh cilantro leaves
- 1 tsp. low-sodium soy sauce
- 2 tbsp. lime juice

For the Curry:
- 1 tsp. canola oil
- 1-lb. boneless, skinless chicken breast,
- 1 cup green beans, cut into 2-inch segments
- 1 cup water
- Juice of 1 lime
- 1 tsp. brown sugar

Directions:
To Make the Curry Paste
1. In a small bowl, add the chilies and cover with hot water. Leave to soak for 10 minutes.
2. Toast the coriander seeds on the side until fragrant, shaking the pan constantly to prevent burning. Transfer immediately to a blender
3. Drain the chilies and add them to the food processor, then add the lemongrass, shallot, garlic, ginger, cilantro, soy sauce, and lime juice. Grind into a fine paste, adding 1 or 2 tablespoons of water if needed. Use immediately, or transfer to an airtight container and store refrigerated for up to three days.

To Make the Curry
1. Over medium heat, preheat the oil. Add the curry paste, and cook, stirring constantly, for about 30 seconds, until fragrant. Add the chicken breast, and stir continuously until just browned.
2. Add the beans and 1 cup of water. Let it simmer for 5 minutes until the chicken is cooked through and the vegetables are tender.
3. Season with lime juice and brown sugar. Serve over rice or rice noodles.

Lower Sodium Tip: Cut the soy sauce from the curry paste to reduce sodium to 236mg.

Nutrition:
Calories: 149; Total Fat: 3g; Saturated Fat: 1g; Cholesterol: 60mg; Carbohydrates: 9g; Fiber: 2g; Protein: 25g; Phosphorus: 35mg; Potassium: 205mg; Sodium: 280mg

269. Turkey Meatballs and Spaghetti in Garlic Sauce

Preparation Time: 15 minutes
Cooking Time: 20 minutes
Servings: 4
Ingredients:
For the Meatballs:
- ¾ lb. lean ground turkey
- ½ cup bread crumbs
- 1 large egg, beaten
- ½ tsp. onion powder
- ½ tsp. garlic powder

For the Pasta:
- 8 oz. spaghetti noodles
- 1 tbsp. extra-virgin olive oil
- 5 garlic cloves, minced
- 2 cups chopped broccoli Rabe
- ¼ cup shredded Parmesan cheese
- Freshly ground black pepper

Directions:
To Make the Meatballs:
1. Heat the oven to 375°F. Line a baking sheet with parchment paper.
2. Combine the turkey, bread crumbs, egg, onion powder, and garlic powder in a bowl then mix well.
3. Shape the turkey mixture into 2-inch round meatballs, and place them on the baking sheet.
4. Bake for 20 minutes, until browned and cooked through, flipping the meatballs once halfway through cooking.

To Make the Pasta
1. Boil a pot of water then cook the noodles al dente. Drain, reserving about 1 cup of the cooking water.
2. Preheat the oil over medium-high heat. Add the garlic and cook until fragrant. Add the broccoli Rabe and ½ cup of the reserved cooking water to the skillet. Reduce the heat to simmer, cover, and cook for 5 minutes until the broccoli Rabe is fork-tender.
3. Toss in the noodles to the skillet and mix. Add a couple of tablespoons or more of the remaining cooking water to the skillet, to wet the noodles. Mix in the Parmesan cheese and season with pepper. Serve the noodles topped with the meatballs.

Substitution Tip: If you don't have bread crumbs on hand, process a piece of white bread, crust removed, in a food processor until finely ground.

Nutrition:
Calories: 450; Total Fat: 15g; Saturated Fat: 4g; Cholesterol: 100mg; Carbohydrates: 55g; Fiber: 3g; Protein: 23g; Phosphorus: 319mg; Potassium: 354mg; Sodium: 245mg

270.   Rosemary Grilled Chicken

Preparation Time: 5 minutes
Cooking Time: 20 minutes
Servings: 2

Ingredients:

- 1 tbsp. fresh parsley, finely chopped
- 1 tbsp. fresh rosemary, finely chopped
- 1 tbsp. olive oil
- 4 (4-oz.) pieces chicken breast, boneless and skinless
- 5 cloves garlic, minced

Directions:

1. In a shallow and large bowl mix salt, parsley, rosemary, olive oil, and garlic. Place chicken breast and marinate in a bowl of herbs for at least an hour or more before grilling.
2. Grease grill grates and preheat grill to medium-high. Once hot, grill chicken for 4 to 5 minutes per side or until juices run a clear and the internal temperature of chicken is 168°F.

Nutrition:
Calories: per Serving: 218, Carbohydrates: 1g, Protein: 34g, Fats: 8g, Phosphorus: 267mg, Potassium: 440mg, Sodium: 560mg

271. Baked Pork Chops

Preparation Time: 10 minutes
Cooking Time: 40 minutes
Servings: 2

Ingredients:

- ½ cup all-purpose flour
- 1 large egg
- ¼ cup water
- ¾ cup cornflake crumbs
- 6 (3 ½-oz.) center-cut pork chops
- 2 tbsp. unsalted margarine
- 1 tsp. paprika

Directions:

1. Preheat oven to 350°F.
2. Mix and spread flour on a shallow plate.
3. Whisk egg with water in another shallow bowl.
4. Spread the cornflakes crumbs on a plate.
5. Coat the pork with flour then dip in the egg mix and then in the crumbs.
6. Grease a baking sheet and place the chops in it.
7. Sprinkle the paprika on top and bake for 40 minutes.

8. Serve fresh.

Nutrition:
Calories 282. Protein 23 g. Carbohydrates 25 g. Fat 10 g. Cholesterol 95 mg. Sodium 263 mg. Potassium 394 mg. Phosphorus 203 mg. Calcium 28 mg. Fiber 1.4 g.

272.   Braised Beef Brisket

Preparation Time: 10 minutes
Cooking Time: 1 hour and 45 minutes
Servings: 2

Ingredients:

- ½ medium onion, sliced
- 1 stalk celery, diced
- 1 medium carrot, diced
- 1 tbsp. fresh parsley, chopped
- 2 ½ lbs. beef brisket
- 2 tsp. black pepper
- 2 tbsp. canola oil
- 3 bay leaves
- 2 cups reduced-sodium beef broth
- 3 cups water
- 2 tbsp. balsamic vinegar

Directions:

1. Preheat oven to 350°F.
2. Remove the fat and season the brisket with black pepper.
3. Warm up the oil in a Dutch oven on medium-high heat.
4. Sear the brisket for 5 minutes and flip to sear for another 5 minutes.
5. Shift this meat to a plate and add carrots, celery, and onion to the pot.
6. Stir fry for 4 minutes.
7. Add bay leaves, parsley, and meat over the vegetables.
8. Pour in the water, broth, and balsamic vinegar.
9. Bring it to a boil then cook for 1.5 hours on medium-high heat until meat is tender.
10. Slice the meat and serve with the jus.

Nutrition:
Calories 230. Protein 29 g. Carbohydrates 4 g. Fat 11 g. Cholesterol 84 mg. Sodium 178 mg. Potassium 346 mg. Phosphorus 193 mg. Calcium 30 mg. Fiber 0.8 g.

273.   California Pork Chops

Preparation Time: 10 minutes
Cooking Time: 10 minutes
Servings: 2

Ingredients:

- 1 tbsp. fresh cilantro, chopped
- ½ cup chives, chopped

- 2 large green bell peppers, chopped
- 1 lb. 1" thick boneless pork chops
- 1 tbsp. fresh lime juice
- 2 cups cooked rice
- ⅛ tsp. dried oregano leaves
- ¼ tsp. ground black pepper
- ¼ tsp. ground cumin
- 1 tbsp. butter
- 1 lime

Directions:

1. Start by seasoning the pork chops with lime juice and cilantro.
2. Place them in a shallow dish.
3. Toss the chives with pepper, cumin, butter, oregano and rice in a bowl.
4. Stuff the bell peppers with this mixture and place them around the pork chops.
5. Cover the chop and bell peppers with a foil sheet and bake them for 10 minutes in the oven at 375°F.
6. Serve warm.

Nutrition:

Calories 265. Protein 34 g. Carbohydrates 24 g. Fat 15 g. Cholesterol 86 mg. Sodium 70 mg. Potassium 564 mg. Phosphorus 240 mg. Calcium 22 mg. Fiber 1.0 g.

274.   Beef Chorizo

Preparation Time: 10 minutes
Cooking Time: 10 minutes
Servings: 2

Ingredients:

- 3 garlic cloves, minced
- 1 lb. 90% lean ground beef
- 2 tbsp. hot chili powder
- 2 tsp. red or cayenne pepper
- 1 tsp. black pepper
- 1 tsp. ground oregano
- 2 tsp. white vinegar

Directions:

1. Mix all ingredients together in a bowl thoroughly then spread the mixture in a baking pan.
2. Bake the meat for 10 minutes at 325°F in an oven.
3. Slice and serve in crumbles.

Nutrition:

Calories 72. Protein 8 g. Carbohydrates 1 g. Fat 4 g. Cholesterol 25 mg. Sodium 46 mg. Potassium 174 mg. Phosphorus 79 mg. Calcium 14 mg. Fiber 0.8 g.

275.   Onion and Bacon Pork Chops

Preparation Time: 10 minutes
Cooking Time: 45 minutes
Servings: 4

Ingredients:

- 2 onions, peeled and chopped
- 6 bacon slices, chopped
- ½ cup chicken stock
- Salt and pepper to taste
- 4 pork chops

Directions:

1. Preheat up a pan over medium heat and add bacon
2. Stir and cook until crispy
3. Transfer to bowl
4. Bring the pan back to medium heat and add onions, season with salt and pepper
5. Stir and cook for 15 minutes
6. Transfer to the same bowl with bacon
7. Return the pan to heat (medium-high) and add pork chops
8. Season with salt and pepper and brown for 3 minutes
9. Flip and lower heat to medium
10. Cook for 7 minutes more
11. Add stock and stir cook for 2 minutes
12. Return the bacon and onions to the pan and stir cook for 1 minute
13. Serve and enjoy!

Nutrition: Calories: 325, Fat: 18g, Carbohydrates: 6g, Protein: 36g

276.   Thai Steak Salad with Herbs and Onions

Preparation Time: 10 minutes
Cooking Time: 45 minutes
Servings: 4

Ingredients:

- 1 flank or rump steak (600-g.)
- 1 tbsp. peanut oil
- 2 red onions
- 1 piece ginger (20-g.)
- 1 red chili pepper
- 1 cucumber
- 3 handful Asian herbs (30-g.)
- 1 tbsp. rice vinegar
- 3 tbsp. lime juice
- 2 tbsps. fish sauce
- 1 tsp. honey
- Paprika
- Chili powder
- Salt/Pepper
- Meat

Directions:

1. Rinse meat, one flank or rump steak, pat dry and salt. Heat the peanut oil and then fry the steak on both sides for 6-8 minutes over high heat. Remove meat from the frying pan and let it rest.

2. Meanwhile, peel onions and ginger. Halve onions and cut into strips. Chop ginger. Cut chili pepper into half lengthwise remove seeds, wash and cut into fine rings. Clean the cucumber, wash, quarter it and slice it. Wash Asian herbs, shake dry and peel off leaves.

3. Add ginger with vinegar, lime juice, fish sauce, honey, and 2-3 tablespoons water to a dressing, and mix with paprika, chili powder, salt, and pepper.

4. Slice the meat and arrange with herbs, chili rings, cucumber, and onions on a plate and drizzle with the dressing.

Nutrition:
Calories: 390 kcal

277. Steak and Onion Sandwich

Preparation Time: 10 minutes
Cooking Time: 45 minutes
Servings: 4
Ingredients:
- 4 flank steaks (around 4-oz. each)
- 1 medium red onion, sliced
- 1 tbsp. lemon juice
- 1 tbsp. Italian seasoning
- 1 tsp. black pepper
- 1 tbsp. vegetable oil
- 4 sandwich/burger buns

Directions:
1. Wrap the steak with lemon juice, the Italian seasoning to taste. Cut into 4 pieces
2. Preheat the vegetable oil in a medium skillet over medium heat.
3. Cook steaks for around 3 minutes on each side until you get a medium to well-done result. Take off and transfer onto a dish with absorbing paper.
4. Using the same skillet, sauté the onions until tender and transparent (around 3 minutes).
5. Cut the sandwich bun into half and place 1 piece of steak in each topped with the onions.
6. Serve or wrap with paper or foil and keep in the fridge for the next day.

Nutrition: Calories: 315.26 kcal, Carbohydrate: 8.47 g, Protein: 38.33 g, Sodium: 266.24 mg, Potassium: 238.2 mg, Phosphorus: 364.25 mg, Dietary Fiber: 0.76 g, Fat: 13.22 g

278. Grilled Lamb Chops

Preparation Time: 10 minutes
Cooking Time: 6 minutes
Servings: 1
Ingredients:
- 1 tbsp. fresh ginger, grated

- 4 garlic cloves, chopped roughly
- 1 tsp. ground cumin
- ½ tsp. red chili powder
- Salt and freshly ground black pepper
- 1 tbsp. essential olive oil
- 1 tbsp. fresh lemon juice
- 8 lamb chops, trimmed

Directions:
1. Combine all ingredients except chops.
2. With a hand blender, blend till a smooth mixture is formed.
3. Add chops and coat generously with mixture.
4. Refrigerate to marinate overnight.
5. Preheat the barbecue grill till hot. Grease the grill grate.
6. Grill the chops for approximately 3 minutes per side.
7. Serve when done.

Nutrition:
Calories: 227; Fat: 12g; Phosphorus: 36mg; Potassium 194mg; Sodium: 31mg; Carbohydrates: 1g; Fiber: 0g Protein: 30g.

279. Lamb & Pineapple Kebabs

Preparation Time: 15 minutes
Cooking Time: 10 minutes
Servings: 1
Ingredients:
- 1 large pineapple, cubed into 1 ½-inch size, divided
- 1 (½-inch) piece fresh ginger, chopped
- 2 garlic cloves, chopped
- Salt, to taste
- 16-24-oz. lamb shoulder steak, trimmed and cubed into 1½-inch size
- Fresh mint leaves coming from a bunch
- Ground cinnamon, to taste

Directions:
1. Add about one-half of pineapple, ginger, garlic and salt and pulse till smooth in a blender.
2. Transfer the mixture into a large bowl.
3. Add chops and coat generously with the mixture.
4. Refrigerate to marinate for about 1-2 hours.
5. Preheat the grill to medium heat. Grease the grill grate.
6. Thread lam, remaining pineapple, and mint leaves onto pre-soaked wooden skewers.
7. Grill the kebabs for approximately 10 minutes, turning occasionally.
8. Serve when done.

280. Air Fryer Breaded Pork Chops

Preparation Time: 12 minutes
Cooking Time: 10 minutes
Servings: 2

Ingredients:

- Whole-wheat breadcrumbs: 1 cup
- Salt: ¼ tsp.
- Pork chops: 2-4 pieces (center cut and boneless)
- Chili powder: ½ tsp.
- Parmesan cheese: 1 tbsp.
- Paprika: 1½ tsp.
- One egg beaten
- Onion powder: ½ tsp.
- Granulated garlic: ½ tsp.
- Pepper, to taste

Directions:

1. Let the air fryer preheat to 400°F
2. Rub kosher salt on each side of pork chops, let it rest
3. Add beaten egg in a big bowl
4. Add Parmesan cheese, breadcrumbs, garlic, pepper, paprika, chili powder, and onion powder in a bowl and mix well
5. Dip pork chop in egg, then in breadcrumb mixture
6. Put it in the air fryer and spray with oil.
7. Let it cook for 12 minutes at 400°F. flip it over halfway through. Cook for another six minutes.
8. Serve with a side of salad.

Nutrition:
425 calories | 20 g fat | 5 g fiber | 31 g protein | Carbs 19g

281. Pork Taquitos in Air Fryer

Preparation Time: 10 minutes
Cooking Time: 20 minutes
Servings: 2

Ingredients:
Pork Tenderloin:

- 3 cups, cooked & shredded
- Cooking spray

Shredded Mozzarella:

- 2 ½ cups, fat-free
- 10 small tortillas
- Salsa for dipping
- 1 juice of a lime

Directions:

1. Let the air fryer preheat to 380°F
2. Add lime juice to pork and mix well
3. With a damp towel over the tortilla, microwave for ten seconds to soften
4. Add pork filling and cheese on top, in a tortilla, roll up the tortilla tightly.

5. Place tortillas on a greased foil pan
6. Spray oil over tortillas. Cook for 7-10 minutes or until tortillas are golden brown, flip halfway through.
7. Serve with fresh salad.

Nutrition: Cal 253 | Fat: 18g | Carbs: 10g | Protein: 20g |

282. Air Fryer Tasty Egg Rolls

Preparation Time: 10 minutes
Cooking Time: 20 minutes
Servings: 3

Ingredients:

- ½ bag coleslaw mix
- ½ onion
- ½ tsp. salt
- ½ cups mushrooms
- 2 cups lean ground pork
- 1 stalk celery
- Wrappers (egg roll)

Directions:

1. Put a skillet over medium flame, add onion and lean ground pork and cook for 5-7 minutes.
2. Add coleslaw mixture, salt, mushrooms, and celery to skillet and cook for almost five minutes.
3. Lay egg roll wrapper flat and add filling (⅓ cup), roll it up, seal with water.
4. Spray with oil the rolls.
5. Put in the air fryer for 6-8 minutes at 400°F, flipping once halfway through.
6. Serve hot.

Nutrition: Cal 245 | Fat: 10g | Net Carbs: 9g | Protein: 11g

283. Pork Dumplings in Air Fryer

Preparation Time: 30 minutes
Cooking Time: 20 minutes
Servings: 2

Ingredients:

- 18 dumpling wrappers
- 1 tsp. olive oil
- 4 cups bok Choy (chopped)
- 2 tbsp. rice vinegar
- 1 tbsp. diced ginger
- ¼ tsp. crushed red pepper
- 1 tbsp. diced garlic
- ½ cup lean ground pork
- Cooking spray
- 2 tsp. lite soy sauce
- ½ tsp. honey
- 1 tsp. toasted sesame oil

- Finely chopped scallions

Directions:
1. In a large skillet, heat olive oil, add bok Choy, cook for 6 minutes, and add garlic, ginger, and cook for one minute. Move this mixture on a paper towel and pat dry the excess oil
2. In a bowl, add bok Choy mixture, crushed red pepper, and lean ground pork and mix well.
3. Lay a dumpling wrapper on a plate and add 1 tablespoon of filling in the wrapper's middle. With water, seal the edges and crimp them.
4. Air spray the air fryer basket, add dumplings in the air fryer basket and cook at 375°F for 12 minutes or until browned.
5. In the meantime, to make the sauce, add sesame oil, rice vinegar, scallions, soy sauce, and honey in a bowl mix together.
6. Serve the dumplings with sauce.

Nutrition:
Calories 140| Fat 5g |Protein 12g |Carbohydrate 9g|

284. Air Fryer Pork Chop & Broccoli

Preparation Time: 20 minutes
Cooking Time: 20 minutes
Servings: 2

Ingredients:
- 2 cups broccoli florets
- 2 pieces bone-in pork chop
- ½ tsp. paprika
- 2 tbsp. avocado oil
- ½ tsp. garlic powder
- ½ tsp. onion powder
- 2 cloves garlic, crushed
- 1 tsp. salt, divided

Directions:
1. Let the air fryer preheat to 350°F. Spray the basket with cooking oil
2. Add one tablespoon of oil, onion powder, ½ teaspoon of salt, garlic powder, and paprika in a bowl mix well, rub this spice mix to the pork chop's sides
3. Add pork chops to air fryer basket and let it cook for five minutes
4. In the meantime, add one tsp. oil, garlic, ½ teaspoon of salt, and broccoli to a bowl and coat well
5. Flip the pork chop and add the broccoli, let it cook for five more minutes.
6. Take out from the air fryer and serve.

Nutrition:
Calories 483|Total Fat 20g|Carbohydrates 12g|protein 23 g

285. Cheesy Pork Chops in Air Fryer

Preparation Time: 5 minutes
Cooking Time: 8 minutes
Servings: 2

Ingredients:
- 4 lean pork chops
- ½ tsp. salt
- ½ tsp. garlic powder
- 4 tbsp. shredded cheese
- Chopped cilantro

Directions:
1. Let the air fryer preheat to 350°F.
2. With garlic, cilantro, and salt, rub the pork chops Put in the air fryer. Let it cook for 4 minutes. Flip them and cook for 2 minutes more.
3. Add cheese on top of them and cook for another 2 minutes or until the cheese is melted.
4. Serve with salad greens.

Nutrition:
Calories: 467kcal | Protein: 61g | Fat: 22g | Saturated Fat 8g |

286. Pork Rind Nachos

Preparation Time: 5 minutes
Cooking Time: 5 minutes
Servings: 2

Ingredients:
- 2 tbsp. pork rinds
- ¼ cup shredded cooked chicken
- ½ cup shredded Monterey jack cheese
- ¼ cup sliced pickled jalapeños
- ¼ cup guacamole
- ¼ cup full-fat sour cream

Directions:
1. Put pork rinds in a 6 "round baking pan. Fill with grilled chicken and Monterey cheese jack. Place the pan in the basket with the air fryer.
2. Set the temperature to 370°F and set the timer for 5 minutes or until the cheese has been melted.
3. Eat right away with jalapeños, guacamole, and sour cream.

Nutrition:
Calories 295 |Protein: 30.1 g| Fiber: 1.2 g| Net Carbohydrates: 1.8 g |Fat: 27.5 g| Carbohydrates: 3.0 g

287.　Jamaican Jerk Pork in Air Fryer

Preparation Time: 10 minutes
Cooking Time: 20 minutes
Servings: 2

Ingredients:

- Pork, cut into three-inch pieces
- ¼ cup Jerk paste

Directions:

1. Rub jerk paste all over the pork pieces.
2. Let it marinate for four hours, at least, in the refrigerator. Or for more time.
3. Let the air fryer preheat to 390°F. spray with olive oil
4. Before putting in the air fryer, let the meat sit for 20 minutes at room temperature.
5. Cook for 20 minutes at 390°F in the air fryer, flip halfway through.
6. Take it out from the air fryer let it rest for ten minutes before slicing.
7. Serve with microgreens.

Nutrition:
Calories: 234kcal | Protein: 31g | Fat: 9g |carbs 12 g

288.　Pork Tenderloin with Mustard Glazed

Preparation Time: 10 minutes
Cooking Time: 18 minutes
Servings: 2

Ingredients:

- ¼ cup yellow mustard
- 1 pork tenderloin
- ¼ tsp. salt
- 3 tbsp. honey
- ⅛ tsp. freshly ground black pepper
- 1 tbsp. minced garlic
- 1 tsp. dried rosemary
- 1 tsp. Italian seasoning

Directions:

1. With a knife, cut the top of the pork tenderloin. Add garlic (minced) to the cuts. Then sprinkle with kosher salt and pepper.
2. In a bowl, add honey, mustard, rosemary, and Italian seasoning mix until combined. Rub this mustard mix all over pork.
3. Let it marinate in the refrigerator for at least two hours.
4. Put pork tenderloin in the air fryer basket. Cook for 18-20 minutes at 400°F. with an instant-read thermometer, internal temperature of pork should be 145°F
5. Take out from the air fryer and serve with a side of salad.

Nutrition:
Calories: 390 | Carbohydrates: 11g | Protein: 59g | Fat: 11g

289.　Breaded Chicken Tenderloins

Preparation Time: 10 minutes
Cooking Time: 12 minutes
Servings: 2

Ingredients:

- 8 chicken tenderloins
- 2 tbsp. olive oil
- 1 egg whisked
- ¼ cup breadcrumbs

Directions:

1. Let the air fryer heat to 180°C.
2. In a big bowl, add breadcrumbs and oil, mix well until forms a crumbly mixture
3. Dip chicken tenderloin in whisked egg and coat in breadcrumbs mixture.
4. Place the breaded chicken in the air fryer and cook at 180°C for 12 minutes or more.
5. Take out from the air fryer and serve with your favorite green salad.

Nutrition:
Calories 206|Proteins 20g |Carbs 17g |Fat 10g |

290.　Herbed Chicken with Veggies

Preparation Time: 10 minutes
Cooking Time: 20 minutes
Servings: 2

Ingredients:

- 1 cup sliced carrots, fresh or frozen
- 2 cups green beans, fresh or frozen
- ½ cup diced onion
- 8 bone-in chicken thighs
- ½ cup reduced-sodium chicken broth
- 2 tsp. Worcestershire sauce
- 1 tsp. no-salt herb seasoning blend
- 1 tsp. dried oregano
- ½ large chicken breast for 1 chicken thigh

Directions:

1. Spot carrots, green beans, and onions in the moderate cooker.
2. Mastermind chicken over vegetables.
3. Pour juices over the chicken, top with Worcestershire sauce, herbs, and flavoring.
4. Spread and cook on Low heat for 6 hours.
5. Present with white rice or rolls.

Nutrition:
Calories: 205 Fat: 6g Protein: 31g Carbs: 5g

291. Roasted Citrus Chicken

Preparation Time: 20 minutes
Cooking Time: 1 hour
Servings: 2
Ingredients:

- 1 tbsp. olive oil
- 2 cloves garlic, minced
- 1 tsp. Italian seasoning
- ½ tsp. black pepper
- 8 chicken thighs
- 2 cups chicken broth, reduced-sodium
- 3 tbsp. lemon juice
- ½ large chicken breast for 1 chicken thigh

Directions:
1. Warm oil in a huge skillet.
2. Include garlic and seasonings.
3. Include chicken bosoms and dark-colored all sides.
4. Spot chicken in the moderate cooker and include the chicken soup.
5. Cook on low heat for 6 to 8 hours.
6. Include lemon juice toward the part of the bargain time.

Nutrition:
Calories: 265 Fat: 19g Protein: 21g Carbs: 1g

292. Southern Chicken and Grits

Preparation Time: 10 minutes
Cooking Time: 10 minutes
Servings: 2
Ingredients:

- 1 ¾ cups fat-free reduced-sodium chicken broth
- 6 tbsp. corn grits, uncooked
- 1 tbsp. olive oil and 1 small onion, diced
- 1 medium clove garlic, minced
- 1 cup sliced mushrooms
- 1 medium jalapeno pepper, seeded and minced
- 1 medium red bell, chopped
- ¼ tsp. ground cumin and ¼ tsp. black pepper
- 1-lb. boneless, skinless chicken thighs, cut into 1-inch chunks

Directions:
1. Spot soup in a 3-to 5-quart moderate cooker. Gradually include cornmeal, mixing continually, to evade irregularities, put the moderate cooker in a safe spot.
2. Warm oil in an enormous skillet over medium-high heat.
3. Include onion, garlic, mushrooms, jalapeno, and red pepper; sauté mixing as often as possible, for around 5 minutes.

4. Add vegetables to slow cooker, alongside cumin and pepper, blend.
5. Include chicken thighs top.
6. Spread and cook on Low for 6 to 8 hours.

Nutrition: Calories 259 Fat: 9g Protein: 27g Carbs: 17g

293. Chicken Adobo

Preparation Time: 20 minutes
Cooking Time: 1 hour and 30 minutes
Servings: 2
Ingredients:

- 4 medium yellow onions, halved and thinly sliced
- 4 medium garlic cloves, smashed and peeled
- 1 (5-inch) piece fresh ginger, cut into
- 1-inch pieces and 1 bay leaf
- 3 lbs. bone-in chicken thighs
- 3 tbsp. reduced-sodium soy sauce
- ¼ cup rice vinegar (not seasoned)
- 1 tbsp. granulated sugar and ½ tsp. freshly ground black pepper

Directions:
1. Spot the onions, garlic, ginger, and narrows leaf in an even layer in the slight cooker.
2. Take out and do away with the pores and skin from the chicken.
3. Organize the hen in an even layer over the onion mixture.
4. Whip the soy sauce, vinegar, sugar, and pepper collectively in a medium bowl and pour it over the fowl.
5. Spread and prepare dinner on Low for 8 hours.
6. Evacuate and take away the ginger portions and inlet leaf.
7. Present with steamed rice.

Nutrition: Calories 318 Fat: 9g Protein: 14g Carbs: 44g

294. Chicken and Veggie Soup

Preparation Time: 10 minutes
Cooking Time: 30 minutes
Servings: 2
Ingredients:

- 4 cups cooked and chopped chicken
- 7 cups reduced-sodium chicken broth
- 1 lb. frozen white corn
- 1 medium onion diced
- 4 cloves garlic minced
- 2 carrots peeled and diced
- 2 celery stalks chopped
- 2 tsp. oregano
- 2 tsp. curry powder
- ½ tsp. black pepper

Directions:

1. Include all fixings into the moderate cooker.
2. Cook on Low for 8 hours.
3. Serve over cooked white rice.

Nutrition:

Calories220 Fat: 7g Protein: 24g Carbs: 19g

295. Pesto Chicken

Preparation Time: 10 minutes
Cooking Time: 25 minutes
Servings: 2

Ingredients:

- 3 chicken breast fillets
- 6-oz. jar of pesto
- ½ cup reduced-sodium chicken

Directions:

1. Spot chicken bosoms at the base of the moderate oven.
2. Put pesto over the chicken and spread to coat the highest points of the chicken.
3. Pour in ½ cup chicken stock.
4. Cook on Low for 6 to 8 hours.
5. Serve over cooked pasta.

Nutrition:

Calories: 278 Fat: 18g Protein: 28g Carbs: 1g

296. Spicy Coconut Curry Chicken

Preparation Time: 10 minutes
Cooking Time: 1 hour
Servings: 2

Ingredients:

- 2 boneless chicken breasts (fresh or frozen)
- ¼ cup chopped green onions
- 1 (4-oz.) diced green chili peppers
- 2 tbsp. minced garlic
- 1 ½ tbsp. curry powder
- 1 tbsp. chili powder
- 1 tsp. cumin
- ½ tsp. cinnamon
- 1 tbsp. lime juice
- 1 ½ cup water
- 1 (7-oz.) can coconut milk
- 1 cup dry white rice
- Chopped cilantro, for garnish

Directions:

1. Consolidate all fixings except for coconut milk and rice in the moderate cooker.
2. Spread and cook on Low for 7-9 hours.
3. In the wake of cooking time, shred chicken with a fork, mix in coconut milk, and dry rice.

4. Turn the moderate cooker to High and cook for an extra 30 minutes, or until the rice has consumed the fluid and is cooked.
5. Serve hot and decorate with cilantro.

Nutrition:

Calories: 270 Fat: 19g Protein: 20g Carbs: 7g

297. Mixed Pepper Paella

Preparation Time: 10 minutes
Cooking Time: 40 minutes
Servings: 2

Ingredients:

- 1 tbsp. extra virgin olive oil
- ½ chopped red onion
- 1 lemon
- ½ chopped yellow bell pepper
- 1 cup homemade chicken broth
- ½ chopped zucchini
- 1 tsp. dried oregano
- ½ chopped red bell pepper
- 1 tsp. dried parsley
- 1 cup brown rice
- 1 tsp. paprika

Directions:

1. Add the rice to a pot of cold water and cook for 15 minutes.Drain the water, cover the pan and leave to one side.
2. Heat the oil in a skillet over medium-high heat. Add the bell peppers, onion, and zucchini, sautéing for 5 minutes. To the pan, add the rice, herbs, spices, and juice of the lemon along with the chicken broth.
3. Cover and turn the heat right down and allow to simmer for 15-20 minutes.Serve hot.

Nutrition:

Calories 210, Protein 4 g, Carbs 33 g, Fat 7 g, Sodium (Na) 20 mg, Potassium (K) 33 mg, Phosphorus 156 mg

298. Chickens' Rice

Preparation Time: 10 minutes
Cooking Time: 35 minutes
Servings: 2

Ingredients:

- 1 lb. chicken parts
- 1 cup uncooked rice
- ½ cup chopped onion
- 1 tsp. black pepper
- 1 tbsp. poultry seasoning
- 1 tsp. onion powder
- ½ tsp. garlic powder
- 1 tsp. crushed bay leaves (optional)

- 4 cups water
- 1 tbsp. vegetable oil

Directions:

1. Put the bay leaves, chicken part, poultry seasoning, black pepper, onion powder, onions, and garlic powder into a Dutch oven; cover with water.
2. Cook until the chicken is tender.
3. Debone the chicken and discard the skin. Reserve 2 cups of the chicken broth as well as the chicken meat.
4. Put the 2 cups of broth, vegetable oil, rice, and chicken in a large pot and boil over medium-high heat.
5. Reduce the heat and allow it to cook for approximately 25 minutes.
6. Serve hot.

Nutrition:

Calories 212, Carbohydrates11 g Dietary fibers 1 g Phosphorus 218 mg, Potassium 283 mg, Protein 21 g Sodium 76 mg

Chapter 13: Soup Recipes

299.   Red Pepper & Brie Soup

Preparation Time: 10 minutes
Cooking Time: 35 minutes
Servings: 2
Ingredients:

- 1 tsp. paprika
- 1 tsp. cumin
- 1 chopped red onion
- 2 chopped garlic cloves
- ¼ cup crumbled brie
- 2 tbsps. extra virgin olive oil
- 4 chopped red bell peppers
- 4 cups water

Directions:

1. Sauté the onions and peppers for 5 minutes over medium heat. Add the garlic cloves, cumin, and paprika and sauté for 3-4 minutes. Add the water and allow it to boil before turning the heat down to simmer for approximately 30 minutes.
2. Allow to cool slightly. Transfer the mixture to a food processor and blend until smooth. Pour into serving bowls and add the crumbled brie to the top with a little black pepper. Enjoy!

Nutrition: Calories: 152 Protein: 3g, Carbs: 8g Fat: 11g, Sodium: 66mg, Potassium: 270mg, Phosphorus: 207mg.

300.   Turkey & Lemongrass Soup

Preparation Time: 5 minutes
Cooking Time: 40 minutes
Servings: 2
Ingredients:

- 1 fresh lime
- ¼ cup fresh basil leaves
- 1 tbsp. cilantro
- 1 cup canned and drained water chestnuts
- 1 tbsp. coconut oil
- 1 thumb-size minced ginger piece
- 2 chopped scallions
- 1 finely chopped green chili
- 4 oz. skinless and sliced turkey breasts
- 1 minced garlic clove, minced
- ½ finely sliced stick lemongrass
- 1 chopped white onion, chopped
- 4 cups water.

Directions:

1. Crush the lemongrass, cilantro, chili, 1 tablespoon of oil and basil leaves using a pestle and mortar to form a paste.
2. Heat a large pan/wok with 1 tablespoon of olive oil on high heat.
3. Sauté the onions, garlic, and ginger until soft.
4. Add the turkey and brown each side for 4-5 minutes.
5. Add the broth and stir.
6. Now add the paste and stir.
7. Next, add the water chestnuts, turn down the heat slightly and allow to simmer for 25-30 minutes or until turkey is thoroughly cooked through.
8. Serve hot with the green onion sprinkled over the top.

Nutrition:
Calories: 123, Protein: 10g, Carbs: 12g, Fat: 3g, Sodium: 501mg, Potassium: 151mg, Phosphorus: 110mg.

301. Paprika Pork Soup

Preparation Time: 10 minutes
Cooking Time: 35 minutes
Servings: 2
Ingredients:

- 4 oz. sliced pork loin
- 1 tsp. black pepper
- 2 minced garlic cloves
- 1 cup baby spinach
- 3 cups water
- 1 tbsp. extra-virgin olive oil
- 1 chopped onion
- 1 tbsp. paprika.

Directions:

1. In a large pan, add the oil, chopped onion, and minced garlic.
2. Sauté for 5 minutes on low heat.
3. Add the pork slices to the onions and cook for 7-8 minutes or until browned.
4. Add the water to the pan and bring to a boil on high heat.
5. Season with pepper to serve.

Nutrition:
Calories: 165, Protein: 13g, Carbs: 10g, Fat: 9g, Sodium: 269mg, Potassium: 486mg, Phosphorus: 158mg.

302.   Mediterranean Vegetable Soup

Preparation Time: 5 minutes
Cooking Time: 30 minutes
Servings: 2

Ingredients:

- 1 tbsp. oregano
- 2 minced garlic cloves
- 1 tsp. black pepper and 1 diced red pepper
- 1 diced zucchini
- 1 cup diced eggplant
- 4 cups water
- 1 tbsp. extra-virgin olive oil
- 1 diced red onion.

Directions:

1. Soak the vegetables in warm water before use.
2. Sauté chopped onion and minced garlic.
3. Sweat for 5 minutes on low heat.
4. Add the other vegetables to the onions and cook for 7-8 minutes.
5. Add the stock to the pan and bring to a boil on high heat.
6. Stir in the herbs, reduce the heat, and simmer for a further 20 minutes or until thoroughly cooked through.
7. Season with pepper to serve.

Nutrition: Calories: 152, Protein: 1g, Carbs: 6g, Fat: 3g, Sodium: 3mg, Potassium: 229mg, Phosphorus: 45mg.

303.   Tofu Soup

Preparation Time: 5 minutes
Cooking Time: 10 minutes
Servings: 2

Ingredients:

- 1 tbsp. miso paste
- ⅛ cup cubed soft tofu
- 1 chopped green onion
- ¼ cup sliced Shiitake mushrooms
- 3 cups renal stock
- 1 tbsp. soy sauce.

Directions:

1. Take a saucepan, pour the stock into this pan and let it boil on high heat. Reduce heat to medium and let this stock simmer. Add mushrooms to this stock and cook for almost 3 minutes.
2. Take a bowl and mix Soy sauce (reduced salt) and miso paste together in this bowl. Add this mixture and tofu in stock. Simmer for nearly 5 minutes and serve with chopped green onion.

Nutrition:
Calories: 129, Fat: 7.8g, Sodium: 484mg, Potassium: 435mg, Protein: 11g, Carbs: 5.5g, Phosphorus: 73.2mg.

304.   Onion Soup

Preparation Time: 15 minutes
Cooking Time: 45 minutes
Servings: 2

Ingredients:

- 2 tbsp. chicken stock
- 1 cup chopped shiitake mushrooms
- 1 tbsp. minced chives
- 3 tsp. beef bouillon
- 1 tsp. grated ginger root
- ½ chopped carrot
- 1 cup sliced portobello mushrooms
- 1 chopped onion
- ½ chopped celery stalk
- 2 quarts water
- ¼ tsp. minced garlic.

Directions:

1. Take a saucepan and combine carrot, onion, celery garlic, mushrooms (some mushrooms), and ginger in this pan.
2. Add water, beef bouillon, and chicken stock to this pan. Put this pot on high heat and let it boil.
3. Decrease flame to medium and cover this pan to cook for almost 45 minutes.
4. Put all remaining mushrooms in one separate pot.
5. Once the boiling mixture is completely done, put one strainer over this new bowl with mushrooms and strain cooked soup in this pot over mushrooms.
6. Discard solid-strained materials. Serve delicious broth with yummy mushrooms in small bowls and sprinkle chives over each bowl.

Nutrition:
Calories: 22, Fat: 0g, Sodium: 602.3mg, Potassium: 54.1mg, Carbs: 4.9g, Protein: 0.6g, Phosphorus: 15.8mg.

305.   Steakhouse Soup

Preparation Time: 15 minutes
Cooking Time: 25 minutes
Servings: 2

Ingredients:

- 2 tbsp. soy sauce
- 2 boneless and cubed chicken breasts.
- ¼ lb. halved and trimmed snow peas
- 1 tbsp. minced ginger root
- 1 minced garlic clove
- 1 cup water
- 2 chopped green onions
- 3 cups chicken stock
- 1 chopped carrot
- 3 sliced mushrooms.

Directions:

1. Take a pot and combine ginger, water, chicken stock, Soy sauce (reduced salt), and garlic in this pot.
2. Let them boil on medium heat, mix in chicken pieces, and let them simmer on low heat for almost 15 minutes to tender the chicken.
3. Stir in carrot and snow peas and simmer for almost 5 minutes.
4. Add mushrooms to this blend and continue cooking to tender vegetables for nearly 3 minutes.
5. Mix in the chopped onion and serve hot.

Nutrition:

Calories: 319 Carbs: 14g, Fat: 15g, Potassium: (K) 225mg, Protein: 29g, Sodium: (Na) 389mg, Phosphorous: 190mg.

306.   Pesto Green Vegetable Soup

Preparation Time: 10 minutes
Cooking Time: 15 minutes
Servings: 2

Ingredients:

- 2 tsp. olive oil
- 1 leek, white and light green parts, sliced and washed thoroughly
- 2 celery stalks, diced
- 1 tsp. minced garlic
- 2 cups sodium-free chicken stock
- 1 cup chopped snow peas
- 1 cup shredded spinach
- 1 tbsp. chopped fresh thyme
- Juice and zest of ½ lemon
- ¼ tsp. freshly ground black pepper
- 1 tbsp. Basil Pesto.

Directions:

1. Heat the olive oil.
2. Add the leek, celery, and garlic, and sauté until tender, about 3 min.
3. Mix in the stock, and bring to a boil.
4. Stir in the snow peas, spinach, and thyme, and simmer for about 5 min.
5. Allow it to cool and stir in the lemon juice, lemon zest, pepper, and pesto.
6. Serve immediately.

Nutrition: Calories: 170, Sodium: 333mg, Total Carbs: 8g, Fiber: 1g, Protein: 3g.

307.   Chicken Noodle Soup

Preparation Time: 10 minutes
Cooking Time: 25 minutes
Servings: 2

Ingredients:

- 1 ½ cups low-sodium vegetable broth

- 1 cup of water
- ¼ tsp. poultry seasoning
- ¼ tsp. black pepper
- 1 cup chicken strips
- ¼ cup carrot
- 2-oz. egg noodles, uncooked.

Directions:

1. Gather all the ingredients into a slow cooker and toss it.
2. Cook soup on high heat for 25 minutes.
3. Serve warm.

Nutrition:

Calories: 103, Protein: 8g, Sodium: 355mg, Potassium: 264mg, Phosphorus: 128mg, Calcium: 46mg, Fiber: 4.0g.

308.   Cucumber Soup

Preparation Time: 10 minutes
Cooking Time: 0 minutes
Servings: 2

Ingredients:

- 2 medium cucumbers, peeled and diced
- ⅓ cup sweet white onion, diced
- 1 green onion, diced
- ¼ cup fresh mint
- 2 tbsp. fresh dill
- 2 tbsp. lemon juice
- ⅔ cup water
- ½ cup half-and-half cream
- ⅓ cup sour cream
- ½ tsp. pepper
- Fresh dill sprigs for garnish.

Directions:

1. Combine all ingredients in a food processor.
2. Puree the mixture and refrigerate for 2 hours. Garnish with dill sprigs. Enjoy fresh.

Nutrition:

Calories: 77, Protein: 2g, Carbohydrates: 6g, Fat: 5g, Cholesterol: 12mg, Sodium: 128mg, Potassium: 258mg, Phosphorus: 64mg, Calcium: 60mg, Fiber: 1.0g.

309.   Beef Stew with Apple Cider

Preparation Time: 15 minutes
Cooking Time: 10 hours
Servings: 2

Ingredients:

- ½ cup potatoes, cubed
- 2 lb. beef cubes
- 7 tbsp. all-purpose flour, divided
- ¼ tsp. thyme
- Black pepper to taste

- 3 tbsp. oil
- ¼ cup carrot, sliced
- 1 cup onion, diced
- ½ cup celery, diced
- 1 cup apples, diced
- 2 cups apple cider
- ½ cups water
- 2 tbsp. apple cider vinegar.

Directions:
1. Double boil the potatoes (to reduce the amount of potassium) in a pot of water.
2. In a shallow dish, mix half of the flour, thyme, and pepper. Coat all sides of beef cubes with the mixture. Add the oil and cook the beef cubes until brown in a pan over low heat. Set aside.
3. Layer the ingredients in your slow cooker.
4. Put the carrots, potatoes, onions, celery, beef, and apple.
5. Mix the cider, vinegar, and 1 cup water in a small bowl.
6. Add this to the slow cooker.
7. Cook on low setting for 10 hours.
8. Stir in the remaining flour to thicken the soup.

Nutrition:
Calories: 365, Protein: 33g, Carbohydrates: 20g, Fat: 17g, Cholesterol: 73mg, Sodium: 80mg, Potassium: 540mg, Phosphorus: 234mg, Calcium: 36mg, Fiber: 2.2g.

310. Roasted Red Pepper Soup

Preparation Time: 30 minutes
Cooking Time: 35 minutes
Servings: 2
Ingredients:
- 4 cups low-sodium chicken broth
- 3 red peppers
- 2 medium onions
- 3 tbsp. lemon juice
- 1 tbsp. finely minced lemon zest
- A pinch of cayenne peppers
- ¼ tsp. cinnamon
- ½ cup finely minced fresh cilantro.

Directions:
1. In a medium stockpot, consolidate each one of the fixings except for the cilantro and warmth to the point of boiling over excessive warm temperature.
2. Diminish the warmth and stew, ordinarily secured, for around 30 minutes, till thickened.
3. Cool marginally.
4. Utilizing a hand blender or nourishment processor, puree the soup.
5. Include the cilantro and tenderly heat.

Nutrition:
Calories: 265g, Fat: 8g, Carbs: 5g, Sugars 0.1g, Protein: 29g.

311. Yucatan Soup

Preparation Time: 10 minutes
Cooking Time: 20 minutes
Servings: 2
Ingredients:
- ½ cup onion, chopped
- 8 cloves garlic, chopped
- 2 Serrano chili peppers, chopped
- 1 medium tomato, chopped
- 1 ½ cups chicken breast, cooked, shredded
- 2 six-inch corn tortillas, sliced
- Nonstick cooking spray
- 1 tbsp. olive oil
- 4 cups chicken broth
- 1 bay leaf
- ¼ cup lime juice
- ¼ cup cilantro, chopped
- 1 tsp. black pepper.

Directions:
1. Spread the corn tortillas on a baking sheet and bake them for 3 minutes at 400°F.
2. Place a suitably-sized saucepan over medium heat and add oil to heat.
3. Toss in chili peppers, garlic, and onion, then sauté until soft.
4. Stir in broth, tomatoes, bay leaf, and chicken.
5. Let this chicken soup cook for 10 minutes on a simmer.
6. Stir in cilantro, lime juice, and black pepper.
7. Garnish with baked corn tortillas.
8. Serve.

Nutrition:
Calories: 215, Protein: 21g, Carbohydrates: 32g, Fat: 10g, Cholesterol: 32mg, Sodium: 246mg, Potassium: 355mg Phosphorus: 176mg, Calcium: 47mg Fiber: 1.6g.

312. Zesty Taco Soup

Preparation Time: 10 minutes
Cooking Time: 7 hours
Servings: 2
Ingredients:
- 1 ½ lb. boneless skinless chicken breast
- 15 ½ oz. canned dark red kidney beans
- 15 ½ oz. canned white corn
- 1 cup canned tomatoes, diced
- ½ cup onion
- 15 ½ oz. canned yellow hominy
- ½ cup green bell peppers

- 1 garlic clove
- 1 medium jalapeno
- 1 tbsp. package McCormick
- 2 cups chicken broth.

Directions:
1. Add drained beans, hominy, corn, onion, garlic, jalapeno pepper, chicken, and green peppers to a crockpot.
2. Cover the beans-corn mixture and cook for 1 hour at a high temperature.
3. Reduce the heat to low and continue cooking for 6 hours.
4. Shred the slow-cooked chicken and return to the taco soup. Serve warm.

Nutrition: Calories: 191, Protein: 21g, Sodium: 421mg, Potassium: 444mg, Phosphorus: 210mg, Fiber: 4.3g.

313. Italian Wedding Soup

Preparation Time: 15 minutes
Cooking Time: 25 minutes
Servings: 2

Ingredients:
Meatballs:
- 1 lb. ground beef or ground pork
- ½ cup crushed pork rinds or almond flour
- ½ cup grated Parmesan cheese
- 1 tsp. Italian seasoning
- ¾ tsp. salt
- ½ tsp. pepper
- 1 large egg.

Soup:
- 2 tbsp. avocado oil
- ¼ cup chopped onion
- 4 celery stalks chopped
- 1 tsp. salt
- ½ tsp. pepper
- 3 cloves garlic minced.
- 1 tsp. dried oregano
- 6 cups chicken broth
- 2 cups riced cauliflower
- 2 cups packed spinach leaves
- Additional salt and pepper
- Parmesan for sprinkling.

Directions:
1. Combine the ground meat, crushed pork rinds, cheese, Italian seasoning, salt, and pepper in a large mixing bowl.
2. Put the egg and mix well using your hands.
3. Refrigerate until soup is ready.
4. Preheat the oil over medium heat until shimmering in a large saucepan or stockpot.

5. Toss in the onion, celery, salt, and pepper and fry until vegetables are soft and tender (7-minute) Then, add the garlic and cook for 1 minute.
6. Stir in the chicken broth and oregano and simmer for 10 minutes.
7. Put in the cauliflower rice and the meatballs and cook for about 5 minutes.
8. Combine the spinach leaves and cook until wilted, 2 minutes more.
9. Season to taste.
10. Serve and enjoy.

Nutrition:
Calories: 303, Sodium: 0mg, Total Carbs: 5.73g, Fiber: 1.86g, Protein: 29.48 g.

314. Creamy Broccoli Soup

Preparation Time: 15 minutes
Cooking Time: 10 minutes
Servings: 2

Ingredients:
- 1 tsp. extra-virgin olive oil
- ½ sweet onion, roughly chopped
- 2 cups chopped broccoli
- 4 cups low-sodium vegetable broth
- Freshly ground black pepper
- 1 cup Homemade Rice Milk or unsweetened store-bought rice milk
- ¼ cup grated Parmesan cheese

Directions:
1. In a medium saucepan over medium-high heat, heat the olive oil. Add the onion and cook for 3 to 5 minutes, until it begins to soften. Add the broccoli and broth, and season with pepper.
2. Bring to a boil, reduce the heat, and simmer uncovered for 10 minutes, until the broccoli is just tender but still bright green.
3. Transfer the soup mixture to a blender. Add the rice milk, and process until smooth. Return to the saucepan, stir in the Parmesan cheese, and serve.
4. Substitution Tip: You can use this recipe to make several varieties of green soups. Experiment substituting spinach, a mix of arugula and kale, or microgreens, for a twist on the ordinary that suits your tastes.

Nutrition: Calories: 88; Total Fat: 3g; Saturated Fat: 1g; Cholesterol: 6mg; Carbohydrates: 12g; Fiber: 3g; Protein: 4g; Phosphorus: 87mg; Potassium: 201mg; Sodium: 281mg

315. Curried Carrot and Beet Soup

Preparation Time: 10 minutes
Cooking Time: 50 minutes
Servings: 2
Ingredients:

- 1 large red beet and 5 carrots, chopped
- 1 tbsp. curry powder
- 3 cups Homemade Rice Milk or unsweetened store-bought rice milk
- Freshly ground black pepper
- Yogurt, for serving

Directions:

1. Preheat the oven to 400°F.
2. Wrap the beet in aluminum foil and roast for 45 minutes, until the vegetable is tender when pierced with a fork. Remove from the oven and let cool.
3. In a saucepan, add the carrots and cover them with water. Bring to a boil, reduce the heat, cover, and simmer for 10 minutes, until tender.
4. Transfer the carrots and beet to a food processor, and process until smooth. Add the curry powder and rice milk. Season with pepper. Serve topped with a dollop of yogurt.

Substitution Tip: Carrots are high in potassium. If you need to reduce your potassium further, use 2 carrots instead of 5. The soup will be a little thinner but still have a carrot flavor and just 322mg of potassium.

Nutrition: Calories: 112; Total Fat: 1g; Saturated Fat: 0g; Cholesterol: 0mg; Carbohydrates: 24g; Fiber: 7g; Protein: 3g; Phosphorus: 57mg; Potassium: 468mg; Sodium: 129mg

316. Golden Beet Soup

Preparation Time: 10 minutes
Cooking Time: 35 minutes
Servings: 2
Ingredients:

- 3 tbsp. unsalted butter
- 4 golden beets, cut into ½-inch cubes
- ½ sweet onion, chopped
- 1-inch piece ginger, minced
- Zest and juice of 1 lemon
- 4 cups Simple Chicken Broth or low-sodium store-bought chicken stock
- Freshly ground black pepper
- ¼ cup pomegranate seeds, for serving
- ¼ cup crème Fraiche, for serving (see Substitution tip)
- 10 sage leaves, for serving

Directions:

1. In a medium saucepan over medium heat, melt the butter.
2. Add the beets, onion, ginger, and lemon zest, and cover. Cook, stirring occasionally, for 15 minutes. Add the broth, and continue to cook for 20 more minutes, until the beets are very tender.
3. In batches, transfer the soup to a blender and purée, or use an immersion blender.
4. Return the soup to the saucepan, and season with pepper and lemon juice.
5. Serve topped with pomegranate seeds, crème Fraiche, and sage leaves.

Substitution Tip: You can buy crème Fraiche at many grocery stores, or make your own. If you don't have crème Fraiche, a dollop of whole-milk yogurt is a fine substitute.

Nutrition: Calories: 186; Total Fat: 11g; Saturated Fat: 7g; Cholesterol 26mg; Carbohydrates: 17g; Fiber: 3g; Protein: 7g; Phosphorus: 125mg; Potassium: 557mg; Sodium: 148mg

317. Asparagus Lemon Soup

Preparation Time: 10 minutes
Cooking Time: 25 minutes
Servings: 2
Ingredients:

- ½ lb. asparagus
- 1 tbsp. extra-virgin olive oil
- ½ sweet onion, chopped
- 2 cups low-sodium chicken stock
- ¼ cup Homemade Rice Milk or unsweetened store-bought rice milk
- Freshly ground black pepper and Juice of ½ lemon

Directions:

1. Cut the asparagus tips from the spears and set them aside.
2. In a small stockpot over medium heat, heat the olive oil. Add the onion and cook, stirring frequently for 3 to 5 minutes, until it begins to soften.
3. Add the stock and asparagus stalks, and bring to a boil. Reduce the heat and simmer until the asparagus is tender, about 15 minutes.
4. Transfer to a blender or food processor, and carefully purée until smooth. Return to the pot, add the asparagus tips, and simmer until tender, about 5 minutes.
5. Add the rice milk, pepper, and lemon juice, and stir until heated through. Serve.

Cooking Tip: Make this soup up to three days in advance and store it in the refrigerator. When ready to serve, heat in the microwave or on the stove top.

Nutrition: Calories: 145; Total Fat: 9g; Saturated Fat: 1g; Cholesterol: 0mg; Carbohydrates: 13g; Fiber: 3g; Protein: 8g; Phosphorus: 143mg; Potassium: 497mg; Sodium: 92mg

318. Cauliflower and Chive Soup

Preparation Time: 10 minutes
Cooking Time: 20 minutes
Servings: 3

Ingredients:

- 2 tbsp. extra-virgin olive oil
- ½ sweet onion, chopped
- 2 garlic cloves, minced
- 2 cups Simple Chicken Broth or low-sodium store-bought chicken stock
- 1 cauliflower head, broken into florets
- Freshly ground black pepper
- 4 tbsp. (¼ cup) finely chopped chives

Directions:

1. In a small stockpot over medium heat, heat the olive oil. Add the onion and cook, stirring frequently, for 3 to 5 minutes, until it begins to soften. Add the garlic and stir until fragrant.
2. Add the broth and cauliflower, and bring to a boil. Reduce the heat and simmer until the cauliflower is tender, about 15 minutes.
3. Transfer the soup in batches to a blender or food processor and purée until smooth, or use an immersion blender. Return the soup to the pot, and season with pepper. Before serving, top each bowl with 1 tablespoon of chives.

Cooking Tip: If you're using a traditional blender, work in batches, and place a clean kitchen towel over the top of the lid as you blend to prevent splashing hot soup. Fill the blender only to the safe-fill line, and be very cautious as you go, as hot liquids can be dangerous to work with.

Nutrition:

Calories: 132; Total Fat: 8g; Saturated Fat: 1g; Cholesterol: 0mg; Carbohydrates: 13g; Fiber: 3g; Protein: 6g; Phosphorus: 116mg; Potassium: 607mg; Sodium: 84mg

319. Bulgur and Greens Soup with Soft-Boiled Egg

Preparation Time: 10 minutes
Cooking Time: 20 minutes
Servings: 1-2

Ingredients:

- ½ cup bulgur
- 2 eggs
- 2 cups Simple Chicken Broth or low-sodium store-bought chicken stock
- ½ bunch mustard greens, thick stems removed, coarsely chopped
- Freshly ground black pepper
- 1 scallion, thinly sliced
- 1-inch piece ginger, julienned
- 1 celery stalks, thinly sliced

Directions:

1. In a small pot, add the bulgur to 2 cups of water and bring to a boil. Cover, reduce the heat, and simmer for 10 to 15 minutes, until the bulgur is tender. Drain the bulgur and set it aside.
2. Place the whole eggs in a small bowl. Bring a pot of water to a boil, and carefully pour the water over the eggs. Let sit for 8 minutes, or longer if a more-set egg is desired. Carefully peel the eggs and set them aside.
3. In a medium stockpot, bring the broth to a simmer. Add the mustard greens, season with pepper, and cook until tender, 3 to 5 minutes.
4. Divide the bulgur between four bowls, and add 1 cup of broth to each bowl. Divide the mustard greens between the bowls. Add 1 egg to each bowl. Top with scallions, ginger, and celery. Serve.

Substitution Tip: If you can't find mustard greens, feel free to substitute any other type of green. Turnip greens, collard greens, or spinach all work well. If you are using a green with thick stems, like turnip or collard greens, remove the stems before cooking.

Nutrition:

Calories: 257; Total Fat: 7g; Saturated Fat: 2g; Cholesterol: 208mg; Carbohydrates: 34g; Fiber: 8g; Protein: 18g; Phosphorus: 315mg; Potassium: 661mg; Sodium: 186mg

Chapter 14: 4-Week Meal Plan

Day	Breakfast	Lunch	Dinner
1	Garlic Mayo Bread	Mint Couscous	Lemon Sprouts
2	Strawberry Topped Waffles	Lettuce Hot Dogs	Lemon and Broccoli Platter
3	Cheese Spaghetti Frittata	Tofu & Quinoa Salad	Chicken Liver Stew
4	Shrimp Bruschetta	Easy Pasta with Vodka & Tomato Sauce	Mushroom Cream Soup
5	Strawberry Muesli	Spaghetti with Pesto & Chicken	Garlic Soup
6	Yogurt Bulgur	Broccoli Salad	Simple Lamb Chops
7	Bacon and Cheese Crust less Quiche	Slow Cooked Chuck	Garlic and Butter-Flavored Cod

1st Week

Day	Breakfast	Lunch	Dinner
1	Mushroom Crust less Quiche	Baked Tuna	Tilapia Broccoli Platter
2	Maple Glazed Walnuts	Vidalia Onion Pie	Parsley Scallops
3	Ham and Cheese Strata	Runza Lamb Pocket	Blackened Chicken
4	Breakfast Salad from Grains and Fruits	Quick BBQ Chicken Pizza	Spicy Paprika Lamb Chops
5	French toast with Applesauce	Butter Crab Risotto	Steamed Fish
6	Bagels Made Healthy	Kale, Apple & Goat Cheese Salad	Mushroom and Olive Sirloin Steak
7	Cornbread with Southern Twist	Pinto Bean Burger Patties	Kale and Garlic Platter

2nd Week

Day	Breakfast	Lunch	Dinner
1	Grandma's Pancake Special	Jalapeno Popper Mushrooms	Blistered Beans and Almond
2	Very Berry Smoothie	Cranberry Glazed Turkey Meatballs	Eggplant Crunchy Fries
3	Pasta with Indian Lentils	Kine Wontons	Oregano Salmon with Crunchy Crust
4	Pineapple Bread	Vegan Mac-and-Cheese	Broiled Shrimp
5	Parmesan Zucchini Frittata	Beef & Pepper Meatloaf	Shrimp Spaghetti
6	Texas Toast Casserole	Curried Rice Salad	Teriyaki Tuna
7	Fluffy Homemade Buttermilk Pancake	Stuffed Zucchini	Very Wild Mushroom Pilaf

3rd Week

Day	Breakfast	Lunch	Dinner
1	Blueberry Muffins	Pad Kee Mao	Lemon Pepper Trout
2	Easy Turkey Breakfast Burritos	Tuna Dip	Salmon Stuffed Pasta
3	Loaded Veggie Eggs	Lemon Dill Rice	Tuna Casserole
4	Diet Breakfast	Curried Pork Empanadas	Oregano Salmon with Crunchy Crust
5	Breakfast Burrito	Baked Haddock	Sardine Fish Cakes
6	Maple Pancakes	Herbed Chicken	Cajun Catfish
7	Mini Frittatas	Pesto Pork Chops	Teriyaki Tuna

4th Week

Conclusion

As you can see, Renal Diet Cookbook is dedicated to serving you with top-quality products that promote a healthy lifestyle. Our comprehensive cookbook for kidney patients provides the best information on what foods are safe and what foods are harmful to people with kidney failure.

Each recipe has been carefully crafted by a team of experts who have the knowledge and experience to make sure you get the most out of every meal. All of the recipes in this cookbook have been carefully adjusted to ensure that they contain low levels of sodium, potassium, and phosphorus. This is important because these foods provide the necessary vitamins and minerals for people with kidney failure.

Truly, kidney patients need a culinary advisor. If you're looking for extra nutrients and a convenient way to eat healthier, check out our Renal Diet Cookbook today! Now that your kidney disease has been stabilized, you should focus on making sure that you consume a healthy diet. We've included plenty of recipes in the "Renal Diet Cookbook" to help you do just that.

You can find out more information about each recipe by reading the ingredients listed on the nutrition facts panel. If the ingredients contain salt, high sodium foods are not recommended for the person taking dialysis. Check with your doctor or dialysis provider before making any changes to your dialysis regimen. The recipes in "Renal Diet Cookbook" are not intended to replace medical advice or professional care from a physician or other appropriate health care professionals.

After using the Renal Diet Cookbook, you will be able to make your meals as quickly and easily as you can with a normal cookbook. Getting the right nutrients is important for anyone with kidney disease or diabetes. But it's much more important when you must live on a kidney diet, or have retinopathy or diabetes.

The Renal Diet Cookbook is organized by days of the week, so you can easily and quickly find the recipes you want. The Renal Diet Cookbook also contains special tips, tricks, and helpful hints that will help ensure your success. Foods high in protein, low in salt, and high in vitamins A and C are used to create tasty and healthy foods! Use the Renal Diet Cookbook to plan your menu each week. Work all of the different recipes into your meal plan, and you will be amazed at how great your kidney diet can really be! There are lots of ways to customize all of the recipes in the Renal Diet Cookbook so that they fit your needs.

After spending many years on dialysis, you may have heard of a renal diet. Renal diet is a dietary guideline that helps its users maintain a steady blood sugar level. While you can follow a renal diet alone, the diet is often combined with daily medications to control complications of renal disease. We've put together this guide to renal diet so that you can learn more about the dietary guidelines and whether they are right for you.

Printed in Great Britain
by Amazon

78334105R00068